Arthur Hugh

The Growth of a P

Arthur Hugh Clough

The Growth of a Poet's Mind

Evelyn Barish Greenberger

Harvard University Press
Cambridge, Massachusetts
1970

To Danny and Lotta
with gratitude and love

Acknowledgments

This study could not have been undertaken or completed without the support of many people and institutions. It was financially assisted by the Fulbright Commission, the American Association of University Women, and the Grant-in-Aid Fund of the English Department of Cornell University, and I am grateful to them.

I wish especially to thank Miss K. L. Duff for her kindness in making available to me the manuscripts in her possession, and for permission to print material including the two poems that Clough submitted in competition for the Newdigate Prize, in Appendix B. These were first printed in the *Review of English Studies* and in *Victorian Poetry*. Dr. R. W. Hunt of the Bodleian Library and Mr. Vincent Quinn of Balliol College Library have made valuable suggestions regarding other manuscript sources. I am grateful to Miss Margaret Crum and Mr. D. H. Merry of the Bodleian Library for their assistance, and also to Mr. M. Bull, Miss P. Brown, Mr. W. G. Harris, and Mr. D. S. Porter of the same library. I owe thanks for permission to consult the resources of the Beinecke Library, the British Museum, Dr. Williams's Library, the Houghton Library, Oriel College Library, and the Pierpoint Morgan Library, and for permission to reproduce manuscript material from the Bodleian and Beinecke Libraries. Quotations from Frederick L. Mulhauser, ed., *The Correspondence of Arthur Hugh Clough,* and H. F. Lowry, A. L. P. Norrington, and F. L. Mulhauser, eds., *The Poems of Arthur Hugh Clough,* are reproduced by permission of the Clarendon Press, Oxford.

The advice and suggestions of Professor Gay Wilson Allen, of New York University, have been invaluable. I am also most grateful to Professor William Buckler, under whom I first entered Victorian studies, and also to Dr. C. M. Ing, of Lady Margaret Hall, Oxford.

I am happy to acknowledge my debts to Professor Edward Spofford, of Cornell University, and to Mr. John Williams, of the Manchester Grammar School, for their translations of Clough's Greek and Latin references. I wish also to thank Miss Felicity Collins, Mr. David W. Jones, Mr. David Mordovanec, and Miss Claudia Kramer for their assistance in checking the manuscript.

I am especially grateful to my colleague at Cornell, Professor W. David Shaw, for his stimulating criticism of the manuscript. To Mr. J. B. Bamborough, Principal of Linacre College, Oxford, I also owe many thanks. To my husband, Daniel Greenberger, the manuscript owes more of good sense than I can estimate; any errors are all my own.

Evelyn Barish Greenberger

Ithaca, New York
February 1969

Contents

Arthur Hugh Clough

The Growth of a Poet's Mind

1837

For as it is quite certain that the beautiful things we conceive are far more beautiful than any real things existing, at least in our world—that is, Ideal Beauty is greater than Real Beauty; so also it is unquestionable that Ideal Beauty cannot be adequately expressed by real existing things.

Clough's first undergraduate essay; Bodleian manuscript

1850

Actual life is unknown to an Oxford student, even though he is not a mere Puseyite and goes on jolly reading parties—Enter the arena of your brethren and go not to your grave without knowing what common merchants and sollicitors, much more sailors and coalheavers, are well acquainted with. Ignorance is a poor kind of innocence.

Clough to J. C. Shairp; Correspondence

Introduction

Arthur Hugh Clough was trained by Thomas Arnold, Headmaster
of Rugby, to believe with Algernon Sydney that "there are but two
things of vital importance—those which he calls religion and politics,
but which I would rather call our duties and affections towards
God, and our duties and affections towards men; science and literature are but a poor make up for the want of these."[1] Preeminently
a poet of his age, and one who made that age his conscious subject
more than most of his contemporaries, Clough clearly took that
dictum seriously, and his political and religious prose reflects the
reality of his interest. Yet this corpus of writing, although important
to the understanding of his poetry, has not yet been thoroughly
studied. After a long hiatus several books have recently appeared on
Clough, but none has made his prose its focus, and several major
questions about the development of his thought on these central subjects remain unanswered.

One recent study, for example, has ascribed the seeming anomalies
and contradictions in Clough's behavior and poetry to his being essentially "uncommitted";[2] another, sympathetic to Clough and more
or less in reply, has offered "positive naturalism"[3] as the rubric under
which the poet's essentially positive response to life could be asserted.
But no work yet, for reasons which will be discussed further below,
has undertaken a systematic and careful study of Clough's prose
writings on political and religious matters, although it is here that
his thought on these subjects can be most readily grasped and its
development traced. This the present study intends to do. It begins

1

with a study of the essays Clough began writing as an undergraduate in 1837 and ends with his writings in America in 1853, concluding at that date both because Clough wrote relatively little thereafter and because his political and religious ideas had by then completed the cycle of their development. (The remaining eight years of his life were devoted first to the establishment of his marriage and an adequate income, then to the added and demanding work of assisting Florence Nightingale, and finally to the illness which brought him death in 1861 at the age of forty-two.) The present study attempts to trace through the years the rise and fall of certain of Clough's governing ideas, and to distinguish between those which were contingent and those which were basic to his thought. Some material not previously published appears here; other prose works that have been misdated, not properly understood, mistitled, or ignored are also discussed. This work hopes to correct certain misconceptions, to sort out the specific steps—not all of them clear-cut—by which Clough's ideas took shape, and to trace the development of his ideas on these two central subjects through the crucial period of his life, the years between eighteen and thiry-four.

The Clough that emerges from this study is not a strikingly new one, unrecognizable to his former admirers and defenders. But neither is he the weak-willed wanderer, crying for the moon of belief, whom a century of disparagement (to paraphrase Walter Houghton) long painted.[4] He is not the "heavy moving vessel" full of mental inertia whom Mrs. Clough and Walter Bagehot described after his death,[5] nor an uncommitted, Oedipally conflicted quietist. The mind that emerges from this study is one always serious in purpose and principles which moves, by a necessary process of growth, and impelled by its ideals, from an undergraduate period of naïveté and abstraction, through an era of activity and polemics, to a temporary stage of reaction, disappointment, and some bitterness, to a final period of acceptance and of a greater wisdom which predicated itself not on revolutions, moral or political, but on the twin realities of the social structure and the possibilities of individual virtue. Clough was for a time somewhat more radical politically than has hitherto been suggested, and he suffered from sanctions both internal and social rather more than his widow or subsequent

biographers wished or have been able to stress. He learned much
from these experiences. His poetry, particularly his three major narrative works, is deeply informed by what he learned, and it traces
the curve of his intellectual development more closely than we have
until now been in a position to perceive. The man who wrote *Epi-
Strauss-ium* in 1845, for example, is not quite the same as the author
of the *Easter Day* poems written four years later,[6] nor, contrary
to one critic's view, do they say the same thing about the sources
of religious hope.[7] And in like fashion, the differences between *The
Bothie* and *Dipsychus* may be grasped at a deeper level when we
understand better the assumptions about life and society that shaped
them.

The reasons for the continued obscurity of some portions of
Clough's writing and thought are not far to seek. The most obvious
reason is that there has never been a critical edition of his prose.
The standard edition of 1869, which I will discuss further below
and on which until recently scholars have had to rely, was a selection,
"relentlessly" edited by his widow, as Stanley T. Williams wrote,[8]
and it is marred by amateurism and deliberate suppressions. All
other editions were based on this text until Trawick's edition appeared in 1964;[9] this too, however, is only a selection. Unfortunately
it both repeats certain previous errors of Mrs. Clough and adds
new ones, while its critical apparatus is very meager.[10] However,
it is unfortunately the only text in print and therefore has been
cited the first time I refer to a work for the benefit of the reader
who does not have access to the original sources or the *Poems and
Prose Remains.*

In addition to the writings printed by Trawick and Mrs. Clough,
and to Clough's voluminous unpublished correspondence, the present
study draws on prose manuscripts or contemporary journals for some
thirty-nine pieces of varying length and significance.[11] A portion
of the material extracted here (or printed in full—see Appendix B)
is totally new to print or has not been collected since its first
appearance in a contemporary journal. Other of these thirty-nine
pieces have been discussed elsewhere, primarily in two works (only
one of which, however, is in English): these are *Arthur Hugh
Clough: The Uncommitted Mind,* by Katharine Chorley, and *Ar-*

thur Hugh Clough, by Paul Veyriras.[12] I have not sought, in studying Clough's prose, to be encyclopedic; I have sought to present a discussion which should be sustained, thorough, and interpretive.

In matters of spelling and punctuation my practice has been silently to regularize trivial matters in accordance with American usage when preservation would be meaningless or merely annoying, for example, Clough's habit of following a comma by a dash. But any practice which might seem to some to express a tone of voice or characteristic quirk of style (such as the poet's tendency to punctuate by a series of dashes when writing informally, or to abbreviate in an odd but intelligible manner, as in "Xty" for Christianity) I have preserved. On the few occasions when a true crux appears, I have suggested a reading but not concealed the difficulty. In general, I do not attempt to re-edit the prose, and emendations have been made only when they are relevant to the argument in hand. These comments, however, do not apply to the poetry and other material of Appendix B, in which I have accepted the responsibility of an editor for presenting a full and critical text.

Because they have been so influential, Mrs. Clough's edition and the "Memoir" she included in it need some comment. Her work is the more unfortunate because it has helped to create not the picture she wished to present of her late husband's ultimate happiness, his serenity, domestic tranquillity, and moral depth, but rather the reverse. The image of Clough that has survived and been reproduced, ever larger and larger, is that of a man whom one biographer called a "nonstarter"; another sees a subject governed by hesitations and an Oedipus complex. Because he was an inward man who rigorously examined his reasons for action, his positive acts have been overlooked and he has been called "uncommitted," although the reverse is true. Such judgments have aptly been called "tiresome" by Professor Walter E. Houghton, but for various reasons they have persisted, and the effect has been to make Clough appear the ineffectual victim of one destructive force or idea after another.[13]

The basic source for this tradition is the "Memoir" written by Mrs. Clough and containing a number of accounts of the poet written by friends of his youth.[14] Mrs. Clough had loved her husband, but she was a young and conventional widow who had not known Clough in his more radical days and had probably heard him speak of them in terms of scorn. Thus, for example, writing to her during his period of reaction, he told her of having engaged at a dinner party "in a contemptuously triumphant putting down of a hopeful radical . . . who still would hold to his belief in progress, democracy, and that sort of thing." In the same month he mentioned a pamphlet whose radical tendencies had drawn attack, and remarked, "I shouldn't write it now . . . I am wiser."[15] Moreover the friends who contributed to the "Memoir" were very unlike Clough. Neither W. G. Ward nor John Conington shared Clough's more radical religious and political ideas, while the largest contributor, John Shairp, a professor of English, was entirely out of sympathy with Clough's ideas. When he had been shown the manuscript of *Amours de Voyage,* considered by some to be the poet's masterpiece, Shairp had condemned its ideas as "unhealthy" and projecting a "state of soul . . . I do not like." In language so emotional it burst finally into meter, he exclaimed "No, I would cast it behind me and the spirit from which it emanates and to higher, more healthful, hopeful things purely aspire."[16] Clough's closest friend and the only one whose career closely paralleled his in commitments and suffering was Tom Arnold (Matthew's older brother); he was apparently not asked to contribute.

But the bulk of the "Memoir" was Mrs. Clough's own work. She, who once primly wrote her fiancé that she had "a sense of what is fitting"—unlike him—and was not allowed by Clough to forget it, had no reason to stress ideas that most people felt had been wrongheaded and that her husband himself had later renounced. With the recent publication of Phyllis Grosskurth's biography of John Addington Symonds, we can for the first time directly see Mrs. Clough's efforts at suppressing anything in the poet's life that would cause scandal. Symonds, whom she had asked to help edit the *Poems and Prose Remains,* tried to persuade her against her course. " 'I say either a truthful biography or none,' " he wrote a friend, and to her he urged that " 'The mass of the remains are already known—accepted: the additions . . . will not, I sincerely believe, scandalize many whose opinion is at all worth having.' " But Blanche was " 'very timid,' " and like many seemingly timid people she had her way. " 'The memoir is written,' " he eventually reported, " '—inadequately, but still written—by Mrs. Clough . . .' "

With great perception he remarked that Clough's life " 'in some sense must have been mutilated. Mrs. Clough of course does not give me this impression or suspect it.' "[17]

Symonds, who had not heard of Clough until 1861, was of course in no position to know the extent of Clough's early involvement with radical ideas, his success in those days, or the real mutilation his hopes and even identity suffered after his voluntary exile from Oxford in 1848. These were undoubtedly among the points and details Symonds referred to which Mrs. Clough did not wish to make public.[18] In her memoir, the widow wrote of the period which he had described to her as that of his "very great force," merely that he had been excellent as a tutor, saying firmly, "But little need be said of this period. He led a quiet, hardworking, uneventful, tutor's life, diversified with . . . reading parties . . . He took a warm and increasing interest in all social questions, and in every way he seems to have been full of spirit and vigor."[19] Sandwiched between "reading parties . . . spirit . . . and vigor," her phrase "social questions" might even have been taken to mean parties and society. There is no question that Clough's early politics was one of the aspects of him that his widow was least willing or able to clarify; she reprinted almost none of his relevant writings. The selections she included gave no evidence that he had ever held unconventional political ideas: only his late (1853) and conservative essay-review of Charles Eliot Norton's book, in which Clough tacitly repudiated his earlier opinions, was included. It is possible that Mrs. Clough was unaware of the extent of her subject's quondam interest in socialism. The letters to *The Balance,* for example, in which his opinions are most fully developed, were anonymous and may not have been known to his survivors. But it is not impossible that she deliberately suppressed this side of Clough's life, just as, according to one biographer, she "almost hysterically" suppressed the sexually frank "Natura Naturans" and as she suppressed improprieties in the little lyric, *Solvitur Acris Hiems,* and in *Dipsychus.*[20]

Until very recently, scholars have not questioned the image she left of him in this regard. Even in the latest studies it is still commonplace to say that Clough's political opinions in 1853 were similar to or only a little different from those of 1848.[21] The truth is, as examination of the documents will show, that while in 1848 he could be accused of being sympathetic even with communistic ideas (though this was an exaggeration), by 1853 he publicly announced a keen distrust of democracy.

In a similar way, Mrs. Clough omitted the very telling correspondence between her late husband and Edward Hawkins, Provost of Oriel, after Clough had resigned from the college on religious grounds. Those letters suggest how sharply and finally Clough's resignation put him beyond the pale of the Establishment, and how unhesitatingly an officer of the Establishment, as Hawkins must be reckoned, felt he must refuse his help to a heretic like his former Sub-Dean when that man sought a teaching post even in a purely secular institution. "I presume," he wrote Clough, " . . . the Principal of the College [at Sydney, Australia] would not teach Divinity, or any particular Xtian tenets; but still it appears to me that no one ought to be appointed to such a situation who is at all in a state of doubt and difficulty as to his own religious belief."[22] No responsible position could be got without Hawkins's support, and he knew it. He judged Clough to be a man of high personal morality, and he assured him his opinion of him personally had not changed. But Hawkins represented both society and the Anglican Establishment, and others would have done the same. Hawkins acted no less punitively because he acted impersonally, and there was no further correspondence between himself and Clough. But of that relationship Blanche wrote only that "in speaking of [Hawkins] he always expressed a strong sense of the uniform kindness he had received from him under these trying circumstances."[23] And she omitted the letters that suggested the depth and specific consequences of the break. Although Clough no doubt repressed any resentment he may have felt and perhaps was magnanimous enough to feel none, Hawkins was not "uniformly kind"—he could not be in his position. To mention, however, Hawkins's refusal to assist Clough at a crucial point in his life—and Hawkins was still very much alive and influential at Oxford in 1868—would be to imply the seriousness of Clough's exile and suffering, and this Blanche had determined not to do. Symonds perhaps was right in perceiving that Clough had been mutilated; it was true in the sense that he had lost his sense of himself as a powerful man; but this was not a view his widow could have accepted.

Not surprisingly, there runs throughout the "Memoir" a pervasive tone of regret for what Clough might have been and for his presumed failure. Although the 1951 edition of Clough's poetry is nearly 600 pages long, including the notes (many of these containing suppressed material), Mrs. Clough felt called on to excuse her husband for having "left so little behind him." This she explained on two counts: the "physical conformation of [his] brain" which let him do only one thing at a time, and his "inertia." Still speaking in his defense, Blanche called him a "heavy moving vessel," and a man of "excessive conscientiousness," one who "had no natural aptitude for making money" and "could not use . . . half-hours to write well-paid reviews *or even poetry.*" (Italics mine.) He was "incapab[le] of treating the common themes of poetry in the usual manner," thereby diminishing his range of subjects.[24] Mrs. Clough's tone is more damning than she probably realized, and it reveals her disappointment as well as a real lack of insight into her husband as a poet. Ignoring that tone, however, one sees a man who had determined that though he had gone wrong he would not now sell himself cheap, nor turn to hack work, ready, like those his wife had heard of, to write up books "or even poetry" in "half hours." Even if Mrs. Clough's temperament and education had not led her to be shocked almost out of love with her fiancé—and all men—when she had first read some of his manuscripts (without his permission),[25] even if she had been preternaturally broadminded and unlike other women of her background, it would still be unfortunate that the tone in which Clough has been discussed ever since should have been set by one too closely involved with her subject to be objective.

The result, to be sure, was a more manageable Clough and one who needed less explaining. If the tenor of his life at Oxford had been pleasant and liberal but not really radical, then his later acceptance of conventional views was less striking. If the particular fact were not known that he could not get a crucial recommendation he had assumed would be given him, if it were not made public that he had been dismissed from University Hall (those responsible came from Mrs. Clough's own social circle), then the embarrassment of committing his suffering to public and hostile eyes while interested persons were still alive might be avoided. The widow knew that her husband had altered his opinions before they were married, but she was defensive about the failure of his poetic voice after their marriage. She could not regard or portray her late husband, who had suffered so much, as having been diminished through their relationship. Undoubtedly she felt that his alterations were the result of personal growth; if they were for the worse, they came from ill-health and not disappointment.

Unfortunately, the omissions and suppressions both in Clough's canon and biography tend to make him appear less of a man, one who not only suffered less, but felt and cared less deeply than he had done in reality. The total impression the "Memoir" and *Poetry and Prose Remains* gave was probably not what its sponsors intended. With so much omitted, his life after the extraordinary promise he had shown at Rugby could only seem a long anticlimax, punctuated by "poetry of doubt." In fact, as we shall see, he fulfilled that promise, after a temporary setback, until his departure from Oxford in 1848, and continued to fulfill it in a different way afterwards. Yet many studies of Clough since have been unbalanced because they begin on the premise, deduced from the "Memoir," that Clough was a failure, and set out to discover why. As a result, an inordinate amount of stress, for example, is often given Clough's life at Rugby under Arnold: this was certainly a significant period and Arnold was a great force upon him, but Clough grew beyond much of that influence, and attention has been diverted from its more proper sphere, Clough's achievements as a grown man. The same can be said of another overworked biographical crux, the religious and academic problems of his undergraduate years.

More recent critical studies have done much to right the balance of judgment. Walter Houghton has claimed a place for Clough as "one of the best of the Victorian poets,"[26] and the studies by Paul Veyriras and Michael Timko, although not as widely known perhaps as Katharine Chorley's biography,[27] have presented a far more rounded picture of the man and the positive aspect of his thought. Nevertheless, due no doubt in part to the hindering absence of a complete edition of Clough's prose, the development of Clough's ideas on the central issues of politics and religion has not yet been traced with full accuracy. It is important to know, for instance, that Clough's late position in 1853 neither just "carried on" from his *Retrenchment* pamphlet of 1847 nor showed merely a "slight retreat"[28] from it but expressed the deep revaluation of six sometimes very difficult and surprising intervening years. We need to know, too, not only of the influence of Arnold and Carlyle, important as they were to Clough, but of his reading of other thinkers such as Friedrich von Schlegel and Emerson. Something of the period and the assumptions of Clough's class must also be known lest we assume too easily, with another writer, that Clough was much concerned with the concept of "Liberty" or could have made it—or any other "natural right"—a crucial or culminating value.[29] What we must try to do, if we would fully understand Clough, is to look at the whole body of his writings on these subjects, trying to compare them, to estimate their differences from each other, and to place them as much as possible in the context of Clough's interests and the influences on him. Clough tried to be the "honest man" he once described, whose "first thought . . . on entering into a new position is to discover the obligations it entails on him. I receive a certain pay; do I do the work it is given for? I have fellow men to serve and assist me; do I pay them the wages of their work?"[30] Like his "transcendental man of business," who loved truth and abhorred illusion, Clough was ready "to admit, *if* things are bad, that they are so [and] to go thoroughly into the accounts of the world and make out once for all how they stand."[31] Such figures may well stand as models for students of Clough.

From this study, then, we can hope to follow the growth of Clough's thought in the context of his period. Ultimately, however, the justification of such a pursuit as this must be that it leads us back to his poetry, for it is on this that our interest in Clough will always rest. His quest to discover his "duties and affections towards God and . . . men," explicit in his prose, is transmuted into the very bone and sinew of his poetry. "What we call sin," Clough wrote in *Dipsychus,* "I could believe a painful opening out / Of paths for ampler virtue."[32] His intellectual and moral opening out, sometimes painful, sometimes exhilarating, is my subject here: its culmination in the "ampler virtue" of his poetry is reason enough for studying it.

CHAPTER I

The Higher Line

"It continues to strike me," Clough wrote from London in 1850, almost fourteen years after he had first gone up to Oxford, "how ignorant you and I and other young men of our set are. Actual life is unknown to an Oxford student, even though he is not a mere Puseyite and goes on jolly reading parties . . . Ignorance is a poor kind of innocence."[1] He made a similar but more detailed attack on his training, and especially the influence of Arnold, in the "Epilogue" to *Dipsychus,* which he began to write shortly thereafter. And certainly Clough's undergraduate essays do reflect in some degree the character he sketches there: the ignorance which is a "poor kind of innocence," the priggishness that Dipsychus's uncle attacks, the "notion of the world being so wicked" and of Arnold's students "taking a higher line, as they call it,"[2] are all apparent in these youthful pieces.

Yet to say only these things, to point only to the essays' naïveté or their reliance on arguments from authority, would be to speak partially of the young Clough. He, as a mature and in some ways disappointed man, was writing in 1850 in reaction against Arnold and his earlier self, and true to Arnold's influence, he was one of his own harshest critics. But if in Clough's undergraduate prose we see the naïve boy with abstract and moralistic ideas about society and himself, yet we also see being formed the person whose basic ideals, whose love of honesty and of the highest standards, never changed. The questioning mind, the humanitarian spirit, the profound moral awareness, at once sympathetic and without cant or illusion, which mark his maturity can here be seen awakening and beginning to stir. If we would understand Clough's later irony, we ought first to know better the mixture of moral ignorance and intellectual integrity from which it grew. And if we would understand the nature of his political and religious thought, both as an undergraduate and later, we need to know something of the influences which formed it. A discussion of some of the major elements of these influences and of the essays themselves, will follow.

America

Studies old and new make it clear that one may justifiably infer that the pattern of intellectual and physical deracination which Clough's mature career expresses was, if not determined by a similar pattern in his youth, at least paralleled by it. There were essentially three major formative forces operating on him as a youth: his life at home till he was nine, the presence of Arnold at Rugby, and the influence of Ward at Balliol. Through each of them Clough experienced at first or second hand what it was to be somehow an alien, at odds to some degree through nationality, politics, or religion, or all three, with the norms of the surrounding social structure. From Arnold and Ward he could have learned the joy of the fight, the satisfaction of being an Abdiel—the Miltonic figure revered by Arnold[3]—to the forces of darkness around him. No doubt in some measure he did learn it. But from his immediate family and its circumstances he probably learned rather the inwardness of that condition which later characterized him, the sense of isolation upon it was founded. Later he became a leader, respected and loved by his peers and elders alike; but from his youth he could tolerate and indeed to some degree sought an intellectual and personal distinction from the crowd which reminds one of his mother's insistence during his American childhood that her offspring "remember they were English."[4]

The Cloughs traced their descent from a Sir Richard Clough who had gained wealth in the sixteenth century as the Antwerp agent of Sir Thomas Gresham, but Clough's father, a younger son, had by necessity become the first of his family to leave the neighborhood of the ancestral home in Denbighshire. A descendant of generations of Tory clergymen and country gentlemen, James Butler Clough moved to Liverpool to set up as a cotton trader. Later, when Arthur was four, he moved to Charleston, South Carolina. The pattern was a common one, as Frank Thistlethwaite has shown, for English businessmen of the period.[5] Filling entrepreneurial roles in America, where the social structure was highly permeable, they frequently moved rapidly to the top. But for Clough's father what was essentially an act of social descent was not recompensed, it seems, by any sense of personal fulfillment or financial success. It was not common for his compatriots to feel completely at home in the American culture, but they tended to be Whigs and Dissenters who had experienced jural biases against them in England, came themselves from the merchant classes or lower, and were ready to make the most of the highly competitive mores in the country to which they had come. James Butler Clough differed from many of these not only in background but in politics and religion, for he was both a Tory and an Anglican. He did not put down strong roots in his new home, but in 1836 removed his family back to England. By temperament easygoing and gregarious, he appears to have been ill-suited in every way for the competitive and unstable business in which he was engaged, and after a long period of uncertainty he went bankrupt in 1841. Clough seems to have felt that his father's failure was a reflection not so much on himself as on the viciousness of the competitive system from which his training and nature were alien, and he voiced his perception in *Jacob,* regarded by the poet's sister as a kind of memorial of their father:

> But I have had to force mine eyes away,
> To lose, almost to shun, the thoughts I loved,
> To bend down to the work, to bare the breast,
> And struggle, feet and hands, with enemies;
> To buffet and to battle with hard men . . .
> How is it? I have striven all my days
> To do my duty to my house and hearth,
> And to the purpose of my father's race,
> Yet is my heart therewith not satisfied.[6]

James Butler Clough died three years after his bankruptcy, in 1844.

The political and religious peculiarities which distinguished the Cloughs from their American milieu were not overcome but reinforced by the personality of Clough's mother. A withdrawn woman of high moral ideals and intense, rather Evangelical religious opinions, Mrs. Clough avoided society when her husband was away on his frequent business trips, and kept her two children close to herself and her intellectual and moral training. Clough himself was remembered by his sister as a rather shy boy, more given to reading by himself or spending his time with his father than playing with his American contemporaries, as no doubt his mother, who wished her children to "remember they were English," desired. She and her husband were, her daughter recalled, "too English to let their children go to a school in Charleston, which . . . was perhaps a pity"; and they were too English to mix freely in the life of the place.[7] The "marginality," the quality of standing somewhat apart from whatever social structure he might be in, which marks so much of Clough's later career, perhaps has some of its roots in the marginality of his family's position, in which these expatriates' proud remembrance that "they were English" involved also their realization that the Cloughs' links to the sources of power and prestige in the England from which they had sprung were as attenuated as were their voluntarily limited links to America.

Arnold

Clough was sent to school in England at the age of nine, a not uncommon experience for the children of English entrepreneurs but one that again set him apart from his fellows, and exiled him from his family's love and support for the rest of his childhood and early youth. He saw his mother and sister only once in the next eight years, and his father only twice. The first departure in 1828, as his sister Anne wrote, "was practically the end of Arthur's childhood."[8]

Clough flourished at Rugby, however, where he arrived in 1829 and which, under the headmastership of Thomas Arnold, was gaining new prestige among the great English public schools. And Arnold in turn came to love him only after his own children, showing him special favor, and on his departure for Oxford writing to his uncle Alfred, a don at Jesus College:

I cannot resist my desire of congratulating you most heartily on the delightful close of your nephew's long career at Rugby, where he has passed eight years without a fault . . . he has gone on ripening gradually in all excellence intellectual and spiritual, and from [the school] he has now gone to Oxford, not only full of honors, but carrying with him the respect and love of all whom he has left behind, and regarded by myself, I may truly say, with an affection and interest hardly less than I should feel for my own son. I only hope, and indeed nothing doubt, that you will have the same pleasure in watching his career in Oxford that I have long had in watching it at Rugby.[9]

Within Arnold's assumptions, "eight years without a fault" was a justified statement. Clough had been outstanding in every way. He had been editor of the Rugby Magazine, a pet project of Arnold's that had been founded by the boys according to Bamford "to spread the worth of Rugby" and of their headmaster when he had been under attack from local conservatives.[10] An athlete, the tall and strong youngster was long remembered as a superb goal keeper at the school where Rugby was invented. Most important, he had been Head of the School, an honorary position to which Arnold appointed a leading boy whom he wanted to set the school's standard. Clough threw himself heart and soul into his position of moral leadership. "I verily believe," he wrote midway through his last year, with all the intensity of adolescence, "my whole being is regularly soaked through with the wishing and hoping and striving to do the School good, or rather to keep it up and hinder it from falling in this, I do think, very critical time, so that all my cares and affections, and conversation, thoughts, words, and deeds look to that involuntarily."[11] As he had put it a few months earlier to his sister Anne: "I am trying if possible to show them that good is not necessarily disagreeable, that a Christian may be and is likely to be a gentleman, and that he is surely much more than a gentleman."[12]

In spite of the sanctimonious note, this is a vital passage for the understanding of Clough's later development. He went on: "It is a weary thing to look around and see all the evil, all the sin and wickedness of those with whom one must . . . strive at least in all indifferent things to please and conciliate; and truly my dear Annie if there was only man to work in the good cause, one might well despair, but we know it is not so, and so we must hope even against hope."[13]

Almost all these ideas, of course, were Arnold's, even to the phrasing, for Clough listened so intently to the Headmaster's words that he could and did repeat his Sunday sermons almost verbatim when he wrote to former Rugbeians who had gone up to the university.[14] Academically, he was also superior, He won award after award at Rugby between 1829 and 1837, and in 1836 won Balliol's single competitive scholarship, then as now one of the University's most desirable awards. On his last prize-day, Arnold publicly congratulated him, an honor he had never before accorded a student, and every boy in the school is supposed to have contrived to shake Clough's hand at parting.[15] Two fags, it is said, were needed to help him remove his prize books.[16]

The headmaster by whom Clough was so honored was a man widely known and respected in the England of the 1830's, but his forte was rather his capacity for leadership, for teaching, and to some degree for polemics rather than for profound or original thought. The ideas and principles he passed on to Clough sprang to a considerable extent from a group at Oxford known as the Noetics, to which Arnold had belonged during the second decade of the century. The Noetics (originally a pejorative nickname, Greek for "intellectual") flourished at Oriel College during the first two or three decades of the century.[17] As the era went on and they rose to higher positions within or without the university, their circle of influence widened, and they formed the nucleus of the Liberals at Oxford, the group whom John Henry Newman called "the leaders, if intellect and influence make men such," of the university in the 1840's and responsible, therefore, for his being driven out of Oxford. "The party grew," he wrote, "all the time that I was in Oxford even in numbers, certainly in breadth and definiteness of doctrine, and in power. And, what was a far higher consideration, by the accession of Dr. Arnold's pupils, it was invested with an elevation of character which claimed the respect even of its opponents."[18]

16

(Clough and his friend, A. P. Stanley, were the two pupils of Arnold whom Newman probably knew best.)

When Disraeli, writing *Coningsby,* wanted to send Oswald Millbank, son of a captain of industry and a paragon of moral and intellectual enlightenment, to the university he made him an Oriel man. Oriel was the Noetics' center, and as dons there they numbered among themselves three Provosts or Provosts-to-be of Oriel: Eveleigh, Copleston, and Edward Hawkins; a future Archbishop, Richard Whately; the future Headmaster of Rugby and Oxford's Professor of History, Thomas Arnold; the future Regius Professor of Divinity, R. D. Hampden, whose appointment caused one of the major controversies of the Tractarian movement; John Davison, and Blanco White, the interesting clergyman who began his career as a Spanish Roman Catholic priest and was converted successively to Anglicanism and finally Unitarianism. The great Biblical scholar Joseph Milman is sometimes considered to have been a Noetic, although he belonged to another college, and some historians include the Cambridge theologians Thirlwall and Hare as having been in sympathy with them in their attacks on authority and interest in reform.[19] The discussions at Oriel tended to be battlegrounds on which less intellectually able or competitive dons felt uncomfortable, and the disgruntled saying of their opponents was that their common room "stunk of logic."[20]

Newman (himself a former pupil of Richard Whately) founded his antipathy to the party on the grounds that they were rationalists. When it was clear after many attacks and counter-attacks that Hampden and his supporters could not be dislodged from positions of influence, Newman in 1841 crossed his Rubicon and published *Tract 90.* He justified its attempt to make Anglicanism as identical as possible with Roman Catholicism by saying that wherever his work led, his opponents' position led to atheism. Rationalism, he wrote, "is the great evil of the day . . . I am more certain that the Protestant [spirit] which I oppose leads to infidelity than that which I recommend leads to Rome."[21]

The Noetics always denied the charge of rationalism but overtly championed the cause of reform on many fronts. Born in the eighteenth century, to some extent they may be said to have used certain eighteenth-century intellectual principles to destroy that century's heritage at Oxford of intellectual sloth and decay. Their primary intellectual and moral principle was to rely less on tradition than on conscience guided by reason and on Scripture itself rather than Church authority. In this they followed the famous eighteenth-century divine, Bishop Joseph Butler, whom Newman himself revered and whose works, especially his *Analogy,* were required reading well into the nineteenth century for all theological students.[22] Butler, attempting to answer the Deists by using their own weapons, had gone so far as to declare that "Reason can, and it ought, to judge not only of the meaning but also of the morality" of Scripture.[23] The Noetics in turn found this a sanction for following free inquiry wherever it might lead. They supported the new methods of scriptural exegesis which German scholars had been developing, although it was becoming evident that in disentangling the strands of Scripture and applying historical tests to it theologians might ultimately cast doubt on the literal veracity of prophecy, revelation, and miracles.[24] On at least two occasions when their scholarship was attacked—once when Milman called Abraham an Arab sheikh, and again when Hampden was accused of unorthodoxy, partly for showing the medieval origins of many Church doctrines—Arnold defended his friends against the charge of rationalism in terms that were essentially Butler's. He said in a famous phrase that the scholarship Pusey abused as "Rationalism," was simply "the moral reason acting under God and using, so to speak, the telescope of faith for objects too distant for the naked eye to discover."[25]

They tended to be Whigs, university reformers, anti-Sabbatarians, and supporters of the Catholic Emancipation Bill. Historical issues loomed large in their debates, and the Noetics identified themselves as Protestants, sons of the Reformation, and supporters of the Revolution of 1688, all points that distinguished them from the larger group of Oxford clergy called, as Newman noted, the "two-bottle orthodox."[26] Perhaps the most far-reaching practical reform they urged from early days was the admission of Dissenters to the university, a measure narrow enough in one view but in which were implicit major social, religious and political changes, for the hegemony of the Anglican Church in religion and higher education existed in a symbiotic relationship with the hegemony of the aristocracy in politics. To grant university degrees to Dissenters would mean permitting them ultimately to compete on equal terms at the centers of political and social power.

Arnold was at one with his fellow Noetics on all these issues, although as time went on he became more involved in matters of social reform outside the university and parted company with Whately in particular on the issue of a Church-State. Wishing to help Christianize England as he was trying to Christianize the public schools, Arnold's basic aims, if not his doctrinal standpoint, were clear. His theory of history regarded reform as "identical with Christianity itself," Stanley wrote, and to reform of all kinds he bent his efforts.[27] Powerful and impulsive in temperament, he was given to polemics. (He once wrote his sister "I must write a pamphlet in the holidays, or I shall burst."[28]) When the revolution of 1830 broke out in France he called it "the most blessed . . . in history"[29] but he came to fear a similar one for England, and he would have broadened the Noetic tolerance of Dissent into a Christian *societas,* influenced in this, as Basil Willey has shown, by Coleridge.[30] Rich and poor would be brought into communion within the church, rather than having their distinctions reinforced by their separate religious structures. The sufferings of the poor should be alleviated: the new Poor Laws (necessary in themselves) humanized, the soul-destroying ugliness of the new jerry-built urban housing, justified by laisser-faire, eliminated; ministers of the Church should not only visit the urban poor (a rare occurrence) but should be trained in the principles of political economy that they might explain to the working-class the "true causes" of their misery.[31] Like Carlyle, he saw that laisser-faire was an excuse for the aristocracy as well as the middle class to ignore its duties to govern with due concern for the workers, and in telling them so he drew their wrath.[32]

He was continually embroiled in arguments and attacks, which he met, even courted, with energy. Many of his proposals made sense, but he lacked tact, and once ruefully wrote that "if I had two necks I should think that I had a very good chance of being hanged by both sides."[33] It was not tactlessness alone, however, that brought opposing factions together against him. He regarded the end more than the means, and real and seeming contradictions mark his thinking throughout; one need not accept Strachey's well-known prejudices to perceive Arnold's faults.[34] Perhaps Archbishop Whately summed it up best when he wrote to a mutual friend in an unpublished letter dated 1833 that Arnold for all his "enormous energies" in his *Principles of Church Reform* was "as indolent as anyone in accurate reasoning but he has not the advantage of being sensible of this."[35] He demanded the right of free inquiry, but he desired to establish a Church-State. He had little respect for the manners and morals of the Catholic countries, but he wanted to erect roadside shrines in England (an idea Newman found an easy target for satire in *Loss and Gain*[36]). He urged the toleration of Dissent, but he would have excluded Unitarians and Roman Catholics from his *societas,* as well as Jews. To the latter he would have denied citizenship, and he joined the governing body of the only university in England that admitted them, with the purpose of making the study of Christian theology a prerequisite for the degree. When his motion failed and the Old Testament in Hebrew was made an alternative to the Gospels, he resigned.[37] His orthodoxy was questioned by his opponents, and not wholly without reason. As a young man he had hesitated for a year before taking orders, in a "morbid" state of depression, because he doubted the Trinity. He took Keble's advice, however, and repressed his misgivings by force of will and a "holy life"[38]—an episode which James Martineau and others have regarded as a "speck" on his consciousness that colored his thought thereafter.[39] He was reported by F. W. Newman to have doubted the authenticity of the Creation and Fall, of the First Gospel and of the Synoptic Gospels. He doubted Daniel as well, "for those times a very serious step."[40] His desire for communion with the poor did not, he thought, in any way threaten the social structure (although public opinion turned his proposals for lay deacons into the accusation that Dr. Arnold would have taken communion at the hands of his butler):[41] he insisted that he sought to preserve social distinctions while merely removing the abuses of wealth and authority.[42] He taught his students that American notions of individual liberty were barbarous, and he regarded the democratic reputation of the clergyman Horne Tooke with horror.[43] Human vice was a sanctioned target, but the English social structure was not.

The inconsistencies in general in Arnold's thought are well known and do not need to be established here; even his most recent expositor, on the whole a defender of Arnold, grants the inconsistencies of his "concessive" religious liberalism.[44] F. J. Woodward in particular has discussed the confusion in the Headmaster's thought between truth and goodness, values which sometimes appear to be identical and sometimes distinct. "He set up his own standard of goodness," she writes, "and did not care whether truth contradicted it or not."[45] In his own time, W. G. Ward said something similar: Arnold "*makes* the system first [of religious doctrine through his reading of Scripture,] and then he praises it."[46] What I wish to point out here is a discrete but similar problem, his tendency to see history as both a path to and a locus of truth, for this had a bearing on Clough's writings and was a confusion from which Clough had gradually to disentangle himself in a process that weakened his own grounds for faith. "There are men," Clough wrote of Arnold in a much quoted passage whose balancing qualifications, however, tend to obscure its biting irony, "too . . . practical to be literally, accurately, consistently theoretical; too eager to be observant, too royal to be philosophical . . . born to do, they know not what they do."[47] Such, as Clough said, was Arnold.

Clough did not write this, however, till 1849, more than a decade after he had left Rugby. Arnold's teachings about truth, in particular, seem to have played a considerable part in Clough's early intellectual development, and it may have been in the process of coming to grips with and ultimately rejecting these that Clough first began to grasp the nature of Arnold's intellectual failings. For in Arnold's thought, unlike that of the other Noetics, truth was not merely an abstract ideal under whose sanction intellectual inquiry should be pursued, but a value he wished in some way to realize, "grasp," or make concrete. In theory, Arnold's religious beliefs required no external proof, but in practice, with their barrenness of doctrine and the weakened position Scripture held in them, any evidence of the existence of God's providence was welcome. His thought ultimately evolved a system, whose circularity he did not perceive, in which truth, history, progress, reform, and Christianity demonstrated each other, and the existence of each was ultimately contingent on the existence of one or more of the others. Abstract truth, like the knowledge of goodness or God, was known intuitively through the conscience. But history was of immense importance: its study was "simply a search after truth" and this and progress also were revealed when history was "read aright." In that historical search, "by becoming daily more familiar with it, truth seems forever more within your grasp."

Clough came to doubt that history revealed the truth in any coherent way after a year and a half of study at Oxford, but to his former Headmaster history not only made truth seem graspable but "pointed the way to that higher region within which she herself is not permitted to enter."[48] In a certain sense, Arnold agreed with the "common" notion that "history is philosophy teaching by examples." Writing prefatory remarks to his bitter attack on the Tractarians (in which he compared them to the assassins of St. Paul among other historical miscreants), he justified his harshness in advance by saying that "history does furnish . . . when read aright . . . a mirror to reflect the true character of existing parties and so, to determine our judgment in taking part with one or another." Again he says, it is a "mirror" by which "to fix first the true standard of all political enterprise and then to judge of parties."

Moreover, history "shows that the world has on the whole advanced." Progress is the message to be learned when it is seen that "the heresy of one period becomes the orthodox faith of another." Reform, which was like progress in being "identical" with Christianity, was also the equivalent of truth. "It is false to say that the reform, or the truth, of a later age undoes . . . the reforms and the truths which have preceded them . . . [They hold them in honor] . . . but . . . farther reforming and developing some further truth."[49] Thus truth is both absolute and a continuous, relative process.

But although there might exist one region of absolute higher truth in which it mingled with goodness, reform, progress, Christianity, and so on, in practice Arnold was prepared to sacrifice truth to other values. First, and on principle, he affirmed that while he loved truth and justice better than any other virtues, they were as "idols" compared to his faith in the person of Christ—who embodied all virtues;[50] then, too, in practice, he was prepared to compromise the undeniable truth of the Anglican doctrines because it was necessary to save Christianity and the Church Establishment in England by merging with Dissenters.[51] And elsewhere he conceded that there might be more than one kind of truth—that a political as well as a moral one may exist, although the former is "less worthy"—and that a good deal depended on the human being's character, for truth required a "strong mind" to be appreciated keenly.[52]

Thus truth should be sought in history, but history would always reveal it, being the story of progress, reform, and Christianity. Not only did history have laws, but these " 'contain . . . no single paradox,' " and all were "in accord with Christian and Biblical ethics."[53] If inconvenient facts, like inconvenient compromises, cropped up, the "mirror" was simply turned to omit them: if Christianity had triumphed, truth, ipso facto, had triumphed also. When Clough, trained in this reasoning, discovered how relatively little Christianity had in fact triumphed, and when he began to realize the contradictions history yielded, Arnold's logic collapsed and with it all metaphysical certainty that aspired to base itself on rigorous logic. Had Arnold not presumed to cite a locus of truth, had he not, more importantly, felt the need so to locate it, Clough would have been less disturbed. As it was, he was left at twenty with the feeling that to attempt to discuss a certain class of ideas was both foolish and dangerous, and we see in his essays the gradual process by which his trust in this certainty was gradually eroded.

Balliol

In studying Clough's undergraduate essays, two points should be kept in mind: first, that they were written "under correction," on set topics, for personal presentation to the tutor to whom Clough read them; and second, that Balliol College and its Master, Dr. Richard Jenkyns, were different in almost every way from Rugby and Dr. Arnold.

Perhaps the fact about Balliol of most significance to this study is that at the time Clough reached the college it had behind it, and still clung to, a long tradition as a "stronghold of the most reactionary Toryism" and a seat of conservative religious views.[54] When Clough came up in 1837 Balliol had already begun to attain the intellectual preeminence it later held at Oxford, but the measures most directly responsible for that achievement, liberal in tendency, had been carried against the opposition of the Master of the college.[55] Clough came much into contact with Jenkyns, for he personally supervised most of Clough's English essays. Academic achievement was valued at Balliol, but the association of the principle of free intellectual inquiry with Whig politics which had prevailed at Oriel in Arnold's day did not exist at the other college.

Positively or negatively, his college could not but have a strong effect on a young man, particularly one of Clough's impressionable age and nature, for at Balliol some hundred-and-twenty-odd men lived intimately together for three or four years, sometimes for life, daily facing each other across the table at meals, sharing library and common room facilities, and in continual contact in tutorials and lecture rooms.[56] The university at large counted for relatively little: lectures were usually college lectures, and friends, if not from Rugby, were usually college friends. The tone of the place, intellectually speaking, was set by the dons, and Clough, with the special privileges and notice given a scholar, lived closer to his teachers than he had done at school, where one master had sometimes to deal with a form of forty or fifty boys.[57] The contact between Clough and his Balliol teachers was prolonged, profound, and came at a time when his mind was ready to be formed.

The Tory and Royalist ties at Balliol kept up by the Master, Dr. Jenkyns, were old ones and Jenkyns, who was a conservative, a "high-and-dry Churchman," and a snob, mentally associated the Arnoldians with heresy.[58] Thus he resisted a liberalizing proposal at Balliol in 1839 because "nothing was less to his liking than a measure which seemed to advertise Balliol as a refuge for the heretic and the Arnoldian." He was a shrewd judge of men, though himself possessing only "moderate" capacities; he did not agree with his younger colleague, the brilliant but erratic W. G. Ward, a tutor who had a close friendship with Clough, to whom Jenkyns said regarding his published defense of Newmanism, "Your book is like yourself, fat, awkward, and ungainly."[59] Jenkyns did not hesitate to join the other Heads of Houses in 1841 in condemning Newman's *Tract 90,* or to agree in deposing Ward from his tutorship when the opportunity arose.[60]

Jenkyns assigned and listened personally to twenty-one, or approximately two-thirds, of Clough's compositions. He appointed four fellows to share in the supervision of the others: John Carr, E. C. Woollcombe, P. S. H. Payne, and Archibald Tait.[61] All of them were undoubtedly "sound," if perhaps not quite so orthodox as the Master, for, as Mallet wrote, Jenkyns may have occasionally yielded to the reformers' pressure but "he appeased the conservatives by choosing for his prime ministers such men as . . . Tait and Woollcombe," who were acceptable to all parties in the common room.[62] Of Tait's soundness his subsequent career is testimony enough, for he went on (with Clough's testimonial, among others) to become Headmaster of Rugby and eventually Archbishop of Canterbury, England's highest ecclesiastical post. He was, while at Balliol, Ward's major opponent in the Balliol Senior Common Room and instrumental in the official actions later taken against both him and Newman.[63]

His own slight stuffiness, and the attitude of Clough's set toward him, is preserved like a fly in amber by some byplay that appears at the end of Clough's fourteenth essay, which Tait had assigned on the formidable topic, "The Prevalence Under Different Circumstances of Different Systems of Philosophy, Considered as an Index of the Character of any Age or Nation." The tutor was not satisfied with the result, and, beside his initials, commented, "somewhat wanting in clearness." Beneath that, and beside *his* initials, is the critique of "A. P. S.," probably Arthur Penrhyn Stanley, Clough's close friend and also a pupil of Tait: "O my dear dean, how like you." It is a little tickle at pomposity.

Less is known of the other three tutors, but there is no reason to suppose that they were any more liberal than Tait, who himself (after being converted to Anglicanism) began as an Arnoldian, like Ward, but in his years at Balliol moved further and further to the right in his opinions.[64] John Carr, who left the college in 1838, was, Benjamin Jowett wrote later, "a refined gentleman and scholar," but he was a little eccentric and "could hardly have been said to have studied with a purpose." P. S. H. Payne was "noble and simple" in character, but he "died early." E. C. Woollcombe, who had just received his B. A. in 1837, supervised only one of Clough's compositions and probably exercised a minimum of influence on him directly.[65]

All of them, however, joined in creating an intellectual and social atmosphere that could hardly have been more different from that of Rugby. In place of Arnold's dictum that the principles of advance and reform in their most perfect state were identical with Christianity, Clough now met Tories ready to quote Johnson's saying that the first Whig was the Devil. Instead of Sunday sermons whose effect no boy ever forgot, there was a free and easy atmosphere in which a don like the Rev. William Tuckwell, or "Tommy" Short, Newman's former tutor, might ride out on Sunday to preach his own or listen to a friend's sermon in a nearby village, enjoy the sight of the Master's pretty daughters (if he had any) in their pew, and then go on to a good dinner and an afternoon of whist—at which the visiting fellow clergyman who was too anxious to talk about religion was considered a bore.[66] And Clough knew after only a few months at Balliol that "anything so 'ungentlemanly' and 'coarse' and 'in such bad taste' as 'Evangelicalism' would never be able to make very much way" at Oxford, and thought for this reason that Tractarianism was the only thing that could, in "an age of activity and shaking-up" have done such "a vast deal of good at Oxford."[67] (It should be noted that in the same paragraph he nevertheless described the Newmanites as "savage and determined enemies.")

Clearly, what was expected of Clough under these circumstances was not expressions of political or religious liberalism—or, indeed, of any opinions on topical questions. What was wanted, as a glance at the titles of his essays will show (see Appendix A), was that he should learn to think clearly and analytically while making his own the broad moral principles and established opinions that were generally accepted on such traditional questions as the character of Venice (a common symbol of depravity), or the morals of the

French and ancient Athenians (not as reliable and steady as the Romans), or the relative values of commerce and agriculture. Above all, he was asked to read and write about Aristotle, "the wisest of the Greeks" (in Jenkyns's words), who was studied at Balliol even to the exclusion of Plato—whom Clough read of his own volition.[68] The real battles that were going on in the university were not expected to come to the surface in Clough's essays, and it is to his credit that he found in these time-worn topics material for his thoughtful and often deeply felt compositions. This, in part at least, explains why we see so little directly of Newman's or Carlyle's ideas. There are other important reasons also, which will be discussed below, but certainly Clough was aware of both these men and their writings, as we know from his correspondence, and no doubt the nature of his audience had a part in his excluding from his set essays references to or reflections of these contemporary thinkers.

A new source of information about Clough's behavior as an undergraduate has recently come to light in the Balliol College Examination Register, discovered among the College's Buttery records in 1963. Jenkyns began to keep this register in 1833, the year when for the first time three tutors (Tait, Ward, and Scott) agreed jointly to take responsibility for supervising the work of undergraduates.[69] In this record the Master entered a list of all undergraduates together with a terminal record of their work in the five subjects they studied: Divinity, Greek, Latin, Logic and Mathematics, and Exercises (English and Latin essays), with a separate column for "Morals." At the end of every academic year he noted which men had won prizes and honors both within and without the college, and which fellows had been university examiners. From this record it is apparent that Clough's conduct, even in what are known to have been periods of serious depression, was always "exemplary." Other students might seem "careless in minor points," or "inattentive in lectures" to the Master's observant eye; even Benjamin Jowett, who was considered so brilliant that he was elected to a fellowship before he was of age to hold it, was so criticized, while Matthew Arnold (whose English essays showed "promise") was wanting in "diligence"; but Clough was a model of regularity and steadiness, at least in outward appearance.[70] He was, as J. A. Froude once told him, a man whose thoughts were "inwards," and his inner turmoil did not express itself through the loss of his habitual reserve.[71] This register with its careful record of all the honors awarded to Balliol men points up Clough's failure, noted by other scholars, to win any of the several prizes for which he was eligible, or to become, in the Whatelian phrase he liked, a "prize gooseberry." (See Appendix B for texts and discussions of two recently found MS poems which prove that Clough twice entered works in competition for the Newdigate prize.)[72] Jenkyns's comments in his register on Clough's exercises are relevant, and his opinion, which was probably representative of that of other judges who read Clough's work, has been preserved there. Clough's writing, Jenkyns thought, suffered from a lack of facility, a want of ease and elegance. "Good—full of thought," reads a typical comment, "but sometimes obscure and unpolished in style"; or more tersely, "good—in matter." Towards the end of Clough's years at Balliol the Master was able frequently to record an "improved" or simply a "good," but never did he commend in him, as in others, "polish and elegance," or "neatness of style."[73]

His criticism is not unfair. Nothing was less epigrammatic than Clough's prose style; it shows great effort and careful thought, and sometimes rises to a certain nobility, but there was nothing consciously "polished" about it. It never fell into glibness or superficiality, but there was perhaps some justification in Matthew Arnold's later attack on Clough's writing for its want of "the *beautiful*."[74] Yet this weakness, or rather this trait, was, I believe, innate in Clough and was also part of his power as a writer. Even at his most light-hearted, Clough could never write well without conviction, and he could not write at all without having something to say. The polished style and neatly turned phrases that Jenkyns preferred and which depend on the refinement and restatement of premises which the writer assumes to be generally accepted were foreign to Clough's whole outlook. Like his transcendental man of business, demanding to see the world's accounts that he might scrutinize their honesty, he drove himself from the beginning, both by inclination and through the training he had had from Arnold, to examine and lay bare the logic of the opinions he held. If intellectual rigor were not always compatible with grace, Clough from his earliest efforts showed which quality he would pursue.

The Essays

The history of Clough's undergraduate essays is not that of the fading of the light within, as Clough seemed to think at the time, but of the fading of the influence of Arnold, and the subsequent sense of bewilderment and loss as Clough struggled to incorporate within himself the guidance that had hitherto been, if anything, too ready and too explicit. Biographers have already suggested in general terms the negative effects of Arnold's training;[75] here we can see in some thirty-four of Clough's own essays, written between 1837 and 1841 and not hitherto adduced in evidence, the process of the young man's reaction.[76] It is clear from them that Clough did indeed pass through a period of great personal strain: it is evident too that he emerged from this struggle a person whose significant attitudes and ideas differed markedly from those he had held four years earlier. He is less happy, less confident, less ready with solutions, programs, and goals; he is also in a real sense more intelligent because more independent, more capable of genuine if realistically limited judgments and authentic responses. He lamented that he "went wrong"[77] and one can not but sympathize with the evident agony of spirit and paralysis of will suggested in some of these essays. But one can not regret the loss of his "higher line"[78] so long as the "higher line" was so clearly mediated to him by Arnold and dependent on metaphysical assumptions which Clough had never before closely examined, and which appear to have crumbled when he did so.

Many, though not all, commentators have agreed that Clough as a youth was deeply concerned with the existence of truth, and that his loss of belief in its immanence under the attacks of his tutor W. G. Ward was a serious blow to him.[79] These essays reflect nothing directly of Newmanistic arguments. They do not argue for the authority of Rome, or take sides on the issue of tradition versus scripture, or consider the validity of Anglican doctrine, or refer to the medieval origin of church teachings, as Hampden had done, or in any way attempt to prove or disprove religious faith or church doctrine. But they do exhibit strikingly both Clough's early assumptions about truth's immanence and his later disillusion with those assumptions. They also give us new insight into what were

29

probably initially Ward's own arguments on the subject, arguments which seem to have had a significant and permanent effect on Clough's thought. Because his changing views on this subject seem to have been central to—indeed generative of—his other intellectual changes, the following discussion will focus on his treatment of that subject, and his specific social and political views will be discussed conjointly with that development.

Clough's views on truth showed Arnold's influence most clearly during his first year at Oxford. The first three or four essays of the eight he wrote that year (1837–38) brim over not merely with confident assertions about truth's existence but with specifically Arnoldian formulations, as he argues from the physical to the metaphysical world, identifies material and spiritual progress with Christianity, treats history primarily as a pedagogical or theological means of reinforcing religious faith, and easily identifies himself with those who confidently perceive "comforting" truths and look forward to seeing "truth higher and greater still." At the same time, he is full of strictures against sin, and he inveighs against frivolity with all the severity of the Headmaster who set himself to fight the "evil" he saw almost everywhere in the boys at Rugby.[80] Thus, asked in his second essay to consider the effects on literature resulting from the invention of printing, Clough held that because printing had been developed in the Christian era, literature had developed a progressive tendency. Classical learning, by comparison, was full of "wasted acuteness" and "rhetorical frippery." "Places of study," he complained, had in Roman times aptly been called places "of 'play' or 'recreation'." Today, things were different, and much better. "Let us compare all this," he wrote, intending no irony, "with our own busy world of reports of philosophical and learned societies, communications, discoveries, and so forth, and with [that] universal and constant spirit which has been infused, it would seem through Christianity, so completely into the modern mind, of *looking forward to truth higher and greater still,* and 'forgetting those things that are behind' " [Italics mine; No. 2].[81] Clough never defined the truth of which he spoke so confidently, but it is evident that, as with Arnold, it meant seeing in the world around him God's providential scheme, the continued triumph of progress, "reform," and moral virtue. Technological change was providentially inspired if its results were humane; if not, "reform" was needed. The opposite of truth was utilitarianism which based itself not on God's will but on material fact, and he inveighed against it and also against "physics," "love of gain," frivolity, and drunkenness. Art, of course, was the servant of morality.

Writing on "The Effect of Dramatic Representations on the Taste and Morals of a People," the youth held that the drama was an inferior kind of art and not likely to appeal much to people of "pure and refined" tastes who would naturally prefer poetry, which was closer to "Ideal Beauty." The only good thing he could find to say about the drama, in fact, was that the response of a theater audience did remind him of "how solemn a thing" it was to listen to a "large congregation" singing hymns. He himself was too high-minded to enjoy comedy. "Indeed it seems a question," he wrote, "what sort of comic representations are allowable properly in a Christian land, or what good can be done by them to the minds of a Christian people further than that merely of relaxation. That vices and sins should be checked in this way . . . seems hardly right . . . it seems clear that to any sincere Christian mind the contemplation of his neighbor's sin cannot but be painful, and therefore cannot be truly laughable" (No. 1).

In a couple of years Clough changed his mind, but by then, just as he had learned that truth was not so readily perceptible as he had once thought, so he had realized that it might be his own, and not his "neighbor's sin" that comedy meant him to "contemplate."

At least three of Arnold's favorite themes appear in this same first essay: the need to raise the poor into some kind of "moral union with their richer brethren," the assumption that man can attain the truth to a significant degree, and the deprecation of what Arnold called "godless utilitarianism."[82] Knowledge of the truth about God's intentions for man would, Clough explained in this essay, combat the false and shallow ideas of progress which constituted utilitarianism. The drama might not be the highest form of art, but perhaps, he imagined, by giving the masses contact with beauty it could uplift them and "raise the minds of the people generally above that love of gain which seems to be eating the very vitals of the nation and also in the poorer classes to present some enjoyment great enough to lead them to prefer it to drunkenness, and of such a nature as to elevate them into some moral union with their richer brethren" (No. 1). The working classes did in fact have their own theater, but the bawdy penny-gaffs Mayhew described a decade or so later in a book that Clough took with him to America, *London Labour and the London Poor,* were very far from anything that Clough, shut in by the same isolation of class culture against which he was protesting, could possibly have imagined or prescribed.[83] As for utilitarianism, Clough held that "it is a great matter to have the spirit of utilitarianism and of love for gain suppressed, and to suppress this there is no fitter engine than taste" (No. 1). Men should learn, he said severely, "that there are better things even in this world than railroads and steam engines." The "better things," of course, were paths to the higher truth: "It is a truth and a most comforting one that the use and cultivation of those faculties, which God has given us for the perception of beauty and of truth not only *can* be sanctified to his glory but moreover *are of themselves* conducive to the health and well-being of our spiritual nature" (No. 1).

In his second essay, Clough again set "the knowledge of Truth and the possession of the power of attaining it" in contradistinction to utilitarianism: progress was good, but the mechanization attending it had an evil side, for it "has led to an overweening and unworthy attention to physics, and a habit of asking in every study, 'what is the use of it,' as if *the knowledge of truth and the possession of the power of attaining it* were not in itself 'its own exceeding great reward': and as if God could not be glorified in the cultivation of the faculties he has given unless they were put to some practical operations." [Italics mine]

For Clough at this period, to attain truth meant, in effect, to attain spiritual insight into such matters as moral action, beauty, and providence: in short, it meant to be emotionally convinced of the value and meaning of ideals already intellectually accepted. It was a circular process, and his remarks on history during this year bear this out. Adopting an essentially Arnoldian position, Clough held that history existed not for its own sake, but for the purpose of teaching faith. Its "use" was, among other things, "the establishment in the minds of men of faith and confidence in the systems handed from their fathers and love and attachment to them." (To ask, "what is the use of it" was evil only, apparently, in the mouth of a utilitarian.) Therefore myths and legends tending to establish such faith and confidence had a rightful place in history—as long as enough time had passed to make them "authoritative." (This concept was promulgated earlier by B. G. Niebuhr, the German historian who was influential on Thomas Arnold. Niebuhr's ideas reappear in one of the notes to Clough's Newdigate poem, "The Judgement of Brutus" [see Appendix B], which he wrote within two or three months of Essay No. 8.) "The traditions we find existing, whether orally or in song or in sacred writings," Clough went on, were "benefits" to the cause of ancestral reverence, and might be included in histories once "time and tradition had done their duty in clothing them with a hallowed and authoritative character" (No. 8). Clough did not go so far as to say that myths ought to be taught as truths, but neither did he "strive to keep up" the "division" between them; the end was more important than the means.

A similar kind of intellectual carelessness for probability was the result on other occasions of this kind of teleological thinking. Thus he held that "the law of nations is a law essentially, almost exclusively Christian" (No. 4), and presumed in a later essay that the "noble" Stoics, whom he admired, could not have achieved their virtue without the benefit of Christian revelation. Therefore, they must have been strengthened in their resolution and comforted in their suffering "by the sight of the cheerful submission and the lively belief of the Roman Christians" (No. 12).

During his second year, however, Clough's essays begin to sound a different note. Previously they spoke in the voice of one consciously, even aggressively, taking pleasure in a sense of moral superiority to a life conceived through the medium of abstractions such as progress, ideal beauty, and sin. The syntax was highly latinate and spontaneity was lacking: one knew neither who the speaker was nor what he cared about, unless one were persuaded of the existence of an author who held to "comforting truths" and thundered his

33

assurance in clause after clause that "by [Christianity] alone" could man "set aright the relations" between man and man, and between man and God, and learn to strive to widen the division between good and evil (No. 4). A distinct change from this tone occurs sometime in the fall of 1838 and makes itself felt in two stages: first in a new sense of personal uncertainty and then in the articulation of that uncertainty on the intellectual level.

The experience of the self and the self-doubts which had hitherto been masked or repressed begin to be spoken of first in the fall of 1838 when Clough refers to the difficulties in real life, "in the rough unyielding material of action duly to set forth the expression of the lofty ideal within, itself so easily forgotten" (No. 9). In a passage unconsciously revealing his own inner conflicts with phantasy, mood swings, and the tendency to withdraw,[84] he writes that "men do not err usually from any excess of caution, but from an evil habit of mind which is confident in deciding, and timid in action. We yield ourselves up to our imaginations: and while it is yet in our power to decide for or against, we yield ourselves to the contemplation of the hopeful view . . . a reaction at once takes place, and we again obey slavishly those gloomy and desponding views with which our imagination now presents us" (No. 9). This understanding of internal conflict, as well as the manifest depression described, is something new in Clough's essays. The material is not yet used imaginatively; there is no narrative distance: it is the stuff of accidental confession, but honest confession nevertheless. To Arnold, no doubt, such expression would have indicated moral weakness: truth needs a "strong mind" to receive it, and the tone of introversion and the sense of helplessness evident here and in some of the succeeding essays does not bespeak a will ready to hold only the impression of the good and reject that of the bad. Yet it is just this new note and, indeed, this new material treated with increasingly aware and shaping objectivity which is sounded more and more significantly in Clough's prose and poetry alike. At the same time, the tone of irony so characteristic of the mature Clough but quite lacking in the letters of the preceding year has begun to make its appearance. "I hoped very much," he writes from Oxford to an anti-Newmanite friend about his own contacts with the Tractarians:

you would come here after your degree was done, but if you continue to rest on Milton's Xtn Doctrine for one leg and Calvin's Institutes for the other I recommend [you] to walk away on them as fast as you can and as far as you can from this Seat and Citadel of Orthodoxy. It is difficult here even to obtain assent to Milton's greatness as a poet, quite impossible, I should think, if you are unable to say that you 'do not know anything about his prose writings' . . . Were it not for the happy notion that a man's poetry is not at all affected by his opinions or indeed character and mind altogether, I fear the Paradise Lost would be utterly unsaleable except for waste paper.[85]

If we look to Clough's reading to account for his intellectual and emotional changes at the period, we will not find a great deal to instruct us. He is familiar with the classical authors of his syllabus, with Butler, with Wordsworth, and with other poets, and by the spring of 1839 he had read Friedrich von Schlegel's *Essai sur la langue et la philosophie des Indiens* in its French translation, and possibly also his *Philosophy of History,* which will be discussed below.[86] None of these, however, would account for the quality or degree of the dilemma of which Clough's contemporary poetry speaks so eloquently and which is articulated also in his essays. There is a considerable amount of other evidence, including Clough's letters and Ward's own testimony, which points at Balliol's Logic tutor as being the author of at least some of the young poet's disturbance.[87] Scholars have long taken into account what by Ward's own later confession was an attempt to convert his students, especially Clough, to the Newmanism to which he himself was converted in 1838; he is said to have urged his pupils to follow him, insisting they "Believe in nothing or believe in the one true Church."[88] From Ward's letters to Clough, not published until 1952, we learn that the tutor's involvement with his student was even more intense than it was pictured in the nineteenth century: one cannot but infer from his nearly hysterical demands for a list of "assurances" about whom Clough shall see, how long (three to four weeks) he shall visit him during vacation, etc., that Ward loved Clough intensely and jealously, although not in the literal sense homosexually, and that Clough, for his part, seems to have tried with kindness both to keep him at arm's length and to help him in some fashion better to understand and control his conduct.[89] The emotional burden was certainly too great, and to it must be added his worries about his father's imminent business failure and the "cloud of degree" hanging over him, concerns which became articulate in the fall of 1839.[90] However, there is no evidence of Tractarian thought in Clough's published work, and the specific content of that influence has been a puzzling issue. The consensus has therefore been that Ward's intellectual influence was negative to Clough's faith and to Arnold's training, but little more could be said on the subject. Clough's essays, however, unlike his letters which generally shun substantive discussion of issues, give us new insight into some of the specific elements of Ward's thought which the younger man incorporated into his own. Naturally, they do not mention directly the tutor whose ideas were unpopular with Jenkyns and his subordinates, but they do follow quite closely one of the arguments Ward was formulating against Arnold and his view of history as capable of revealing truths to mankind. This issue was a central one, for not only was history a bulwark to faith, but the methods that attacked it could also be turned against the Bible itself—and then indeed the Tractarian arguments from tradition and Church authority would be left in command of the field. Scripture was in a vulnerable position, and in fact B. G. Niebuhr, the great German historian whom Arnold revered, had already canceled his Biblical researches, carried out by historical methods, in part because his findings seemed to promise a threat to religious faith.[91] Ward, however, secure in Tractarianism, did not hesitate to point out the weakness of hoping to find truth from the study of history. Specifically he rejected Arnold's wish to found a political science on its basis. Arnold "*makes* the system first, and then he praises it" Ward wrote scornfully of the other's presuming to find doctrine in Scripture.[92] " 'There is not a fact in history,' " he held, quoting another writer, " 'which is not susceptible of as many different explanations as there are possible theories of human affairs . . . History by itself, if we knew it ten times better than we do, could prove little or nothing; but the study of

it is a corrective to the narrow and exclusive views which are apt
to be engendered by observation on a more limited scale.' "[93] He
used a similar argument later, holding that to try to prove the truth
about early Christian doctrine through historical researches would
be a superhuman task. "Nor can it be said that [the seeker's] per-
plexity would remain but for a short time; for our own parts, we
should be inclined to say that, on a very moderate computation,
five times the amount of man's natural life might qualify a person,
endowed with extraordinary genius and power of research, to have
some faint notion (though this we doubt) on which side truth lies."[94]

These arguments, as we shall see, appear directly in Clough's
thirteenth and seventeenth essays, and the color of their pessimism
is washed across the others as well. Ward resolved his own epistemo-
logical dilemma by acts of faith, by his desire obediently to submit
to Church authority, and ultimately by his conversion to Roman
Catholicism. What he could not discover for himself he would accept
on the authority of men and institutions more divinely guided than
he: man could judge his teachers, he reasoned, but not what they
taught; he particularly attacked Arnold for believing in the Trinity
but not that he was "defend[ed] on earth" by "holy angels."[95] Passionate acts of faith, the longing to swallow the camel as well as
the gnat which characterizes Ward's mode of belief, were out of
character for Clough, and the older man's desperate terror of having
nothing in which to believe was not shared by Clough. Such a condition was painful, and he was to know its full extent, but he would
not attempt to minimize or deny it falsely by willing to know what
his conscience should of its own accord tell him. The "intuitions,
idealities, etc., etc." with which he resisted Newmanism were in
fact anything but unstable, for they remained with him the rest
of his life. Nothing in Ward had power over their integrity, and
while logic could move him, anxiety or the inability to tolerate philosophical ambiguity could not.

But that Ward could and probably did give him new questions
one may see in an essay written in January 1839. Writing on "The
Philosophy of History," Clough no longer regards history as an instrument of his teleology meant to teach men "faith and confidence
in the systems handed from their fathers and love and attachment

to them" (No. 8). On the contrary, history was now to be studied not to discover God, but man. He rejected the idea that a historian might, by *a priori* reasoning about the "course and successive stages of society," become the "highest and paramount authority" on the "great questions of life." He reiterated the traditional view that history had lessons to teach man, but now he maintained also that the study of history led to "the general study of human character in its social development" and that this aimed at answering two questions of primary importance: 1) What are the purposes of Human society, and 2) how can we attain those aims? "Political truth" rather than "higher" truth was now his aim. "The study of man's nature, of his faculties and duties, is the true method of search for political truth," Clough wrote, almost as if offering the argument on this "very important subject" which Ward in his review of Arnold's *Sermons* had hoped to include "in a future number."[96] Man's attention should be turned to "the course and progress of society . . . the various effects and tendencies of agriculture, manufacturers . . . commerce and communication." But to these studies, he concluded, "the philosophy of history is utterly unequal . . . truths of such consequence . . . should not be left to rest on such uncertain foundations as the inductions of the historian" (No. 13). Almost as if summarizing the direction his own thought was to take, he concluded prophetically that to the theoretical approach to history must be added "the life and character obtained by the transition to the concrete from the abstract."

Although Ward was probably largely responsible for the negative attitude Clough now maintained towards the subject, it is possible that he may in some measure have been responding also to the work of Friedrich von Schlegel. We know that he had read Schlegel's *Essai sur la langue et la philosophie des Indiens* in its French translation before April 18, 1839,[97] for he cites it as one of his authorities in the MS poem, "Salsette and Elephanta," which he submitted for the Newdigate prize that year.[98] In all probability, Clough was also familiar with Schlegel's *Philosophy of History,* which had been available in English in the Bodleian Library since 1835, for not only does Clough's essay titled "The Philosophy of History" reflect both in its title and content the basic assumptions of Schlegel's theories, but other essays as well show close parallelisms with the German's interpretations of classical history.[99] Friedrich von Schlegel, the famous German literary historian and Sanskrit scholar, brother of Auguste, had in his old age produced a two-volume Leibnizian *systema theologicum,* as J. B. Robertson wrote, consisting of *The Philosophy of Life* (1827) and *The Philosophy of History* (1828).[100] Dissatisfied with the course of German religion (he was himself a Roman Catholic convert), which he saw as tending towards either pantheism or rationalism, and perhaps disturbed by his own findings in comparative religious studies, Schlegel made it his mission to produce a philosophical system which would "restore . . . the lost image of God" to man by reconciling historical, metaphysical and scientific truths under one truth inductively perceived. His method involved the broadest of generalizations, and major unorthodoxies. One of the basic concepts on which he based his remarkably ambitious aim was that, contrary to received opinion, there had been revelations of God's truth to man, admittedly in "primitive" form, at a time previous to the Judeo-Christian era. This revelation to the Indian and Chinese cultures had since become mixed with the "slime" of idolatry,[101] but it alone could account for the spirit Schlegel saw breathing, for example, through the Hindu Vedas of whose Brahma he wrote, nearly ecstatically, "It is HE . . . It is God himself."[102] He too, going further than Arnold, viewed history not merely as a potential source of God's revelation of truth to man but specifically raised it to the level of Scripture, conscience, and science (or nature) as sources of truth. Of him one might say, as Ward said of Arnold, that he made his system first and then praised it: the scope and tone of his scheme may be glimpsed in such statements as:

The most important subject, and the first problem of philosophy, is the restoration in man of the lost image of God . . . To point out historically in reference to the whole human race, and in the outward conduct and experience of life, the progress of this restoration in the various periods of the world, constitutes the object of the philosophy of history . . . To point out the progressive restoration in humanity of the effaced image of God, according to the gradation of grace in the various periods of the world, from the revelation of the beginning, down to the middle revelation of redemption and love, and from the latter to the last consummation is the object of this philosophy of history.[103]

Even without Ward's influence Clough might well have been given pause by such assertions. Certainly, if Schlegel is the model he has in mind in his thirteenth essay when he writes that "truths of such consequence . . . should not be left to rest on such uncertain foundations as the inductions of the historian," one can understand and sympathize with his conclusion. (These "uncertain foundations" were also attacked by a reviewer in the Tractarian journal, in which Ward published, *The British Critic*.[104])

Early in May of the same year, Clough had another opportunity to comment on the study of history, and again his views both differ from those of the preceding year and suggest the tutelage of Ward. Asked in his seventeenth essay to discuss the effects on Greek morals and culture of the Peloponnesian war, Clough's tone in his prefatory remarks is valedictory and a trifle sad: he disclaims not only responsibility for realizing faithfully the truths of the historical question he is about to discuss but also the possibility that historical studies in general could provide man with truths in any significant way. His argument parallels Ward's closely. The ordinary man's imaginative reconstruction of the past, Clough now thinks, is likely to be enticing but false, and honesty would compel him to admit this if he should look back over his past errors of interpretation:

While the due appreciation of the past can belong to no one but a man endowed with the most exalted perceptions of abstract truth, the peculiar nature of historical evidence lays us open to crude results and premature deductions in their most enticing and plausible forms. Each succeeding year may furnish us with a new and lively picture of Greek morals and manners, and the experience of the last suffice but to convince us that all we had before imagined was unreal and unfounded. We must either sacrifice the certainty of complete truth to obtain the freshness and vigor of genuine perception, or resign this latter advantage for those cold and half-realized assertions, which one day we believe we shall recognize as the whole and perfect truth (No. 17).

With these words, Clough recognizes the dilemma that Arnold and Schlegel faced before him but chooses a different solution, determining to put his faith not in "enticing" perceptions that might become invalid within the year, but in facts, "cold, half-realized assertions," that may be less satisfying than "genuine" insights, but also less ephemeral and more reliable. The "day" in which he hopes to know the "whole and perfect truth" would not be a day in ordinary time, but at least in the meanwhile he should not delude himself. He cannot help hoping; he still has "hauntings of a purer mind," as he describes them in a Wordsworthian way in "Salsette and Elephanta," written in the preceding months: "[which] yet, as wilful children, when they roam, / Turn oft their hesitating glances home," but he knows his state of innocence is past. The "primeval Truth divine" he dwelt on there, and of which Schlegel had also written, now "gleamed" only "faintly."[105]

The passage from the essay just discussed is the last generalized statement Clough makes about the possibility of knowing abstract truth in this world. When in later years he writes "It fortifies my soul to know / That, though I perish, Truth is so,"[106] he speaks, to use an Emersonian term, in the optative mood and not the declarative. He still believes in the *nous,* in the ultimate intelligibility of all things in accordance with God's will, but not in his—or for all practical purposes, any man's—capacity to perceive it while still in what he had learned to call, perhaps from Ward, this "state of probation" (No. 28). When he does speak of truth it is most often in a negative context, as something ignored by the majority of men, or else as a superior kind of fact, a generalized concept relating facts or giving insight into them. Thus in a late essay written in the autumn of 1840 he distinguishes between "mere facts" and "real truths," but these truths are now insights not into God's providence but into underlying psychological and moral motivations in human behavior: and he finds history to be superior in a limited way to biography not because it teaches man to revere tradition but because it conceptualizes human action and makes it comprehensible. "What biography yields to history," he writes, "is the vivid picture of the influence of the age on men. From . . . [the family memoirs of the Romans] we derive amid . . . every possible misstatement of mere fact a real picture nevertheless of real truths—representations whose truth the event established of pride, patriotism, obedience to discipline, submission to authority—all those other qualities which distinguished early Romans and left to their late posterity the empire of the world" (No. 30).

And in a work from the same period on "The Art of Rhetoric," Clough makes man's fallen state and his failure to follow the truth the reason for the degradation of rhetoric itself. Once it had aimed at "the mere conveyance from one mind to another of the knowledge or perception of truths relating to the nature of actions." In that golden age, "in a pure state . . . men could not otherwise act than from intellectual conviction that such and such action was in accordance with justice and with the will of God" (No. 32). Now, however, the art of rhetoric rested on the opposite assumption, or "the presupposition that [the state of ideal innocence] exists no more . . . the course of our vessel is guided . . . by the chance winds of heaven and the varying currents of the deep" (No. 32). In the same vein, writing in May 1840, he holds that it would require a mind "superhumanly strong" and a "love of truth beyond the love of mortals" to live uncorruptedly in the corrupt world. He therefore finds the contradiction between Plato's ideal of the philosopher-king and the actuality of Plato's own retirement from the world to be entirely reasonable. Using the metaphor of the sea, as he does also in the essay on rhetoric (No. 32) and often in his poetry to describe the threatening and morally dissolving forces of life, Clough writes of Plato that it was "enough for him . . . if in the general tempest he could find some little creek or haven in the which to shelter his bark and look on in sorrowful contemplation. Madness would it be and worse than madness were he to leave his hard-gained harborage to join in unequal conflict with the mid-sea's winds and waves" (No. 28).

This description of Plato's condition evidences one of two concomitant developments which appear in these essays roughly at the same time as Clough's sense of the immanence of truth begins to fade: the pragmatism which has often been noted in Clough's thought,[107] and the seemingly contradictory but actually complementary depressiveness and genuine *angst* evident also in such verse as "Blank Misgivings of a Creature Moving about in Worlds not Realised."[108] The two tendencies exist side by side and in dialectic with each other: their synthesis is in his poetry, and the period 1839–41 was indeed one of Clough's most fruitful ones poetically.

Clough's growing pragmatism is expressed in different ways and on different subjects, but essentially it is based on a newly humanistic attitude, seeking to understand man's purposes and proper sphere of action not on the basis of teleological assumptions but through the study of man himself and the recognition that man's ground of being must be known through experience rather than through contemplation of the light within. One of the earliest assertions of this viewpoint is made in his eleventh essay, written in November 1838, near the beginning of his second year. In it his world is still a purposive one where good and evil demand choice and where poetry has a course of development and an "object" also—to lead man to a "higher and healthier frame of mind." But it is also a world in which patterns of development in human affairs require purely human study. The possibilities seem new and fascinating. Luxury, leisure, civilization, and "self-contemplation" have produced new studies: moral and natural philosophy (which he had once despised as "physics"); logic, the "not unnatural product of its time"; the study of languages; and, above all, political economy, the study of man in society, which is as important as moral philosophy itself: "Finally come works regarding man in his social character and the development of a new and extensive class of questions not less difficult and not less important than those of moral philosophy itself. The Republics of Plato and Cicero, and the Politics of Aristotle in the old world, and in the new the writings of Grotius and Puffendorf on the Law of Nations and the works of political economists are examples of this branch of literature" (No. 11). The names of the great dramatists and poets, philosophies, and branches of study with their "infinite variety of additions" roll exuberantly across the page, and we become aware that after a year at Oxford Clough has begun to substitute for the negativity which had censured classical "frippery" and hinted at his own more pure and refined appreciation of the Ideal, an enthusiasm for the real and for learning of all kinds.

He recognizes now that "it is useless to have a theoretic knowledge

43

of [the great machine of man's social system] without a practical experience of its working" (No. 13). And in his next essay he again asserts from the point of view of a kind of primitive determinism that neither individuals nor nations can remain uninfluenced by the age in which they live: indeed, the very perception of truth itself now seems to him in some degree a cultural phenomenon. The age, he points out, influences even those very individuals "who betray great pleasure and complacency in any real or imagined liberation from its effects. Still less can we doubt that particular deficiencies and peculiar impulses such as form the distinction of character between nation and nation should lead to the apprehension or rejection of particular portions of truth or of error" (No. 14).

In the same essay (written immediately after his critique of the philosophy of history), he goes so far as to suggest that modern religion is, like the modern philosophy of utilitarianism, equally the "offspring of . . . previous failure[s]": "Were we to proceed to the examination of the various fluctuations of the human mind with regard to religion, whose office in modern times involves that of the ancient philosophies, we should find examples no less striking than numerous . . . [This would illustrate the] common canon that the prevalence of low views and low systems points to the previous failure of others more lofty and more pretending" (No. 14).

From such pessimism he turns in reaction to its antithesis and begins simultaneously in the spring of 1839 to assert the values of the will, of human activity, productivity, and perseverance. Commerce, involvement with others, obedience to discipline, even satire, as an instrument of the moral will, he now stresses. Of the business spirit which he earlier termed the "love of gain which seems to be eating the very vitals of the nation" (No. 1) he now sees broadening and energizing consequences. To be sure, the loss of one's roots through the effects of trade is "pernicious," he writes, possibly thinking of his own father's pathetically unfulfilled life (No. 18). The primary object of trade is money, and money produces an "aristocracy of wealth," under whose blighting influence "self-respect, kindness and nobleness" are "sacrificed," and servility fostered. Yet "commerce has doubtless its benefits: it gives men, if not so much in our times the enlarged and capacious mind free from narrow and exclusive prejudice, yet certainly that wisdom of the serpent which is all powerful in the discovery of means to an end . . . could we once deprive commerce of its selfishness, its natural vigor and activity in the service of noble and disinterested feelings would work effects beyond hope or calculation" (No. 18). He repeats his endorsement of commerce later, again stressing that it encourages men to be active. Aristotle was wrong in censuring trade: "In the vulgar crowd of usurers . . . and petty traffickers [Aristotle overlooked] the elements of the only instrument which could effectively call out the resources of nature and fulfil to its legitimate extent the divine command to subdue the earth . . . A view of society so exclusive of this duty of cultivating our portion of the earth can hardly be considered otherwise than imperfect" (No. 23).

Clough's inability to discipline himself to work seems to have been a severe problem for him and appears to lie behind a rather remarkable essay. Paradoxically, in some ways it is the most Carlylean of all he wrote in style and in what one might call its manifest content; in its latent content, the emotive qualities which occasionally border on hysteria and incoherence, one hears a voice perhaps not really so different from certain of Carlyle's tones but certainly not one whose apparent sense of helplessness Carlyle would have approved. From a period beginning early in 1840, a few months before he was due to take his degree examination, Clough's increased depression is evident in his letters: he wishes the "ordeal" were over, "even though it were in a failure," he wishes for the "pleasant treadmill routine of school" rather than the unstructured situation of a university; he "shrink[s]" at the thought of taking orders, and the examination itself (which he ultimately postponed for another year) is a "cloud . . . right before me."[109] This is the language of his correspondence, in which, true to his personal style, he tries to control his anxiety by expressing the facts of his condition with relatively little directly emotive language. The quasi-anonymity offered, however, by an essay which was to be written in the third person on a supposedly impersonal topic apparently made licit a tone that is at once more powerful in allusion and metaphor, and more painful to read than that of any other prose piece that he wrote at this period. The Germanic inversions add to the Carlylean quality of his approach and suggest the central chapters of *Sartor Resartus*, as he takes up Aristotle's famous dictum that the man who does not need or cannot relate to society is either a beast or a god. Man must live and work in society, Clough writes in February, 1840:

He, once set within these bounds of time and space, is committed to the work: and as wisely may he strive to shake himself loose from existence itself as believe that . . . he can escape the no less wondrous mystery of relation. . . . The earth too, as with a wise solicitude, urges the stranger to his task: she refuses the food he will not with his mates labor for; the shelter and security he will not cooperate to seek: with cold and nakedness, hunger and thirst as her scourges [she forces] him to begin the work and once begun permits him not to intermit (No. 25).

Though engrossed by a "vision of more than material beauty," Clough writes with intensity, he "must go forth among his peers" despite his "heart['s] . . . assurance" that he and others "are creatures depraving and depraved, and that as heat passes unseen from body to body so evil radiates invisibly and ever from soul to soul."

From the same depression and sense of surrounding evil came a striking metaphor of emotional and physical paralysis. "Yet to stand still avails not, nor is possible; it is useless to close fast the mouth that it speak not and, as it were, with hands too thin and small to seek to hide the face and eyes that speak no less." Yet action alone is not enough: action holds its own terrors: "And yet it is far from enough to go forth bodily and readily: we must add to our readiness caution and temper our boldness with discretion. He that does not this may ere long have to fly like Timon from the world he so confidently entered, or worse . . . have to rush in horror and despair from guilt now done and now no more to be undone, seeking with lifted hands for that he shall not obtain, to forget and to exist no more, like Cain from the murder of Abel" (No. 25).

The imagery of fratricide and the most embittered social exile is strikingly out of keeping with the commonplace homily to which it is attached, and the incongruence gives evidence of the emotional pressure behind what was for Clough at this time a highly loaded subject. Ordinarily his prose conceals the emotions and sensitivities which find expression in his poetry: when occasionally they escape into his prose, as in the fragment beginning "An Ill World, Apemantus," (which contains the only other reference to *Timon of Athens* in the prose studied here), or the third "Letter of Parepidemus," the effect, as Clough once imagined his self-revelation would be, is indeed that of "a flood of lava boiling-hot amidst their flowery ecclesiastical fields and parterres.[110]

The end of this strange and tortured essay is as paradoxical, ambivalent, and syntactically confused as Clough himself now was about his subject, the social structure and man's relation to it. To consider society is to recall the Fall with a Miltonic sense of loss. "The structure of human society" is now seen as a "Tower of Babel," and "some timidly shrinking, some hurrying madly forward, some goaded on by the taskmaster, each and all have laid a stone to the pile: few and far between have those appeared who while they labored to subdue the earth . . . retained even as much as a loving memory 'of the light / Full early lost and fruitlessly deplored' which shone at the first around them." Almost as if goading himself onward, Clough ends with a Draconian peroration whose closing lines are almost incoherent: "he who through indolence . . . shows himself incapable of social action sinks to less than man: he who through courage and patience overcomes the evil of his social conditions rises at last to more . . . as we believe in existence, so we also believe in relation independent of those fluctuations and released from those trammels of necessity which render the one alike and the other in this our present state fit neither for beast nor god, for less or more than man."

Clough's new knowledge of his own weakness, however, was not wholly negative in its effects, nor did it exist without its countervailing insights. Although at times one feels that the references to the dulling of conscience (No. 22), or the almost gratuitous comment that no sins are forgiven in this world, no errors even of the "novice" can be "undone" (No. 26), are evidence of a nearly obsessive sense of personal guilt and shame, it appears that at the same time Clough is gaining practical insight into certain human and social phenomena he had previously misunderstood. Thus satire, which by implication he had earlier condemned (No. 1), he now praises for its moral effect as the "means whereby a love of virtue and excellence in circumstances of general depravity has best found a vent. . . . Numbers too careless to heed, and too hardened perhaps to appreciate the more usual and universal admonitions, are by the keen edge of satire roused to a sense of their folly and baseness" (No. 22).

Clough now is able to understand the mode he was to use so well, and able to know that it stemmed from a sense of discord in life: "Midway between the [poet and orator] stands satire, in many ways genuine poetry, yet in its angry indignant spirit giving indications numerous and evident of a position among the jarring and discordant elements of what is technically termed life" (No. 22). Envy he understands now too, and he seems to interpret it through personal reflection. In its most common form it was not the rage of a Miltonic Satan but a more passive emotion, that seeks "To close the eye that it see not, and the ear that it hear not; to harden the heart lest it feel, and to blunt those moral perceptions which would but too truly tell us of that which we might have been or even now might be—this is a task that calls for little effort" (No. 24). He understands by this time "how needful" it seems at times "to acquiesce in the second-best" and how quickly man comes to "deny to others the existence of that higher excellence which we . . . consciously departed from" (No. 24).

Burdened as he was at this time by emotional and intellectual strains, this was not for Clough a period of exploration in social or political questions. His essays touch on such issues as democracy, civil liberties and their acquisition, slavery, and marriage, but these are not central to the essays and his opinions do not depart from those he might have learned from Arnold or Carlyle. Significant in its absence, for example, is any reference to the economic depression of the late 1830's and the subsequent increase of Chartist activity. Once Clough had taken his degree he became a freer agent in several ways than he was at Balliol, and in the forties his adoption of certain relatively radical attitudes, and some Carlylean ones, becomes striking. At this point, however, his debt to the older man is ambiguous. His interest in Carlyle was keen and we know that he read the *Essays, French Revolution,* and *Chartism* as an undergraduate; we may safely assume that he knew *Sartor Resartus,* by which Carlyle had gained fame. The young poet's opinions vary but are generally favorable; indeed they are, for Clough, unusually explicit in their praise: Carlyle's work is "very beautiful," "very fine," "somewhat heathenish"; he feels for it "increasing admiration."[111] But for the most part those ideas of Clough which most parallel Carlyle's—for example the highly qualified sympathy for the masses, and the distrust of egalitarian democracy—may also be found in Arnold's thought and that of other contemporary liberals. Stylistically, except for the twenty-fifth essay, there is no such strong evidence of Carlyle's influence in the period 1837–41 as there is later on, for instance in the *Retrenchment* pamphlet of 1847.

To Clough in these dark days, democracy of the sort suggested by the phrase *vox populi, vox dei* could only be viewed with deep distrust.

If the lives of the great majority express individually desertion of that which is the true and only best, and acquiescence more or less reluctant in some one out of the many mere second-bests—if that which is seen in single men be for the most part revolt from the particular voice of God which speaks in the conscience of each, how can we expect that the combination will give for result that very voice itself? . . . is it not . . . to be thought that this Vox Populi is the voice of him whose name is "Legion," the din from the thousand voices of chaos and outer darkness? (No. 31)

Both Arnold and Carlyle in his *Chartism* were equally suspicious of the principle of egalitarian democracy, but counseled, as Clough now does, that those in power should listen to the demands of the poor and ameliorate the evils of their condition. "If there is indeed all this flux and fickleness, then may we not deem that . . . a cry in which many join and persevere in joining is indeed a real utterance, and if not to be revered as the voice of God, to be respected as the voice of man? . . . do we not come at last to something worthy to be called vox dei?" (No. 31).

In like fashion Carlyle, writing *Chartism* in 1839, had held that the rioting Chartist laborers who were petitioning for the vote should be given not self-government—which could lead only to "rebellion . . . No-Government and *Laissez-faire,*" but "food, shelter, due guidance," and education. "He that will not work," wrote Carlyle in words that Clough was to echo, "let him go elsewhither; let him know that for *him* the Law has made no soft provision . . . Work is the mission of man in this earth." Nevertheless, as Clough after him suggests, the cry of the people could not forever be ignored, and "the central fact forces itself on us, the claim of the Free Working-man to be raised to a level, we may say, with the Working slave; his anger and ceaseless discontent till that be done . . . pacific mutual division of the spoil, and a world well let alone, will no longer suffice."[112]

Abolition was a subject for radical agitation throughout the 1830's, but Clough's opinion on the rights or civil liberties of former slaves are only an extension of those he held on democracy generally, and again one may find parallels in the writings of Arnold and Carlyle.[113] Rome fell to the barbarians, Clough writes, in part because of the evil moral effects of the "admission of emancipated slaves and their children" with all their "slavish arts" to full citizenship. Like Carlyle, who in *Chartism* urged the "right" of the ignorant man to be governed, "gently or forcibly," by the wiser, so Clough wrote that former slaves deserved not "the perilous gift of self-government" but "careful, affectionate guidance," for the "State must number her menials among her sons . . . possessed . . . of peculiar claims on her favor" (No. 34).

In what is perhaps Clough's only remark in these essays about the condition of women, he interestingly links it with slavery, just as the reformers who held forth in Exeter Hall in the 1830's were doing. Aristotle's "fatal error" was to "regard one man as essentially distinct from another, one nation a nation of masters, another of born-slaves, [and allow] self-government . . . only to a few. Therefore with him the relation of marriage is not that of two human beings each with the same object united for mutual encouragement and assistance: slavery with him is a hopeless, eternal subordination" (No. 23). Clough did not favor slavery per se any more than he favored the subordination of women, but he looked, like his mentors, for the "cultivation" of the masses—indeed, held that to be the criterion of human government (No. 23)—before full freedom should be granted them as a privilege, and not a right.

A sense of the distance Clough had traveled in the writings of the four years we have been examining may perhaps best be got from comparing his first and last essays. In both he is asked to discuss the formation of national character and in both he seeks to establish a causal relationship between a nation's culture and its spiritual qualities. There, however, the parallel ends. His first essay, "On the Effect of Dramatic Representations on the Taste and Morals of a People," had envisaged a morally purposive universe influenced by the uplifting power of ideal beauty, the degrading tendency of material pursuits, the solemnity of public worship, and the "comforting truth" that man may perceive truth. None of this teleology appears in his thirty-fifth essay, on "The Causes Which Contributed to Render the Romans a Great Conquering People." Two causes only had formed the Roman character: geography, and the psychological effect of valuing obedience more than civil liberty:

The exceedingly slow growth of civil liberty—the great length of the discipline to which the plebeian estate was subjected . . . was of great advantage to [the Romans] . . . The government was allowed to remain in full strength; obedience never ceased to be regarded as a chief virtue; while on the other hand patience and hope under long disappointment, eagerness to seize and resolution to establish every opportunity, firm determination to yield no step once gained in advance, these and other excellencies were the fruit of their labors in that long contest carried on under the guidance of their tribunes by the body of the people (No. 35).

Clough had begun by defining man's virtue as his achievement of certain spiritual, teleological aims; the last essay concerns itself not at all with where the obedient and determined Roman citizen was going, nor with the ideals, whether of beauty or truth, by which he was influenced: he did not need to fix his gaze on providence; all that mattered was that he should proceed steadily on his way without stumbling. His style in this last essay reflects his new approach: "We may at any rate believe that though the Roman character was a fine character from the first, it was more than any other favored by the sunshine and the storm of fortune . . . in a manner singularly providential" (No. 35). These are the last words

51

of Clough's undergraduate prose compositions. His singularly casual use of the adjective "providential," which with its Christian connotations has to jostle for place at the end of a string of jumbled terms connoting concepts at once deterministic and fatalistic, is perhaps symbolic of the way Clough's understanding of that key word had developed in those three and a half years. The hegemony of the Ideal had given way to that of fact, consciousness of righteousness to consciousness of sin, the immanence of truth to the necessity of duty. "Truths higher and greater still" had less interest for him than "the life and character" present in the world around him and gained by the "transition from the abstract to the concrete."

In general, then, one can say of Clough's undergraduate political and religious views that although they reflect radical changes in him, they are not radical in the common sense. On the whole, they show the influence of Arnold rather more than that of anyone else, but one can say this only with strong qualifications, for they express his reaction against Arnold as well. Carlyle, whom we know from external evidence Clough was reading enthusiastically, seems to have contributed towards Clough's style and ideas on one or more occasions, but the poet chose carefully among Carlyle's notions, adopting the more neutral ones, such as the value of work, but eschewing, for example, his doctrine of the strong man, already incipient in *Sartor Resartus* and the *Essays,* and skirting around their basic élitism just as he avoided Ward's exaggerated and short-lived stress on the holiness of self-denial. He gained from Ward an unanswerable argument against Arnold's historicism and teleology; there are those who feel Clough paid too heavy a price for the destructive logic he probably absorbed from Ward, but to say this is to forget how much in Ward Clough chose to ignore. One cannot but feel that he would have discovered the weaknesses of Arnold's doctrinal position without Ward, as others had done, and that his emotional depressiveness may have been aggravated by his tutor's powerful personality, but is unlikely to have been induced by it. Clough's struggle during this period, as with most students his age, was not purely intellectual but intellectual and personal at the same time: in learning to choose among Arnold's teachings rather than to depend on them indiscriminately, he was learning also to choose his own personal style and to know his own moral being, to leave behind the self-righteous tone Arnold had fostered and the self-congratulatory attitude he later satirized as feeling that one was "not a mere Puseyite" but went "on jolly reading parties." He discovered at the same time that, like other human beings, he had faults which went to the bottom, and that without the crutch of Arnold's moral support he had great difficulty in forming his goals and working towards them—difficulty, if you like, in incorporating an unpunitive superego. Considering the sensitivity of his temperament and the problems in the circumstances in which he in fact found himself, it is not surprising that this period of growth was often a painful one for Clough.

But if he gave up the happy confidence, implanted by Arnold, that God guided his actions and that what he pondered on and concluded to be right was so, he nevertheless gained from Arnold certain basic attitudes that remained with him throughout his life: a commitment to the achievements of the modern world, and a belief that reason and action rather than flight into unreason or the past were ways to meet the world's problems. He kept always, also, the conviction that social relations and the nature of the society in which he lived were his business, that concerning himself with such issues was a primary and not, as the Tractarians would have made it, a secondary way of expressing his relation to God. He had no interest in Arnold's concept of a church-state, but he understood very well the axiom behind it that all political acts are moral acts, and that the two cannot be separated. He had neither the time nor the emotional energy at this time for exploration of social problems. His concept of the class structure and his own relation to it was closer to that of *noblesse oblige* or that embodied in the obligations of the Christian gentleman than to any kind of genuine democratic feeling. Yet for all that, during this period somehow the foundations for his future openmindedness and energetic dealings with the world were laid. From this time on his rhetoric ceases to speak of ideal beauty, or of persons of refined minds, but deals with real issues, and its metaphors and allusions tend to be drawn more and more from the lives of men engaged in their work—cobblers, accountants, builders of houses. He wishes now not to declaim but to essay, not to assert aggressively, but to involve himself personally and speak only from experience. It is this almost tactile sense of experience which informs Clough's best poetry; but he found the style in which he could express it only through the painful process of recognizing how little he knew, either of life or himself, when he had asserted most.

CHAPTER II

Citoyen Clough

The years 1842–1848 were a period of great personal and intellectual growth for Clough. This was the era he later called that of his "great force," when he named himself Carlyle's "Apostle of Anti-laissez-faire,"[1] and when he began to get that practical knowledge of "the great machine of man's social system"[2] (No. 13) which he had known even in 1839 to be essential but of which he had had no experience. In the course of this growth, he emerged from a bachelor of arts with no particular political interests to become one of the leaders of the "magisterial" party whose influence at Oxford on Gladstone's behalf in 1847 was counted of major assistance,[3] and from being an Arnoldian and uncomplaining subscriber to the Thirty-Nine Articles to a man who held that Christianity was no longer his "actuating religion."[4] He could report of his politics at twenty-nine, not without satisfied amusement, that he was known as the "wildest and most *écervelé* republican going."[5] With a reputation for sincerity, originality, and complete commitment to his beliefs, he studied, read, spoke publicly, and wrote to further the opinions which will be the subject of this chapter. These opinions constituted neither literally the "Chartism" to which a contemporary later referred,[6] nor the communism on which two others thought his views bordered, nor indeed the mere Carlyleanism of which some critics have accused him;[7] but the reasons for these allegations need to be examined more closely than has hitherto been done.

Clough's writings on social and political matters during this period, however, cannot be separated from certain aspects of his personal achievements, for to some extent the former were predicated upon the milieu which both surrounded Clough and which he helped to shape. He was elected to a fellowship at Oriel early in 1842[8] after almost a year of poverty, in which he lived on a £100 stipend eked out by coaching.[9] His first duty was to get hold of his responsibilities as a teacher and member of the college, and the first two years of his tenure were busy ones, devoted largely to this work. He quickly became popular in both capacities, and a contemporary, James Anthony Froude, wrote that Clough was "loved and respected by every member of the college."[10] He had been there scarcely half a year when extra teaching duties, marks of success, were calling him away from long college dinners, "which abrupt retirement," he wrote with genial satire on what Carlyle would have called his "gigmanity," "if the reason be enounced with the judicious unostentatious-audible tone serves the purpose of an advertisement, similar to the creaking-booted physician-incipient's periodical retirement from public worship."[11] In the same month he undertook to write the first of the seventy-seven biographical contributions he was to make to a famous classical dictionary.[12] In the summer, he took pupils to the Lake district.[13]

Certain facts have come to light about Clough's income during this period which are noteworthy, for they establish on a measurable basis something of the nature of Clough's personal and professional success at Oriel. His extra work and evident ability did not go unnoticed, and before he had been at the college more than a year and a half, the Provost, the crusty old Edward Hawkins, passed over nine senior fellows to offer Clough the post of College Tutor.[14] Moreover, contemporary documents show that Clough was appointed Sub-Dean in 1847, a position close to the top of the college's hierarchy,[15] further confirmation of the confidence that Oriel, and Hawkins in particular, reposed in Clough in spite of his views. The post quite probably carried with it additional moneys, but of this we have no evidence. Looking merely at his calculable income, one realizes that it was large; a fact of significance, for his earnings directly reflected both his personal and professional success at Oxford. Under the Oxford system a don was free to take on as many private tutorial students as he wished, and each paid him a fee which was additional to the sum the college gave him as a fellow. His students might come from his own or other colleges, and their numbers reflected the tutor's reputation. Some men outside of the college system in fact got their livings, sometimes handsome ones, entirely as private coaches.[16] Clough's "judicious unostentatious-audible" withdrawal from dinners meant he was meeting many such students who were being referred to him by other dons and by his own students. The amount of those fees is not known, but when he was made College Tutor, a post which may or may not have precluded private tutoring, he recieved £300 over his fellowship, which alone brought him £285.[17] To this sum he added two more sources of income. Every summer but one while at Oriel he took five or six pupils on reading parties in the summer; the average fee for each was £30.[18] One hundred pounds, at a conservative estimate, was probably cleared each summer, and in addition he was paid an unknown amount for the seventy-seven articles he contributed over a period of years to the dictionary.

His income, therefore, was between £700 and £800 a year, and this was not merely respectable; it was handsome. A don with few students did not make half so much. In Trollope's novels, written later when money was worth less, £700 was looked on as an excellent income for a well-to-do man; Everett Wharton in *The Prime Minister,* a rich man's son with only only a modest allowance, has £400 annually.[19] By the standards of the day and in the eyes of his fellows, Clough was an outstanding success in his work, and the fact is worth noting.

But while Clough was making headway in his personal career, England was undergoing one of the worst economic crises of the century, the so-called Hungry Forties, of which a trade unionist wrote during a depression in 1884 that though his fellows might think they suffered now, "never, in [their] darkest hours" did they suffer "a tenth part of the hunger and starvation which the atrocious Corn Laws inflicted upon [their] forefathers."[20] It is not necessary here to deal in detail with a history well known to students of the period, but it was an era as turbulent as any in England's modern history, and Crane Brinton has written of the twenty years between 1832 and 1852 that during them the British upper classes were never entirely free of the fear of a violent revolution.[21] The bad harvests and American bank failures with their English repercussions of the late 1830's had been succeeded by severe and deepening economic depression. The Chartists, a working-class party which eventually numbered millions among its petitioners, had sprung up in 1838 to secure what would have been revolutionary power for the masses. "The House of Commons is the People's House," its first manifesto read, in aggressive, Cobbett-like tones which are also rather moving, "and *there* our opinions should be stated, *there* our rights should be advocated, *there* we ought to be represented, or we are SERFS."[22] The Anti-Corn Law League, founded in 1839 to repeal the importation duties which artificially maintained the price of wheat, thereby keeping wages and manufacturing costs up while benefiting the landowners—and penalizing the middle-class businessman—was also agitating more and more fiercely.[23] Strikes, riots, lockouts, even murder, became part of the political picture throughout industrial England.[24] Many of the poor starved to death in the miserable cellars and back alleys of cities like Manchester and Liverpool, flooded by Irish immigrants, and graphically described by Elizabeth Gaskell in *Mary Barton*. When Clough in the early 1840's helped his sister with her church school in Liverpool, or with her visited the poor to distribute the only supplies—coals, potatoes and flour—that stood between them and starvation, he was learning at first hand what the "Condition of England question" really was.[25]

The workers carried their first Chartist petition to London in 1839, in the belief that Parliament and the Queen must be merely ignorant of their condition and would help if they knew the true facts. They were repulsed, and their second petition was not brought until 1842 in a winter when misery and bitterness were at their greatest. In that year John Bright, for example, later the famous Quaker M.P., having joined with other manufacturers in lowering wages, tried to organize a general lockout: his aim was to provoke a revolution that would force the government to repeal the Corn Laws.[26]

Throughout this period the investigatory commissions set up to inquire into the conditions of labor were publishing their findings, and six full-scale reports came before the public between 1842 and 1845.[27] Their revelations of the grossest kind of abuse of laborers finally shocked the middle classes into taking minimal regulatory action, beginning in 1844 with the Ten Hours Act. But because of religious rivalries there was to be no general public education in England until 1870,[28] and John Stuart Mill said that the English working class was the most uneducated and depraved in Europe.[29] Under the New Poor Laws, so-called "outdoor relief" was no longer available, and no public assistance could be got short of moving into the Workhouse.[30] There were no public medical dispensaries, no public sewage or lighting systems—essentially no health services at all. Cholera swept through London and elsewhere endemically in the 1840's, but although the public could, as it were, hear it coming, and the idea had grown that it had something to do with inadequate sewage, government did nothing about it, essentially on grounds of laisser-faire.[31] Lord Robbins has pointed out that laisser-faire was not held as rigidly as a principle by Bentham and other major political economists as once was thought,[32] but in the popular middle class mind, as Woodward has said, it held sway in part because there was no clearer theory to put in its place[33]—and nothing the holders of power wished to substitute for it. Its wide public acceptance gave government an excuse for that passivity which Carlyle repeatedly attacked as "Do-Nothing" government in *Chartism, Past and Present,* and other works.

The ills of England in the 1840's stood out like the ribs of her starving poor, and men like Arnold, earlier, and Carlyle had their share in gradually rousing the conscience of some members of the public to what was wrong. Disraeli caught the tone of the problem in the subtitle of his novel, *Sybil, Or the Two Nations,* and Gladstone, who had begun his career as a conservative, a defender of slavery in the West Indies,[34] and a protégé of the notorious Duke of Newcastle (whose phrase, "I have the right to do as I like with my own" had made him infamous when he evicted forty tenants for voting against his wishes),[35] was moving steadily toward a more liberal position.

This was not, however, a period when the ordinary citizen, even if he enjoyed the franchise, could hope to rise in politics or effect social changes. "Politics" were decidedly not "for the people" (contrary to the hopeful title of a Christian Socialist journal founded in 1848), and a "man of honor could not make politics a profession unless he had a competence of his own," as Macaulay wrote in 1833.[36] Only one born to wealth and social position could readily see himself as part of the political world. There was little distinction between the Whigs and Tories, representing as they did the same upper class, and differences among them tended to be rather those of faction, blood, or personality, than of ideology.[37] As late as 1840 Lord John Russell, the Whig leader, did not think it more than "convenient" for the government to have a program of its own,[38] and Melbourne remarked in 1839, "I do not dislike the Tories; I think they are very much like the others; I do not care by whom I am supported; I consider them all as one."[39] A minister speaking in the House could refer synonymously to his "friends" and to his "party,"[40] and the myth of an England represented by social equals was maintained in the face of near revolution from the unrepresented. It was unthinkable that the largely illiterate masses should have the vote, unthinkable that men, many of whom ate meat only once a week and subsisted for the rest largely on bread,[41] should be paid to sit in Parliament, or should be free, as the Chartists also wished, to turn governments out at stated intervals.[42] It was unthinkable to treat with their demands, and class divisions made communication almost impossible even when the educated man was willing. Clough's friend, Frederick Temple, for example, once gained admittance to a Chartist meeting only by showing work-hardened hands.[43] Under such circumstances only the self-seeking hack, the Tapers, Tadpoles, and Johnsons of the novels of Disraeli and George Eliot and others,[44] or the more respectable but paid agent sought to meddle in politics in any minor capacity, while the men who themselves sought office had to be financially and socially well supported.

A man in Clough's position, therefore, could identify himself as a Whig or a Tory, but he could no more seek public office, or join the Chartists, than he could fly to the moon. If his opinions, however, were radical in tendency, politically he was almost impotent, as John Stuart Mill's career in the period shows. There was no strong party of the left, and Mill regarded the Radical party as having become by 1840 "a mere *côte gauche* of the Whigs."[45] Individual M.P.s still bore the name Radical, but for all practical purposes the party had ceased to exist, and in Carlyle's view "pacific mutual division of the spoil" was the rule of the day.[46] Mill himself withdrew from politics in disillusionment in 1840 because, in spite of his high reputation and the influential position he had held as the editor of the *London and Westminster Review,* he had, as a reformer, no place to go.[47] What was true of him could only be much more true of a man like Clough. Later Mill came to define himself as a socialist, and it may be that the term in the limited sense he meant it came to be applicable for a time to Clough also. This will be discussed further below; here it is useful to point out that no socialist party, per se, then existed in England, the term itself having only been invented a few years previously in France.[48] There was not even any general agreement as to what socialism meant. Tom Arnold, for example, wrote later that "English social-ism . . . in those days was represented by Robert Owen and the Chartists,"[49] but Chartism had no primary interest in the redistribu-tion of property and explicitly denied any link with socialism. Char-tism, indeed, was not only anti-intellectual and lacking in any ideo-logical basis, but grew overtly hostile to its would-be theoreticians.[50] Owenism, for its part, was essentially a dead movement in the 1840's.[51] The nomenclature of movements for social change, like the anxiety they aroused, was undifferentiated, and as Christensen has written, "Chartism, socialism, communism, infidelity, and even immorality were generally regarded by the upper and middle classes as synonymous—and they reacted accordingly."[52]

It was in an atmosphere, then, of social and ideological flux that Clough began to educate himself in political matters. He, Tom and Matthew Arnold, and Tom Walrond had been in the habit of meet-ing in Clough's rooms and discussing politics. According to Tom Arnold, Clough had been a supporter of Peel in 1842 and an eager reader of *The Spectator,* edited by the Radical Rintoul, throughout the period.[53] However, one of the first datable statements we have appears in a letter of July 1844, occasioned by Gladstone's sponsor-ship of the new railway act.

In 1842 the Chartists had listed as one of the monopolies by which the upper classes oppressed them, "the means of travelling and transit."[54] The railway industry, born in the 1830's, began to boom in the next decade, but no provisions had been made either for protecting the investing public or for bringing the fares within reach of the working class. At one time, "five distinct companies" were formed to build a line between London and Brighton—and "all of [their] shares at some time or another were at a premium."[55] Obviously, many amateurs, like Bonamy Price, Clough's former master at Rugby, were in the highly speculative market, and laisser-faire was the industry's only guide.[56] Gladstone's proposal of 1844 aimed at satisfying the workers' demands for cheaper transportation while curbing this dangerously unregulated competition.[57] Clough summed it up: "I am glad to say that we are offered by the Ministry, auctore Gladstone, a grand anti-laissez-faire Railway Bill, empowering the Board of Trade, when profits rise above 10 per cent on the original shares, to insist on a decrease of fares; also in certain conditions to purchase railways for the Crown; also to insist on certain accommodations for the poorer passengers. I hope it may be passed in its full integrity but there will doubtless be sharp opposition."[58] The bill as passed did little more than insure that the poor should not pay more than a penny per mile when they took special trains provided for them, but that Gladstone, a Tory and High Churchman with manufacturing ties, should even have contemplated the ultimate purchase of an industry by the Crown may be one reason why Clough threw his support behind the Peelite when he stood for Oxford in 1847.[59]

This letter is interesting also because a statement introductory to the passage just quoted is the first of several assertions, overt or implied, of his now stronger interest in Carlyle. "I am considerably inclined," he writes, "to set to work at Political Economy, for the benefit of the rising generation;—and to see if I cannot prove 'the Apostle of Anti-laissez-faire.' "[60] In assuming that Apostleship, he is responding directly to Carlyle's call for such followers.

Clough's relationship with Carlyle's thought is an interesting but complex one. The poet's letters, especially the early ones, are full of references—whose ambivalence tends to be overlooked—to his reading of the older man, and later, during his London years, Clough became a friend of the famous writer. (Carlyle, in fact, got Clough the job at the Education Office for which he returned to England from America in 1853.)[61] And the Carlylean note was often, and overtly, sounded in Clough's prose. It has come to be taken for granted therefore that Clough accepted Carlyle's views more or less in toto, and the issue has not been felt to require close comparative study.

But although one scholar writes briefly in this tenor that "Carlyle was one of his heroes,"[62] after Rugby (and possibly his experiences with Ward) Clough really had no heroes. The Scotsman's influence on the poet was strong, and it will be discussed below, but to avoid distortion of the picture, certain caveats should first be noted. Clough's admiration for the older man was not as uncritical as some studies have suggested, and it is clear that even as an undergraduate Clough chose rigorously, even rather narrowly, from among the ideas and attitudes that Carlyle offered. Thus in a letter of 1841 Clough remarks, "I keep wavering between admiration of his exceedingly great perceptive and analytical power and other wonderful points and inclination to turn away altogether from a man who has so great a lack of all reality and actuality."[63] Two years earlier, while asserting his admiration of Carlyle, he had also demurred that the essayist was "certainly . . . somewhat heathenish."[64] Clough seems to have read most of Carlyle's productions as they appeared, as Veyriras has pointed out,[65] but no wholly unqualified positive remark of his about Carlyle survives. Clough's distrust of "a man who has so great a lack of all reality and actuality" was a significant doubt, and it is a mistake to assume, with one writer, that John Holloway's definition of Carlyle's idealism, or *"anti-mechanism,"* is a sufficient summary of his meaning for Clough.[66] Moreover, it is often impossible to distinguish ideas Clough may have got from Carlyle and which have been ascribed to the Scot's influence, such as his hostility to cut-throat competition, or his trust in the "Ideal" (Essays No. 1 or 2), from those he had already learned from Arnold.

It is necessary also to recognize that Clough failed to adopt several of Carlyle's most strongly emphasized points. The poet never, for example, accepted Carlyle's reverence for heroes or strong men. In his early writings he does not argue the issue; he simply ignores

63

it. Such figures, and such reverence did not interest him. Later, in an unpublished review which will be discussed below, he specifically rejected the concepts of heroism which he feared might lead man to choose glory over common honesty.[67] Another of Carlyle's favorite targets, of course, was the idea of democracy. Democracy in Europe, he wrote, could be but a "zero . . . a regulated method of rebellion and abrogation." It was the "consummation of No-government and *Laissez-faire*,"[68] the expression of the flunky's resentment of Order, and "despair of finding any Heroes to govern you."[69] Clough began by sharing Arnold's (and their class's) distrust of democracy,[70] but until around 1849 or 1850 his attitude grew increasingly egalitarian. And even at his most conservative, there is nothing in Clough of this determined and ingrained hostility to democracy; indeed, the reverse is often in evidence.

In general, then, Clough was unmoved by what might be called the authoritarian aspect of Carlyle's thought. He despised the idea that might could make right,[71] specifically attacking it when he heard it uttered in America.[72] Carlyle's thunder about judgment, the punitive side of his morality, found no response in Clough, just as he lacked Carlyle's passionate faith in Order, his sense that physical and metaphysical problems could largely be solved by the action of Abbot Samsons exerting their Will against Chaos. Oversimplification, judgmental attitudes, authoritarianism—none of these was native to Clough's personality.

But Carlyle nevertheless did have a strong effect on Clough's writing, and perhaps on his acts as well. The influence was evident in Clough's style, varying in degree with the argument and audience Clough was addressing; the *Retrenchment* pamphlet of 1847, for example, is more deliberately Carlylean than the letters to *The Balance* of the year before. Clough also adopted some specific ideas from Carlyle. Indeed, to a certain extent one might say that he helped to form Clough's adult self-image, albeit, at times, by indirection or negatively, forcing Clough to react to Carlyle's own terms and terminology, furnishing him with elements of a vocabulary—the flunky, the apostle—which the poet might adopt or redefine, but with which he had to come to terms.

An interesting passage from one of Clough's letters of 1844 is relevant to this process. "I can feel faith in what is being carried on by my generation," he wrote about his role as a teacher while struggling with religious uncertainties: "I am content to be an operative—to dress intellectual leather, cut it out to pattern and stitch it and cobble it into boots and shoes for the benefit of the work which is being guided by wiser heads."[73] The assumption of the role of simple artisan, honestly doing the work nearest at hand, cannot but recall Carlyle. We may also justifiably hear an allusion to Carlyle's reverence in *Sartor Resartus* for George Fox, "by trade a shoemaker," founder of Quakerism, whose "making to himself . . . one perennial suit of leather" so that he could retreat from the world and meditate was "perhaps the most remarkable incident in Modern History." ("Fox turned from the Clergy," Carlyle wrote, from the idea of man as but a "patent Digester," and the Belly life's "Grand Reality," turned "with tears and a sacred scorn, back to his Leather-parings and his Bible.")[74] But Clough carries the metaphor further, elaborating on it in a way characteristic of his mature style as he decends with it into a deliberate, almost rococo bathos. From the worthy operatve he becomes—or seems to become—that butt of the philosopher's vituperation, the flunky, the man to whom no master is a hero:

Without the least denying Xtianity, I feel little that I can call its power. Believing myself to be in my unconscious creed in some shape or other an adherent to its doctrines I keep within its pale: still whether the Spirit of the Age, whose lacquey and flunkey I submit to be, will prove to be this kind or that kind I can't the least say. Sometimes I have doubts whether it won't turn out to be no Xty at all. Also, it is a more frequent question with me whether the Master whom I work under and am content to work under is not carrying out his operations himself elsewhere, while I am as it were obeying the directions of a bungling journeyman no better than myself. As the great Goethe published in his youth The Sorrows of the Young Werter, so may I, you see, the great poet that am to be, publish my "Lamentations of a Flunkey out of place." You, perhaps, will say the Lamentations are more out of place than the Flunkey. . . . Transmit to him advice and good counsel . . . In the meantime he must dress and put on his livery for dinner—*Exit Flunkey.*[75]

It would be a mistake to take this bathos at its face value; this language of lackeys and flunkies, which comes directly from *Past and Present, Heroes and Hero-Worship,* and other of Carlyle's writings, is complexly ironic. For Clough is expressing here not only his own uncertainty, but at least two other points as well: first, that he is not a flunky at all, but a man capable of following Carlyle's deeper meaning and directing himself to the work at hand; and, second, that in so doing he is comporting himself not like a Hero, or even like a Hero's proper electors and constituents, but like an ordinary citizen, nobody special, yet capable of the more profound heroism of right action. He is the guard who will not sleep in the sentry box, to use one of his own later images, who has seen "higher, holier things" than the self-conscious posturing of a Châteaubriand or Mazzini.[76] We may well see here, if not actual criticism of Carlyle's concept of heroism, at least Clough's deliberate distinction of himself from it, a determination that his personal style shall not be that of self-inflated superiority. And, indeed, in his poetry one of his central aesthetic problems—and achievements—was the creation of a diction adequate to speak for his anti-heroes, men who have too complex a sensibility to find expression in a heroic pose.

Yet Clough undoubtedly gained from Carlyle's exhortations a sense of reinforcement towards action. Being the "Apostle of Anti-laissez-faire" cannot be divorced from Arnold's previous training, or Clough's own earlier interest in Anne's work with the poor, but it was probably strengthened by Clough's sense of Carlylean backing. His activities took at first two forms of action: his participation in the Decade, an Oxford debating group, and his work in the slums of St. Ebbe's for the Oxford Mendicity Society.[77] The latter was direct social work, offered by private citizens at a time when the profession per se did not exist, in response to a crying need.

The documents of the Society show that during 1844 Clough was the only one of his circle to become what was known as a "visitor" of the Society. He had already long been a contributor to the charity, which seems to have been the major one at the university.[78] Founded in 1818 by the Provost of Oriel, Edward Copleston and another man,[79] its subscription list included most of Oxford's best-known names, and Clough's own uncle Alfred had served as chairman of its committee while he was a don at Jesus. It operated on the charity-ticket system, which aimed at relieving the crowds of beggars that swarmed through Oxford, as through the whole country after the Napoleonic wars, by giving them not cash but a ticket which could be exchanged for food and lodging. The organization tried to winnow out the "worthy" from the "undeserving" poor and assured its subscribers that every case was carefully investigated by its visitors.[80] It can hardly have been a pleasant job. When he went to work at the office in the slums of Castle Street in 1844, the calls on the charity had more than doubled in a few years; the number of the destitute was so great that three constables were employed merely to keep the beggars off the streets. As an innovation that year the society ran its own hostel, and purchased "3 iron bedsteads" so that the aged did not sleep on the floor with the others. The committee reported with satisfaction that the applicants "have submitted to all the House Rules, both in washing themselves and forbearing from smoking and drinking; and generally read to one another in the evening. The only refractory case was immediately punished."[81] Clough helped dispense the standard soup-kitchen fare, sitting by nights in the office as the ragged and weary filed past to sleep on bare boards and start again at daybreak. A letter describing his work gives some idea of the manner, at once objective and humane, with which he approached the situation: "I am just returned," he wrote in June, 1844,

from the Mendicity Society's office, where I have administered relief to about six people only, tonight. They used to come by twenties, and one night I remember eighty. Yet even now the hay harvest is so scanty that many who usually have work are thrown out. Sometimes we have very nice people. There was a little boy under thirteen tonight, from Stratford, who was a rather interesting case. They get a pint and a half of broth and a piece of bread for supper, and (at present only) a small piece of bread for breakfast.[82]

It was good but rare training for a man who was to write on political economy, and Clough served through 1848. Most men preferred to shut their eyes, and Clough deserves credit for expressing in his own acts the sense of "reality and actuality" he looked for in others.

Clough's speeches at the Decade were another form of activism, although here the influence of Carlyle was tempered in moral and religious matters by that of Emerson, whom Clough had been reading for some time. His speeches on these matters, however, will be discussed in a subsequent chapter. Clough was later not frightened by the fact that his opinions were not popular at Oxford; no doubt his membership in the Decade accustomed him to criticism. More importantly, however, that membership also gave him a forum that helped him develop his new opinions, as the Decade, now an almost forgotten society, became for Clough and his friends very much what the Oriel Common Room had been for their intellectual forebears, the Noetics.

Founded around 1835 by two former Rugbeians to provide a forum for the discussion of more serious questions than were usually treated at the Union, the Decade flourished for some twelve or fifteen years. It elected to membership the cream of the Union and a select few undergraduates, but most of the group were young B.A.s or fellows.[83] In many qualities—its intellectual *esprit de corps,* its exclusiveness, its liberal tendency, even its nickname (the Decayed)—the group appears to have been formed in the Noetic style. The parallel is borne out in the description written later by the Lord Chief Justice, Lord Coleridge, in a tone of mingled amusement and deep appreciation:

There was a society called the Decade . . . (a Balliol scout . . . persisted in embodying the external world's judgment on it by always calling it the Decayed) which I think did a great deal for the mental education of those belonging to it, of those of us, at least, who came from public schools [Eton in his case] where we were taught to construe, to say by heart, to write verses, and Greek and Latin prose, but where our minds were allowed to lie fallow, and to go on, unclouded by thought, in an atmosphere of severe and healthy unintelligence . . . We met in one another's rooms. We discussed all things, human and divine. We thought we stripped things to the very bone, we believed we dragged recondite truths into the light of common day and subjected them to the scrutiny of what we were pleased to call our minds. We fought to the very stumps of our intellects, and I believe that many of us, I can speak for one, would gladly admit that many a fruitful seed of knowledge, of taste, of cultivation was sown on those pleasant, if somewhat pugnacious evenings.[84]

What they were "pleased to call [their] minds" deserved the name, for among them they numbered Benjamin Jowett, the future Master of Balliol; Matthew Arnold and Arthur Hugh Clough, two major Victorian poets; E. M. Goulburn, future Headmaster of Rugby; A. P. Stanley and William Lake, future Deans of the Church; Coleridge himself, the future Lord Chief Justice; and others who were to be prominent in Parliament and the professions. Few, however, of the Decade's members were Tories, and even these seem to have been "liberal Conservatives," like Gladstone. Illustrative of the tone of the society is the attitude of Clough and Tom Arnold to one such member, Chichester Fortescue, who represented, to Arnold in particular, the epitome of aristocratic demeanor: in later years, when Clough was living discontentedly in London among middle-class Unitarian businessmen, he wrote Tom, "I . . . yearn to the Fortescues, whose faces refute Coningtoniana with a look, or did so at least to you."[85] But even this Fortescue, who was later a member of Gladstone's cabinet, whose family had been founded in the seventeenth century by one Sir Faithful Fortescue, a Royalist cavalier, was "from the first a decided liberal";[86] while the middle-class John Conington (secretary of the society) whom he quelled was not merely liberal but very radical and was "considered a dangerous innovator."[87]

Clough belonged to the Decade from approximately 1843 to 1848.[88] When he spoke it was with unusual power and influence; some of his hearers could repeat his arguments almost verbatim more than twenty years later. Both Matthew and Tom Arnold felt that "no member of the society spoke in so rich, penetrating, original, and convincing a strain as Clough."[89] His friend J. C. Shairp wrote that "what he said and the way he said it were so marked and weighty as to have stuck to memory when almost everything else then spoken has been forgotten." The secretary, John Conington, wrote more than twenty years later: "I can recall his commanding manner, and the stately serene tones in which he delivered a kind of prophecy of the new era which in a few days [with the imminent repeal of the Corn Laws] was to be inaugurated, and told us that 'these men' (the manufacturers) 'were the real rulers of England.' "[90] (Clough's recognition that "these men were the real rulers of England" echoes Carlyle's respect for the Captains of Industry.) Some idea of the reputation of Clough's influence and that of his circle may be got from the words of Stafford Northcote, Gladstone's campaign manager (if so modern a word may be used for a position that then had no name) during the hotly contested election of 1847. The university was privileged to send two members to Parliament, and Gladstone's cause as that of "a possible reformer and . . . a man who thinks," became a rallying point for the younger men, who sank their rivalries and combined against the "high and dry Tories" and the "two-bottle orthodox" of the old school, typified by Heads like Jenkyns and, to some degree, Edward Hawkins. "The effect of the contest," wrote Northcote to Gladstone, "has been good . . . the young men exult, partly in the hope that you will do something for the university yourself, partly in the consciousness that they have shown the *strength of the magisterial party* by carrying you against the opposition of the Heads, and have proved their title to be considered an important element of the university. They do not seem yet to be sufficiently united to effect great things, but there is a large amount of ability and earnestness which only wants direction." [Italics mine.] Northcote mentioned Clough's influence in the "magisterial party" and said that what the "learned veteran" Hallam's "adhesion was in influence among the older men, that of Arthur Clough was among the younger."[91]

The earliest record of a speech by Clough at the Decade is of one made around 1844 in support of Ashley's Ten Hours Bill, an act bitterly opposed by the manufacturing interest and defeated when first brought forward, the battle being fought on grounds of laisser-faire. This seemingly modest piece of legislation would have applied only to the textile industry. It limited to ten hours daily the work not of the "operatives," the men who ran the looms, but of the women and children who tended and supplied them. However, unless the assistants were worked in shifts or at staggered hours, the operatives could not have worked longer than they, and therefore the bill had wider application than prima facie it appeared to have.[92] The manufacturers and such publications as *The Spectator* opposed the measure, admitting that they pursued (on Malthusian principles) a deliberate policy of repressing wages, while trying to compete with the more cheaply staffed continental mills.[93] Their major defense, however, was the principle of unrestricted competition, and it was this that Clough attacked. "In supporting the resolution," Tom Arnold wrote, "he combated the doctrines of *laissez-faire* and the omnipotence and sufficiency of the action of supply and demand, then hardly disputed in England, with an insight marvellous in one who had so little experience of industrial life, and at the same time with a strict and conscientious moderation."[94] Clough's principles were expressed more strongly in his own words in a letter written on June 25, 1844:

I . . . believe that [the worker] has not his proper proportion [of gain], that capital tyrannizes over labor, and that government is bound to interfere to prevent such bullying; and I do believe too that in . . . some way or other the problem now solved by universal competition, or the devil take the hindmost, may receive a more satisfactory solution. It is manifestly absurd that to allow me to get my stockings ½d a pair cheaper the operative stocking weaver should be forced to go barefoot. It is surely not wholly Utopian to look for some system which will apportion the due reward to the various sets of workmen and evade this perpetual struggle for securing (each man to the exclusion of his neighbor) the whole market.[95]

Clough's insight, remarked on by Tom Arnold, is evident here in his capacity to see that inequities were caused not merely by the failure of the upper classes to lead, as Carlyle argued, but grew from denying to labor its positive rights. To men like Carlyle who looked back with longing to the feudal age, the workers' only right was the right to be governed well, to be led, fed, and protected, "gently or forcibly." Teufelsdröckh's creator opposed as soulless the new "Benthamee" attempts to deal systematically with social problems.[96] Clough favored, on Carlylean grounds, recognition of "the social and political importance of the manufacturing interest" and later recalled his championing of it at the Decade:[97] "Your sanguine friend still puts his trust in master manufacturers, as in those olden days when the face of Fortescue shone triumph in the Decade."[98] Yet Clough was also able to see beyond this position to the fact that the classes' interests were not identical, that "bullying" was and would be the rule while one class held all the power, and that

71

only the creation of a more powerful central authority could win for the workers their "due reward." John Stuart Mill argued four years later that competition had in fact always been controlled by custom, that the free operation of supply and demand was a myth, and there "is always a master who throws his sword into the scale, and the terms are such as he imposes,"[99] but these remarks, although embodied in a book which was quickly recognized as a classic, were popularly regarded as revolutionary at the time they were made.[100] Clough deserves credit for the company his ideas kept, particularly when he reached conclusions parallel to but independent of those of Mill.

At the same time as he was giving some of his Decade speeches Clough began to read an odd little American journal called *The Lowell Offering,* extracts from which had found a remarkably wide audience when brought out in England by Charles Knight as *Mind Among the Spindles.* Published intermittently between 1841 and 1850 in Lowell, Massachusetts, by two idealistic ladies who were also mill hands, a Miss Carter and a Miss Harriet Farley (the daughter of a clergyman whose character, she wrote, "is pure as the snow that glistens on an Alpine height"),[101] the journal desired to demonstrate to the public the novel thesis that working women, living alone, could be educated, moral, and happy. Of their production Clough wrote "I have been reading a magazine written by factory girls in Massachusetts—quite as good I think as the Rugby Magazine [of which Clough had been an editor]. They work 12 hrs a day nevertheless like our people and yet have Lyceums and ballrooms and Societies for Mutual improvements and Magazines, and don't seem much worse either for their work or their play."[102] English Radicals, as Thistlethwaite has pointed out, found America during this period an "incandescent example," and thought the American republic under Jackson had been the "hope of the world."[103] Clough's interest in this magazine, which cannot have been more than passing, nevertheless both afforded him a new insight into the possibilities of the life of labor and enables us to infer something of the way in which he was entering into the attitudes of contemporary reformers, and becoming familiar with views more sympathetic to the United States than those, typical of the upper class, expressed by friends like Matthew Arnold or editors of publications like *The Times* and *The Spectator*.[104]

By 1846 Clough's social thoughts had developed sufficiently for him to wish to commit them to paper, and in that year he published six letters, almost short essays, in a new journal called *The Balance*. The opportunity arose through his friendship with Bonamy Price, who was one of the sponsors, together with his "great" Whig and Evangelical friends, of the newly reorganized weekly. Its principles cannot be better described than in Clough's own words, as "Arnoldite out of Evangelical, a somewhat mongrel progeny perhaps, with more of profession than fervor, and the paper is certainly weak, though certainly at the same time well meaning. It wishes to become a sort of Sunday newspaper for all sorts of people, gentle and simple, noblemen and serving man . . . I wrote a letter myself which possibly may appear in its columns next week and possibly not. At Price's persuasion I take it for a quarter."[105] Clough could not, in fact, have taken the paper for much more than a quarter, for it expired after only twenty issues. It seems to have reflected no clear personality of its own, or of its readership, but was always conscious of the fact that it was run by "A Committee of Gentlemen of varying opinions who in the spirit . . . of Dr. ARNOLD" hoped their production would be bought by the "Religious manufacturer" and gentry who would give it to the poor. In format it resembled the more sophisticated *Spectator,* but it differed in its concern, however self-conscious, for labor. Its major innovation was a "Workingman's Column" which was to include "subjects of interest to the artisan and the peasant; the economy of the cottage and the workshop; articles and extracts likely to be read by the laborer, *neutralizing the injurious effects of infidel writings, and exposing the fallacies of the discontented and designing.*" [Italics mine.][106] The column was quietly dropped even before the newspaper itself ended its existence.[107] Clough was to differ radically from this typical middle-class and Arnoldian attitude when he later insisted on presenting the worker as a man with rights rather than as a charity case.

The five letters relevant to our study here (the sixth deals with the militia and will be omitted) are all concerned with the nature of the social and economic conditions and changes which England would or might experience with the coming repeal of the Corn Laws. Through them all Clough is opposed, like Carlyle before him, to the action of unlimited competition, but for the most part the letters reflect Clough's own voice and attitudes, and these often differ from the older man's. Already in *Chartism* Carlyle had tended to see in education alone the means of political change, as Neff has written, and he grew more conservative with the years. By 1849, in *The Nigger Question,* for example, he was advocating that the Jamaican Negroes be forced to work, and slavery reinstituted, so that the whites might prosper and the " 'Slavery of the Wise to the Foolish' " be avoided.[108] Clough, meanwhile, was moving leftward. His proposals, albeit tentative ones, for change through governmental action go far beyond anything Carlyle ever advocated, just as his analysis of the contemporary business scene stresses its murderous competitiveness. But Clough omits Carlyle's reverence for the Captains of Industry, preferring now not to idolize such figures but to identify himself as an employer and proceed to lay upon himself those moral strictures and responsibilities any honest man should feel. Clough does foretell, theorize, and assert certain moral propositions, but we do not feel, as we do after reading Carlyle, that a prophet has spoken for God: rather we have heard a voice developing the argument from certain assumptions that he and we can take almost for granted. Often all sense of moral struggle has fallen away in these letters: the writer is not contending with his audience or his own soul: he is dealing with moral problems and attitudes as if the right were a matter as little debatable as the figures in a ledger, the accountancy once checked. This is not an expression of weakened moral fervor but a preferred polemic position: under such circumstances and with such a tone, questioning those basic assumptions becomes merely irrelevant: to grant that is to emphasize the propriety of getting on with the more difficult matter of turning those assumptions into action, of getting down to just that "reality and actuality" Clough had found wanting in Carlyle.

Whomever *The Balance's* editor might have imagined his readers to be, Clough was clear that his audience was the manufacturing middle class, and in his letters he addressed himself directly to them.

The first appeared on January 23, 1846,[109] and dealt with the imminent repeal of the Corn Laws. John Conington described a speech Clough also made on this subject as having seemed serenely "prophetic"; there is something of that tone in this first letter. England, Clough foretold, was on the eve of a great economic change in which labor would leave the farms and the cities would grow. This opinion, after a long, slow advance, had suddenly spread, like the tide which has surmounted a steep slope and reached level ground: "It may be, though this is a question, that labor will have to remove from the field to the mill, and such transfers are pretty sure to be attended with hardship; but the money which the country saves will ere long be a benefit to all . . . To the nation at large, and in the long run, the change will be economically a blessing; that is, in the matter of pounds, shillings, and pence. We shall stand better in the columns of the national account-book."

Clough sees the issue here as one demanding not indignation but investigation, analysis, and forethought, and he tailors his metaphorical language to suit the marketplace in which his readership was engaged. Granted that a mill girl's life was largely taken up by work over which she had no control: how then and by what standards were she and her employer to determine their behavior? "In how many cottages were changes in moral habits . . . most sudden and most potential, introduced by the invention which discarded the spinning wheel . . . The time of so many men is, in so large a proportion, taken up with employments prescribed and regulated by the economy of the state—we are so many of us exclusively employed in earning food, and shelter, and comforts, by methods thus arranged for us—that in our relation to these employments must consist much of our moral life." Was it a good thing, however? What would happen now to the young girl who would once have "learnt at her mother's side the use of the spinning wheel in some lonely hamlet, perhaps amongst the hills of Yorkshire [but] now, among those same hills of Yorkshire, in some new-built straggling town, or, it may be, as an immigrant in some huge central Manchester, serves in the army of the mill?"

The "proposed change," by increasing trade, Clough agreed "will, indeed, make us richer; but will it make us better, or will it make us worse?" We should not, he insisted, piously "trust to Providence," and believe "that, in all positions, grace 'is sufficient for us.' " The question was, "are we called to do it?" Clough was to be impatient with this Evangelically oriented passivity that used Scripture to cover callousness when he wrote the following year on an epidemic of cholera. Grace was not sufficient in a world increasingly ruled by industrial conditions. "I . . . rate very low the intellect or knowledge of any man, who is not aware that physical well-being, domestic comfort, such an exemption from the miseries and moral degradation of want as shall give a man respect in his own eyes, and confidence in the laws, must be the basis of national morality."[110] But just as no man could in good conscience assert to himself that he was called to a vicious profession merely because "in it I shall get most worldly profit," so England could not conscientiously suppose that repealing the Corn Laws would merely mean getting richer. "Social changes of some kind assuredly there will be; nor will they . . . be unmixedly either good or evil. It is but prudence to think beforehand what they will be on either side, and seek to be prepared to avail ourselves of the good, and provide against the evil." Newman would have dissented from the idea that national morality is founded on physical well-being: this in fact he made a cardinal point of the "Liberalism" he always opposed. But how could he have differed from the qualification with which Clough followed his first point? It was this kind of conscientious moderation that won for Clough the respect of those from whom he differed.

In his second letter he began to attack the basis of "the evil": unlimited competition. Clough was to end his series of letters by asking some pointed questions about the system of free enterprise itself; but he began quietly enough from seemingly innocuous moral premises. Political economy, he pointed out, was a more complex matter than merely the idea of laisser-faire could explain. The interchange of labor was based on an unwritten social compact.

The first thought of an honest man on entering into a new position is to discover the obligations it entails on him. I receive a certain pay; do I do the work it is given for? I have fellow men to serve and assist me; do I pay them the wages of their work? . . . What functions do my fellow citizens perform? What are their wages, and do they receive them?—questions whose true answers can hardly be found, except by a study of the economical system as a whole, by investigation of the wealth of nations.[111]

In order to understand the significance of Clough's views, one should know that, as Mill pointed out two years later, the "law" of competition as it governed supply and demand was generally, if erroneously, considered the only operative one in political economy.[112] Mill had already in 1844 tried to broaden the scope of political economy from being the study "in what manner a nation may be made rich" to one that "informs us of the laws which regulate the production, distribution, and consumption of wealth."[113] It is very likely that Clough, who had read Mill's *Logic* with typically qualified enthusiasm, was following his lead here as elsewhere in broadening the scope of political economy to include the study of the proper distribution of wealth.[114]

The repeal of the Corn Laws, Clough held, raised the question not merely "whether the nation will be richer, but . . . palpably more important, whether a part of the community be not receiving unfair wages." He explained that he used the term "wages"— blandly jabbing at middle-class amour propre—"as Mirabeau used it when he uttered his famous dictum that he knew only three ways of living—by begging, by stealing, and by wages." (Carlyle may have been the first to draw this apothegm to Clough's attention.)[115] "The very peculiar charm" of Clough's conversation, thought Walter Bagehot, the economist and writer on the British constitution, was that without cynicism he "saw what it is considered cynical to see."[116] The alternating idealism and realism in the last few quotations illustrate just that "peculiar charm."

The rest of this second letter is devoted to attacking what Veblen later called conspicuous waste, then more honorifically known as unproductive consumption. "There is . . . a theory" Clough wrote, "which justifies the existence of extravagant and costly habits on the ground of the stimulus which they afford to those who cannot as yet indulge in them, which believes in the wisdom of holding out to the . . . industrious the bait of idleness and luxury . . . We find men continually acting on the belief that it is their duty to be large consumers; to use the expensive where the cheap would

do, to employ labor to frivolous purposes for the good of trade."
The error of this idea was so egregious as "to tempt one to ask
you for a special 'rich man's column.' "

There was in fact such a theory abroad. Mill's *Essays* in 1844
had treated it as an exploded notion,[117] but popularly it still hung
on, and one of Disraeli's workers' chorus in *Sybil,* after she has
finished debating the state of the nation, buys her loaf of bread
"for the sake of trade."[118] Mill granted that some unreproductive
consumption might be necessary for man's well-being, but he distinguished between psychological and economic benefits. Clough followed the same line in his fourth letter: "There are things . . . that
do great moral good, and yet cost much money. And of money
. . . spent in this way, at present let no question be raised. Only,
let none say or suppose that expense of this or any other kind is
a benefit to themselves, or to others, in the mere pecuniary point
of view—that in [the] national economy the thing is a duty."[119]
It was wasteful consumption when "a rich man buys a horse and
never rides it; a lady buys a dress and wears it once." We can
better understand Clough's attacks on contemporary waste when
we remember that at that period the nation supported almost two
domestic servants for every man with an unearned income, and
the desire of wealthy women for those almost unworn dresses had
called into being a labor force devoted largely to clothing them
that exceeded the combined numbers of men employed by the army,
navy, iron mills, and collieries.[120]

Clough admitted that for the rich suddenly to change their habits
would also be unfair to labor, but pleaded with them that "if the
hands already employed can have work of a different, a reproductive
kind found for them, the sooner they take to it the better." To
those who would then ask what should be done with that labor
and money, Clough applied with greater vividness Mill's prescription: capital investment and the support of emigration. "Is there
no capital wanted by manufacturers for new mills, by farmers for
improvements, by mining companies, canal companies, railway companies[?] . . . But it costs so much. Nay, did you not wish to spend
money for the good of trade and the working-classes? What you
have hitherto expended in buying what you confess you were as

well or even better without—that same sum spend now in assisting emigration. Far more good will you do by sending one laborer to Canada or Australia, than by supporting twenty at home as idle footmen, or useless shop-boys."

He had argued rationally and judiciously until now, but in his last paragraph Clough's anger at injustice and hypocrisy came to the surface, and he attacked the complacency of those members of the "enjoying classes" and their apologists among the "Manchester school" of economists who would have liked to see sacrifices made by everyone except themselves: "Yet economists, who against this consumption say not a word, profess that the Ten Hours' Bill is a robbery from the laborers—that the workman's long time and short wages are simply indispensable for laying up a stock for his future employments. Capitalism, who keeps his carriage, will never be able to build mills, unless Labor, who barely keeps himself, saves money to help him."

If times were indeed so hard for the capitalist, said Clough, then "ours is no time for scruples . . . Verily, if this be so—if to limit the hours of labor be to rob the coming generation of the stock that should be laid up for them—a far greater and more guilty robbery do they commit who, on whatever pretext, diminish that stock by consuming for consumption's sake only. If both err and both unwittingly, yet the zeal of mistaken benevolence is hardly to be compared with the complacency of mistaken self-indulgence."

But Clough went even further than this, and in his last two letters he expressed some of those ideas which alarmed men like Church and Price. Over a hundred years before England eventually adopted a national incomes policy, or began seriously to think of regulating trade for the benefit of the whole community, of controlling the rate of industrial growth, or of fixing a minimum wage, Clough's words adumbrated some form of all these measures. Eschewing most of the various schemes of economic controls then being mooted— cooperatives, for example, or profit-sharing, or land reform—his thought centered on a strong central government working through ministries and commissions to regulate the economy in the interests of all.

The more gently to introduce his suggestion that there ought to be a "chamber of commerce, endowed with powers far transcending any now thought of," that could "regulate prices" without "the present 'higgling of the market,' " Clough first put the case for such protection from the side of the entrepreneur. Suppose, he said in his fifth letter, titled "A Few Practical Hints," a builder has erected too many houses. The price might fall "indefinitely"; he might suffer, or all builders might suffer if he undersold them.[121] Is this an example, Clough asks, of fairness and the principle of honesty working through a "law" called laisser-faire, or is it "fair only as winnings won by gambling are fair?" No existing authority could interfere with such a loss. "Is it possible," Clough asks, "that such authority should be called into existence at all?" To attempt regulation of prices piecemeal would introduce "extremest confusion." But *"some chamber of commerce, endowed with powers far transcending any now thought of"* [Italics mine] might end the present system in which we "stifle the murmurs of the ingenuous unmercantile conscience; we strike the bargain, and then go on to boast of it; boast how much we have had done for us; how little we have done in return."

It is noteworthy that Clough in attacking the "law of laisser-faire" does not here employ Carlyle's moral objections to it as dehumanizing and degrading, but chooses rather to question the actuality of the "law" itself. He objects that the so-called law is no such thing, but with a sociologist's instinct sees it as a "mere expedient."

In his next and last letter,[122] Clough puts the case for protecting the laborer and sums up his opposition to laisser-faire. "A slight degree of thought would suffice," he writes drily, to overturn the "fundamental misconception" that "the common rules of trade do in themselves constitute the laws of fairness and honesty." Two years before Mill was to show that competition had never been truly free, and that "there [had] always [been] a master who throws his sword into the scale, and the terms are such as he imposes,"[123] Clough is already saying that "on the contrary, these rules require the continual interference of higher principles, as of equity; that the whole system is a mere expedient, the best, indeed, we can lay our hands on; it serves in nine cases, but in the tenth it fails; an instrument demanding perpetual superintendence; a sort of ruthless inanimate steam-engine, which must have its driver always with it to keep it from doing mischief untold."

E. L. Woodward has pointed out that "in many cases, the argument [about laisser-faire] concealed an admission that a problem was insoluble, or that it must be endured because no one could think of any method of solving it."[124] Clough, however, did not regard social problems as insoluble. The idea that strong economic policies could not exist simply because they never had existed before was anathema to him. The present system, he insisted, "is an expedient, I say, just as trial by jury is an expedient . . . an expedient . . . and an instrument." "If a plan," he insisted, "were brought forward tomorrow which could be warranted more exactly and unerringly just in the rewarding of labor, it would, I believe, be the duty and interest of the nation, in spite of its being less productive, to adopt it." Equity and not cheapness should determine prices; national need and not the profit motive should motivate trade: "It is not, I conceive, true that I am to go to the cheapest shop because it saves me my money; or, if you please, saves money for the nation. I go, or I ought to go, because it is the fairest." And if a central authority such as he conceived might control the building market for the good of all, so the state should be empowered to demand work from its citizens, to "compel shoemakers to make shoes": "The state, I should hold, has a right as perfect to compel shoemakers to make shoes, as it has to exact their respective services from soldiers in the army, sailors in the navy, or judges on the bench. I pay the price because it is part of a system which, on the whole, is the most efficient means for making men work in their trades and getting them their honest return."

Nothing could be more specific as a statement of opposition to the dog-eat-dog philosophy of business ethics. In understanding his bitter opposition to the ethics that governed trade in his time, one should remember not only his own father's experience of failure in the attempt to "struggle, feet and hands, with enemies,"[125] but the way business claimed its apprentices as soon as they were in their early teens. The ordinary merchant entered the business world that was to form his ideas of life at around fifteen—much earlier if he were poor—and unless he were an unusual man he had had little time to develop for himself much knowledge and interest in other matters. Clough angrily rejected the pattern set by the Mr. Dombeys and their henchmen and victims, the Carkers and Little Grinders: "I am not to regard myself as engaged in a petty warfare with all those for whom I work or who work for me. It is not a scramble who shall get most and do least. We are not adventurers, soldiers of fortune, each man for himself, and chance for us all; we are servants to each other, soldiers in a standing army, public functionaries with public duties and public pay." This is the essential code of ethics by which Clough tried to live in a commercial society, a code based on a sense of personal dignity and keen pride. As an undergraduate, criticizing Aristotle's *Ethics* in 1839, he had written, "His system . . . from beginning to end is—in his own words—a δεύτερος πλοῦς [second best].[126] The son of a merchant, speaking to merchants, Clough nevertheless refused to adopt the ethics which Aristotle elsewhere had said were their stock in trade.

Clough's aim in these "Hints" was not to paint either a communistic state or one characterized by "a centralized organization with an all-powerful state owning and running the means of production, distribution, and exchange," to use Robbins's definition of modern socialism,[127] and to term him flatly a "Socialist" might be misleading. He does not yet question the private ownership of property, although he later regarded this as a less than absolute right, but limits himself to envisaging a government endowed with certain broad regulatory powers exercised for the benefit of society as a whole. And his analysis of the situation proceeds as much from moral as from purely economic grounds: to the "law" of laisser-faire which he challenges he opposes the higher laws of justice and equity. How to classify his ideas in view of the contemporary fluidity of parties and ideologies is a difficult question, although they appear to find their closest parallel in those of John Stuart Mill. Unlike Clough, Mill tended to favor cooperative movements rather than a more powerful central government, but he defined himself as a socialist on grounds that in a similar way were primarily ethical: socialism, he wrote, could describe his own aims inasmuch as he looked for the equal distribution of labor and the day "when the rule that they who do not work shall not eat will be applied not to paupers only, but impartially to all."[128] Clough likewise looked for the equalization of labor and held, quoting more directly than Mill, " 'If a man will not work, neither let him eat.' "[129] Lord Robbins has asserted truthfully that Mill's "socialism" would not be recognized as such now. Mill used the term however in an era when no consensus existed as to its meaning and each defined it for himself. Clough may not have been a socialist by our lights, but his thought must be estimated in the terms of his own day, and in grasping some of the complexities of his position then we can better understand the distrust men like Church and Price had for what Church called Clough's unacceptable "degree of socialism,"[130] and why no exploration of these speculations by Clough was permitted to appear in the "Memoir" which Symonds found so "incomplete" and unsatisfactory.[131]

Before considering Clough's *Retrenchment* pamphlet, his last major piece of prose on political issues, it will be illuminating to note the rather different persona he presents in a little known MS called "An Ill World," which Walter Houghton has said is "reminiscent of Swift."[132] Evidently occasioned by the endemic outbreaks of cholera and mounting deaths throughout England which had been foreseen but against which, despite Chadwick's efforts, no preventive measures had been taken, this fragmentary outburst reveals a Clough both angry and ribaldly funny.[133] This is not the thoughtful young don writing letters to *The Balance,* nor is it Carlyle's apostle, but an aspect of the private Clough, the satiric poet who could be proud, emotional, depressive, ribald, and capable of great scorn, letting loose the "flood of lava boiling-hot" which Clough told Anne he usually kept within himself at Oxford, "living in [a] state of suppressed volcanic action."[134] Yet that flood has been channeled, and in this fragment we have a fascinating insight into the poet-reformer deliberately experimenting with the resonances of a literary mask. The mask is that of Timon of Athens, unnamed but presented in a dialogue with the cynical philosopher Apemantus. Clough invents for Timon a calculated spontaneity of anger; the language is a kind of shout, a personal response to a public disgrace, angry, scatological, parodic, and comically exaggerated. Man, he complains, is since the Fall as corrupt physically as morally: "An ill world, indeed Apemantus! an ill world—a most pestilent miasmatic epidemic-breeding atmosphere. Ah mother Eve, Father Adam, ye two between ye let out a most pernicious gas amongst us, a most concentrated, transcendental, sulphuretted hydrogen. That which of cholera is not true, saith the doctor, is, saith Apemantus, in the moral world axiomatic."

As he goes on, the cause of Clough's melancholy becomes more clear. "The air that I inhale, and this water so bright and clear, pellucid, sincere-seeming elemental purity that recreates me—these things are replete with fungoids that once in the human venter do generate, not one way, nor two, but many." He is disgusted to realize that his body is, willy nilly, a host for parasitic germs, a breeding place of disease; but the disgust becomes farce. "O ye foul subtle infusia, how shall we escape you; how live if we do not? For to walk about one mass of engendering fungoids, to be the brothel and public bedchamber perpetuating copulation and recopulation of the progeny of the close-stool—such is our lot, o my brother. Have respect therefore unto dunghills, which in comparison of us are respectable." In the next paragraph the note of parody on an Evangelical sermon being offered against the atheistic Chadwick breaks out more strongly; in his present mood, even the old Arnoldian phrase about choosing the good, which he himself had uttered as an undergraduate, does not escape his fire: "Yet indeed shall no man deprecate nor deodorize us, which is indeed but smooth hypocrisy, nor appoint sewage or sanitary commissioners upon us. He that endureth to the end—for indeed God would have his angels strong-minded. Butter and honey shall we eat—ordure and compost shall he smell, and submit himself to be engendered upon of zoophizta that he may, through much tribulation of nose, enter into the kingdom of good smells, having learnt to reject the evil and choose the good." He refers to the numbers who were perishing of cholera in London: "For indeed God is also glorified in them that perish at London or elsewhere and become as the dung of the Earth. Have patience therefore, o thou semi-fungified Apemantus—for indeed is there an objectivity of smell."

To mention dung, as Clough says in *Dipsychus,* is not "genteel,"[135] but much of his best poetry is based on the saying, in one way or another, of things almost unsayable in his own day. Prose in its form, this little fragment is close to some of his satirical verse in its intensity of feeling, and gives us a glimpse into the "lava boiling-hot" which lay beneath his crust of composure and added motivation to his years of protest.

In 1852, referring to his so-called *Retrenchment* pamphlet, Clough wrote off-handedly to his fiancée: "Have you looked at my sometime pamphlet? . . . I shouldn't write it now, you must know—I am wiser—but it meant something at the time."[136] What that "something" was needs to be examined in a new light, for in this pamphlet, whose actual title is *A Consideration of Some Objections Against the Retrenchment Association,* Clough echoes but also goes beyond Carlyle to advocate principles which neither the Scotsman nor he himself in later years could support; to understand what he meant five years later when he thought himself "wiser" we need to know better what earlier opinions he had corrected.

The pamphlet's immediate occasion was the Irish famine, which had been the great fact of political and economic thought since 1846. The repeal of the Corn Laws was achieved in May of that year, but the freer importation of wheat did not, under Russell's callous mishandling of the problems of disease and transport, prevent continued and even worsening suffering.[137] One of the major obstacles of those who sought to help Ireland, however, from Peel down to Clough, was the difficulty of persuading the English to believe soon enough that the stories of terrible suffering were true. Too many preferred to shut their eyes, partly no doubt out of respect for their purses, partly from distrust of Ireland's reputation for exaggeration.[138] The national conscience was aroused only very gradually by such stories as that of Skibbereen, which caught Clough's attention and to which he refers in his essay. (An Irish magistrate named Cummins who had brought food and clothing to Skibbereen wrote *The Times* that he had been mobbed by some two hundred starving, half-naked figures who had begun to tear the clothes from his back. Gripped about the neck from behind he turned to find himself held by a nursing mother wearing only a sacking loincloth; he had run in terror—but their "demoniac yells" were still ringing in his ears.)[139] Peel's government fell a few months after the necessary repeal had been instituted, and under Lord John Russell, as Cecil Woodham-Smith writes, "Adherence to *laissez-faire* was carried to such a length that in the midst of one of the major famines of history, the government was perpetually nervous of being too good to Ireland and of corrupting the Irish people by kindness and so stifling the virtues of self-reliance and industry."[140]

Clough was always aware in his prose of his relation with the audience he wished to reach; getting "the right tone" to do "some good" through an article might be "*the extreme* difficulty,"[141] but it was worth the trouble. The tone of the *Retrenchment* pamphlet, unlike that of *The Balance* letters, is essentially that of a public polemic, and for this reason draws heavily on Carlyle's stylistic model. The Retrenchment Association had been formed at Oxford to relieve the poor both by collecting funds for them and by urging a policy of restraint on unnecessary spending. Its aims appear to have been attacked, and Clough entered the fray with this pamphlet, written—although not conceived, as he said—in haste and published on April 16, 1847. Like Carlyle's writing, it is characterized by Biblical allusions, declamation, and a plethora of imagery that seethes with life. Like Carlyle, too, he invents a set of characters who "illustrate the points of view . . . he wishes to commend or condemn,"[142] and evokes series of images—"the ghosts of forgotten champagne bottles, the spectra of long-worn-out waistcoats, the simulacra of the fruits and the ices of Whitsuntide '46"—that are precise and vivid. In his prose Bennett and Bickerstaff, the tradesmen, shift places with the Duke of Newcastle, while Oxford's bloods, the "born to be rich, or at least born not to be poor . . . young men of Oxford" placidly "ventilate [their] fopperies arm-in-arm up the High Street."[143] The thoughtful tone of earlier essays is abandoned here, and Clough assumes the role Holloway has described as that of the Victorian Sage, aiming less at logical proof than at "opening the eyes" of his readers, "making [them] see in [their] experience what [they] had failed to see before."[144] He cannot here assume that his luxurious Oxford audience shares his moral assumptions: the undergraduates to whom he addresses himself stand in need of correction and persuasion, and in such circumstances he not only can but should strike the gong loudly. While the sky in Ireland "looks upon famishment and fever . . . let us not scoff at eternal justice," he urges, "over-eating, over-drinking, and over-enjoying" (p. 9).

The typical argument against retrenchment was that "if I save at all, I must save to pay my debts." But, he asks, "is it never added . . . I will therefore not save at all? . . . It is not impossible there are men who will say, What money I have I owe to Bennett or Bickerstaff; however, as Bennett and Bickerstaff are not famishing they may as well wait, and then I shall have my money to take me up to town" (p. 8). A tendency to antithesis, epigram, and even alliteration, all rare in Clough's prose, is aroused by the strength of his feelings: "Surprise Bennett with banknotes, and gratify Bickerstaff with gold . . . I ask you not to be generous before you are just; I only bid you make haste and be just that you may be generous the sooner" (p. 9).

Drumming away at the unproductive consumption he saw around him, Clough evokes Skibbereen as an image of the suffering following on the near-paralysis of trade: "On whom falls the loss? Not on the rich . . . but on those whose labor makes the rich man rich . . . He who at this moment saves money (I say not to send to Skibbereen, but) to lay out in some profitable investment, to lend to master manufacturers for buying cotton, or landlords for draining . . . yes he who buys into the funds does more . . . than he who spends, albeit for the benefit of . . . trade, in wines, and ices, and waistcoats" (p. 5).

Some would reply, Clough foresaw, that the tradesman's workpeople as well as himself would suffer by "retrenchment." Clough effectively used the parable of a stranded ship to illustrate the condition of the nation: "The ship is stranded and short of provisions, but a port full of supplies is at hand; and they who control the matter will not victual the boat's crew that should go to obtain them, because forsooth it would straiten the allowance of their cabin boys, and cooks, and waiters. And that these forsooth may earn their food, and their masters have an excuse for feeding them, these masters bid them continue their functions . . . for their own overeating" (p. 7). He unashamedly repeats himself, casting himself in the accurate but still calculated role of impassioned don hurrying

87

to press, under the force of conscience and public suffering:

> . . . I am running into idle repetitions . . . But . . . you must not insult God alike and man with the spectacle of your sublime indifference. The angels of heaven, . . . as they pass above [Ireland's] devoted shores, in gazing on that ordained destruction let fall untasted from their immortal lips the morsel of ambrosial substance . . .
>
> The term is half over . . . ere I correct the proof sheet, the hot weather may be here. But if I have been obliged to write hurriedly, believe me I have obliged myself to think not hastily (pp. 17, 19).

It is not "the graces and splendors of composition" he has thought of, but "Irish poor men's miseries, English poor men's hardships, and your unthinking indifference" (p. 19). A Jeremiad aimed at a complacent university, this essay's Carlylean prose style is fitting for the prophetic role its author here assumes.

Yet although Clough obviously shares Carlyle's concern for the poor and his anger at the idleness of the rich (basic assumptions, indeed, for anyone writing such an attack), it would be a mistake to ignore portions of this essay which have received less attention but which diverge from a Carlylean stance to differ from him on substantive issues. Carlyle does not call for the redistribution of labor or question the rights of property: his appeals, as Cazamian has said, are all moral appeals, and he insists on moral change as precedent to any change in the social structure.[145] The Biblical allusion he makes to the ownership of the land should not be expanded to infer any hostility to private property per se; it is the idea of "work[ing] well" on the land he wishes to emphasize, and the work he wants to encourage is clearly good stewardship, responsible ownership on the part of his readers. In Carlyle's golden feudal myth Cedric owned the pigs, but Gurth, the peasant who tended them, had his share of "the parings." And he had moreover the "inexpressible satisfaction" of being held in a supportive social structure: "he had superiors, inferiors, equals."[146] The ranks are not to leave their places, but to perform their functions; the governors are paternally and wisely to care for the poor, if need be enforcing true liberty—that of governance—on the foolish.[147] Clough in passing acknowledges the potential value of the upper classes in preserving civilization, but essentially he does not share Carlyle's valuation of a rigid social hierarchy, or the might on which that valuation rests. He is attracted not to power but to the virtues of fairness and self-restraint, which, being in the reach of all, are essentially egalitarian. Labor, Clough says, must not only get what Carlyle called Gurth's share of the "parings" of Cedric's pigs, the pigs also must somehow be redistributed. And the "Institution of Property" when held excessively and unfairly, was no longer to be regarded as an inalienable right.[148]

In 1829 the Duke of Newcastle had won for "his name an unpleasing immortality in our political history" when, after having suborned most of his tenants at a borough election and evicted forty others who opposed him, he defended himself, as Morley wrote, "with the haughty truism, then just ceasing to be true, that he had a right to do as he liked with his own."[149] Clough makes this statement a refrain as he turns his attack to the distribution both of property and labor. "I know not," he writes,

if there be any who venture on the bold declaration, the money is mine, and I will have the good of it; I have got and I will spend; the Irish have not, and they must do without. To these sticklers for the rights of property it is worth putting one question. If you had been wrecked the other day in the Tweed steamer, and had been successful in reaching the place of safety in the rocks, would you, if the articles of food secured there from the waters happened to belong to your own peculiar . . . stores—would you have entertained the thought that to you exclusively belonged the right to enjoy them? This barrel of biscuits is marked with my letters, and was always known to be mine; did I not pay for it? Mine has come, all the better for me, yours has not, all the worse for you (p. 10).

If this argument were offered too often, Clough suggests, there might be a dangerous inquiry into the original means by which property had been secured. The second Chartist petition had alleged that it could "prove" that the aristocracy had usurped the people's ancient rights.[150] While hinting at the same idea, Clough grounds his argument rather on Scripture, saying that the only true hereditary title to property was that bequeathed by God to all his children: "And the earth hath He given to the children of men." Clough would advise these "sticklers for the right of property," "to hesitate ere you venture the question, 'May I not do what I like with my own?' ere you meddle with such edge tools as the subject of property. Someone, I fear, might be found to look up your title-deeds and to quote inconvenient Scriptures" (p. 10).

Still alluding to men like Newcastle, Clough goes on to say that the inviolability of property is no sacred law but an expedient, which should protect only the industrious: "The Institution of Property . . . is all well enough as a human expedient to secure its reward to industry, and protect the provident laborer against the careless and idle" (p. 10). His bias towards the worker is evident. The inalienable right argument is not sufficient to justify the excessive wealth of some: "But for half-million-per-annum fortunes, fifty-mile-long estates, and may-I-not-do-what-I-please-with-my-own proprietors, some other justification, it would seem, must be sought" (p. 10). "Sought and found," Clough insists, in the strain that was to alarm Price, "Found it must be by owners, or looked for it will be by others." "How came you to have money?" he asks, and alludes, as he had done the year before, to Mirabeau's dictum that all money was got by "begging, stealing or serving" (p. 10).

Clough does not wish his challenge to stand unmodified, however, and he adds below that "it is of course utterly foreign to my meaning to do anything but find a secure basis for the rights of property; to impugn them were idle" (p. 10). But the "secure basis" he desires is clearly not to be inferred merely from ownership: "justice as administered by the laws of property must be modified by the equity of a higher though less definite rule" (p. 10). In times of famine, he asserts, "to appropriate is to steal." No more than Carlyle would he destroy the aristocracy. The good they may do in preserving civilization—so the old argument runs, and he does not dispute it— provides the justification for distinctions among ranks. But in principle the equalization of labor is a duty: "So far as . . . without encouraging present idleness and improvidence, without encroaching unduly on provisions for posterity, it were possible to equalize the distribution of labor, so far were that equalisation a duty" (p. 10). "The sons of deceased public servants"—so Clough redefines the aristocracy—"possess no indefeasible title to those lands, and goods, and moneys, which they call their earnings" (p. 15). Just how Clough would have redistributed labor is not made clear; perhaps he had in mind those powers by which, a year earlier, he held a government could "compel shoemakers to make shoes."[151]

Clough's former master at Rugby, Bonamy Price, who had become an active capitalist and railway director, wrote Clough that he regarded the younger man's views as tending toward socialism or communism.[152] (Clough may have anticipated Price's disagreement, for he had not sent him a copy of his pamphlet.)[153] He dissented strongly from Clough's statement that "in great calamities a higher law, 'a law within the law' steps in to supersede that of property." Probably he was also offended by Clough's exhortation to take as "guide" the "apostolic limitation of that primitive-Christian state of things where 'they had all things in common.' "[154] Price demanded, "Are you prepared to defend the legitimacy of the [workers'] demand for a fair day's wages for a fair day's work . . . as being most calculated in the long run to maintain the largest number of men in comfort and abundance?" If that was his line of argument, it was dangerous. "A socialist, a communist would agree so because they believe such a distribution of wealth as this demand implies would cause the largest amount of industry that could be effected by law" (fol. 111). But they would be wrong. "Once make the owners of property," said Price, "feel that they must share it compulsorily with the masses and the desire to work, to accumulate, will be so paralyzed, as to diminish vastly the sustaining powers of the nation" (fol. 111).

The only way to cure economic distress was by "direct calls on the government and by appeals, *moral* appeals, to individuals" (fol. 112). References to "higher laws" would be understood by the poor merely as "an invitation to help themselves, at their discretion" (fol. 113). Price also rejected the distinction Clough (after Mill) had drawn between productive and unproductive consumption: "By drinking Burgundy," the Rugby master insisted, "a man keeps up as much industry as he would by setting men to drain" (fol. 115) — i.e., by investing in capital improvements. Clough's reply was conciliatory in tone. He seems to have regarded communism and socialism as conjointly and favorably characterized by "benevolence" rather than the motive of "greed" he attached to capitalism, but he wanted to avoid argument about their practicality: "if needs be, let the greedy be greedy to the utmost. I do not moot the question whether the actual selfish or selfish-domestic rule be or be not a better means for making people work than a theoretical Communistic or Socialistic system, working by benevolence and public spirit.[155] But he would have established the principle, which clearly Price would have opposed, that "every man has a right to a fair day's wages for a fair day's work—*jure divino* this; *and that proprietors have no jure divino right to their property in its full extent and integrity.* The land belongs to the human race that is and that shall be; and whatever A. B. and C. have got out of it [it] is liable to pay rent or royalties to the true proprietor."[156] [Italics mine.]

If we wish to sum up Clough's political position at this point in his life we will not find a convenient label to attach to it. He himself acknowledged with pleased amusement his reputation as a "republican"; a contemporary loosely termed his views "Chartism"; an older, very orthodox man saw communism in his *Bothie,* written a year later. None of these terms, as we have seen, could be literally applied to Clough. What is clear, however, is that his opinions and activities were notably to the left of those of the not inconsiderable circle he moved in at Oxford. Many of his contemporaries—men like Froude, Jowett, and A. P. Stanley—like liberals of the 1930's or subsequent periods, found it, in this decade of violence and widespread starvation, appropriate to hold reforming political notions. But few went so far as Clough did, or wrote, read, and spoke as actively as he. The closest analogue, as I have suggested above, to Clough's views may be found in those of John Stuart Mill, who in 1848 defined himself as a socialist by criteria which Clough espoused also. Clough was a socialist in the sense that Mill uses the word, but to stress this term, although it would in a limited sense be accurate, might also be misleading, for it might be taken to imply adherence to a party, group, or doctrine which did not then exist and which Clough did not take on himself to supply. What is perhaps more important, then, than the affixing of possibly anachronistic labels is to recognize the seriousness of the leftward tendency of Clough's political activity during the era, the dominance during his young manhood which such issues held in his thought, and the daring which some of his writings exhibit in their willingness to take a fresh look at certain of the country's economic, and by implication at least, social structures.

We have seen now that Church's phrase about "Mr. Clough's Chartism" could not have been intended literally: it connoted rather, for a man of the upper class, views dangerous, like those of the Chartists, to the class structure and to social and economic privilege. It was undoubtedly views such as these that Mrs. Clough was unwilling to discuss, but not least among Clough's accomplishments, we can now see, was his ability to hold and publicize his opinions while winning the respect and liking of men older and more powerful than he who were entirely opposed to his ideas. Successful as a teacher, influential among his peers in local groups, political and otherwise, the kind of leader who gained men's love and respect without making these his object, Clough, whose poetry we read for its complexity and subtlety of perception, was also a man of unusual personal force. The real "problem" in understanding Clough is not finding out why he "failed," but grasping what held him together, perceiving the complexities of his nature, and gaining some notion of the shifts in their equilibrium and the results of those shifts. The study of Clough's prose would be valuable if for no other reason than the way in which it shows us not an "uncommitted," man but a complicated one, partly the "serene," sound, scholarly public figure of the Decade and his friends' early memories, and partly, simultaneously, an emotional, proud, and highly sensitive writer, whose artist's intense awareness of tone and style helped him control the expression of these more private responses. Not least among his creations during this period was his integration of the two, an integration which perhaps reinforced primarily the public side of his character, strengthening and deepening his capacity for work at contemporary social problems. Clough was neither a revolutionary nor a utopian, although he hoped for the best from Europe's revolutions of 1848; but he had a creative man's capacity to look freshly at a familiar object and imagine new possibilities for it and new combinations of forces. He stood midway between those who, like Carlyle or Newman, held that no social advance could be authentic without first improving man's moral nature, and those architects of social change like Owen or Fourier who hoped that by the planning of new towns and new societies man might progress to a "pantisocratic" state of moral perfection. But interestingly, the kind of economic changes Clough hoped for through more powerful governmental controls—rather than the other means, such as association, that were then mooted—were in the mainstream of those measures which Great Britain over the last century, through a variety of manipulative controls, has ultimately come to adopt. Clough wrote little of his best poetry during this period; it is probable that the poet and public man could not find simultaneously powerful expression in him, that one or the other had to be dominant in his consciousness. But it is clear too that the same originality of vision we see in Clough's poetry, the same sense it gives us of anticipating the mood of things to come, we see also in his political thought. "I can feel faith in what is being carried on by my generation," Clough wrote. More than many, perhaps, he was aware of what was being "carried on"; less than most did he distrust the changes that in fact came more slowly than his "generation" then expected. This imaginative openness to new experience, this faith in his own generation, were to be disciplined in the ensuing few years but not checked completely: out of the tension between them and this discipline arose what is probably Clough's best poetry. With the closing sometime between 1847 and 1848 of this period of hopefulness, of untrammeled "great force," we see concluded the first half of Clough's real education.

CHAPTER III

The Morals of Intellect

In the mixture of moral pride and moral courage in Clough's career, there is a strangely tragic quality, a quality that can be seen not only in the half-prophetic, half-joking announcements he made about himself from time to time—announcements that often came true—but also in the very pattern of his development, in which hubris, recognition, and peripeteia follow irrevocably one on another, brought on by a flaw for which Clough was neither entirely blameworthy nor entirely blamefree. He has been compared, by inference, to Oedipus;[1] but he can be compared in another way to the man who by his desire to know the truth and save his city brought destruction upon himself; for, like Oedipus, he saw around him a city which he dearly loved slowly dying,[2] and like him, too, he could neither give up his desire to know "*if* things are bad, that they are so"[3] nor to cease asking those obsessive questions even when he knew that their answers would bring him into exile. He was not the only man to leave Oxford on principle, but he was among the first, and if, en masse, the handful of men who left the city they loved in protest at its "mephitic"[4] atmosphere of enforced conformity contributed to the pressure which ultimately brought about the reforms of 1854—the first major ones since Laud—then in some measure Clough helped preserve its health.

The first acts of the drama, at any rate, had passed, and Clough's hubristic need to know all that could and could not be proved about religious truth had already established itself by 1843. Between that date and 1848 Clough wrestled with his conscience, attempting first to ignore the question of subscription and then to find another form of faith before finally announcing to his friends that Christianity was no longer his "actuating religion," punning to Froude that he was "a heathen man and a (Re)publican"[5] and telling Hawkins that he "deeply repent[ed]" of ever having subscribed at all.[6] Recognition had succeeded the agony, and an exile was to follow for which there could be no reparation. It is that process of recognition that will occupy us in this chapter.

The problem of subscription figured largely not only in Clough's life, but in the lives of many, and had done for centuries. In Clough's day, as William Reginald Ward has written in his richly detailed study, *Victorian Oxford,* "oaths and subscriptions . . . were abhorrent to three great groups, the dissenters, the radicals and the evangelicals."[7] All ministers of the Anglican Church and persons taking their degrees at the two ancient universities had been required by law since 1572 to sign an oath attesting their belief in the Thirty-Nine Articles of the Church. These articles, which owed much to the Confession of Würtemberg, approved by Luther himself, were one of a number of sixteenth-century "Confessions" by which the Reformation had made itself known. The first five articles of the thirty-nine affirmed the basic, "Catholic," doctrines of the faith, but, as Barry has written, most of these confessions were essentially negative and the Anglican document was also. At least ten of the articles were directed against the growing power of Calvinism with its extreme doctrines of predestination, election, and so on; eighteen more are primarily attacks on the "usurpations of Rome" and its claims to authority on the questions of tradition, the Pope, a celibate clergy, propitiary masses, and other familiar points of disagreement.[8] Subscription meant, in effect, that Clough promised to accept as his own this ancient formula with all the prima facie marks of sectarian warfare preserved in its precise restrictions and condemnations.[9] Required subscription had long caused—or been the symptom of—profound schisms in English religious and social life. Dissenters, or Nonconformists, were burdened by handicaps imposed by the Establishment. They were excluded from taking university degrees at Oxford or Cambridge, which impoverished them culturally and to a considerable degree economically, although they came to form the backbone of the middle class. (The alternatives to the old universities were meager and not equivalent. London University, founded in 1828 specifically to admit Dissenters, was still too new and floundering to be a significant force in education. If they wished to leave the country the universities of Scotland might admit them but these institutions in an intensely Presbyterian country had their own strong religious ambience. In England, the opportunities for social advancement to the higher levels, the sense of being part of the mainstream and not "excommunicate"—to use the Unitarian Crabb Robinson's term—the prestige and potentially powerful connections that came with university life were all greatly limited, if not entirely missing, for anyone not a graduate of Oxford or Cambridge.) The Dissenters were taxed to support the Established Church, and their own churches were consequently short-changed. To the working classes, as we have seen, the Established Church seemed to be actually an instrument of class oppression. Even many Anglicans in the nineteenth century found the Articles an obstacle. Arnold, as we have seen, hesitated for almost a year before he could bring himself to subscribe, while Newman composed *Tract 90,* the famous essay of crucial importance to his career, in order, he thought, to show that the Articles were not anti-Roman after all.[10] The major crisis in the life of Clough's former tutor, W. G. Ward, arose when this Tractarian admitted in 1844, in *The Ideal of a Christian Church,* that he had brought himself to subscribe to the Articles only by interpreting them in a "non-natural" sense. His opponents found it hard to answer his challenge, paraphrased by Morley: "Show me how any of the recognized parties in the church can subscribe in a natural sense, before you condemn me for subscribing in a non-natural."[11] Yet Ward lost his M.A. degree for this, and his career at Oxford ended in 1845. Dislike of subscription was widespread among Clough's friends and most of them equivocated. Shairp and Jowett doubted at least some of the articles, and there was scarcely a member of their circle, whether Puseyite or Arnoldian, who could have signed the articles without some quiver of conscience. Yet not to sign, unless one had a private fortune, meant that any man not destined for trade was likely to blight his fortune and render himself, however talented, ineffectual—and, in particular, ineffectual in reforming the very system he disliked. If he had a career to make, he was déclassé before starting. Education and the Church were what these young men had been bred up to, but dissent closed these avenues. Upper-middle class and aristocratic society would look with suspicion on such singularity. A man might still rise in medicine or law, but on the whole these professions (except for the Bar) were a step down for a university graduate.[12]

Clough's resistance to subscription had two major phases. The first occurred in 1843, when Hawkins offered him the position of Tutor, and he faced the fact that if he did not take his M.A., which involved a renewed subscription, the promising career which had only just begun would come to a halt. Clough had no specific objections, but he disliked it on principle:

I have a very large amount of objection or rather repugnance to sign 'ex animo' the 39 Articles, which it would be singular and unnatural not to do if I staid in Oxford, as without one's MA degree one of course stands quite still, and has no resource for employment . . . It is not so much from any definite objection to this or that point as general dislike to Subscription and strong feeling of its being . . . malgré Guy's Hospital Maurice,[13] a bondage, and a very heavy one, and one that may cramp and cripple one for life. What to do, if I don't stay at Oxford, is a very different question.[14]

The problem of subscription is a fascinating one that comes up again and again in Victorian studies, and W. R. Ward has shown in *Victorian Oxford* how it became as much a stumbling block for the Tractarians, who at first had made ammunition of it, as it had long been for the liberals.[15] Part of its interest lies in the fact that it was involved in the gradual but hard-fought establishment of two modern principles: the separation of religion and education, and academic freedom—which, removed from its religious connotations, is, after all, only another aspect of that right of free inquiry for which the Noetics and later the Liberals at Oxford fought.[16] Clough understood these principles and knew what was at stake.[17] Nevertheless, having no clear-cut objections at the time, urged by compelling practical arguments, and also no doubt by his friends, he "signed without demur" in October, 1843.[18] The first phase of his struggle with subscription was over.

He entered now on the period of what he later called his "very great force."[19] The development of Clough's political and religious ideas suggests the struggle of a man tied by a rope on two sides: the more he freed himself in one area of conventional thought, the looser his bonds seemed to become in the other. He plunged into the "thoroughly terrestrial element of college tutorism . . . Mendicity Societies and the like" that was to render him the "Apostle of anti-laissez-faire," and this absorbed him greatly for the next year and a half. Nevertheless, as he wrote, he still considered "the old scruple to be a sort of St. Paul who ought not to be put off by any Felix . . . to a more convenient season," and perhaps the very suppression of his doubts made them keener and more distinct when they again erupted in 1845.[20]

The debacle following Ward's degradation and the conversion of Ward, Newman, and others to Rome made notable changes in the tone at Oxford. The vociferous Tractarian party now stilled, others, to whom, as two contemporary observers wrote in almost identical words, " 'the historic truth of Christianity was . . . an open question,' " began to make themselves heard.[21] Clough was among this group; indeed, he usually figures prominently, sometimes with Froude, when examples of this unrest are offered. It is not generally recognized that Clough's doubts had taken fairly clear shape by 1845, but we are able from the unpublished journal of his sister Anne to learn in some detail the nature of his questions, for she quotes Arthur as her only teacher in these matters. Her journals suggest that Clough may well have read D. F. Strauss's epoch-making *Life of Jesus*[22] in the original German earlier than has been supposed, and it, along with Blanco White's *Life*,[23] seems to have made a strong impression on him. He had known German for some years, and the sudden efflorescence in his arguments of critical views greatly similar to those of Strauss suggests that he did not have to wait until George Eliot's translation appeared in 1846 to make himself familiar with the German's attacks on dogma.[24] At any rate, the Gospels, sacraments, and liturgy were now being criticized by Clough. Summarizing the reading and thinking she had been doing under her brother's guidance, Anne noted in 1845 that she had felt the "tremendous effect" of reading Blanco White's *Life*:

I thought I could not but believe much the same, and this distressed me greatly . . . I longed to talk to Arthur about what was occupying my thoughts but could not. We had spoken a little the Sunday before on the subject of Baptism, which he seemed greatly inclined to regard as merely a sort of form which had been instituted as a sign of admission into the early Christian Church and useful then when outward signs for everything were constantly required—but he seemed half inclined to doubt whether there was any use in continuing it.[25]

Arthur had also criticized the liturgy: "He spoke too of the bad arrangement of the Sunday lessons from the Old Testament and the little advantage people in general derived from the going to Church, and the need there was for a thorough alteration in the church services." In an interestingly naïve reflection of J. W. Beach's thesis that in the nineteenth century Nature increasingly assumed the proportions of religion, Anne concluded by explaining why she was ready to agree with her brother and be "liberalized": "I had felt for some time a sort of freedom growing up in my thoughts. I half fancied from seeing the open mountains, breathing the pure air—and so I had been prepared to be liberalized." Arthur had further told her that "the first three Gospels were not to be altogether depended on." Most unsettling of all to Anne was the Straussian reinterpretation of the doctrine of the Atonement, in which, even at fourth hand, Kant's views are discernible:

About the doctrine of the atonement He [sic] said—what Christ said to Nicodemus of John was the right doctrine, viz. that a change was effected in us by the knowledge of Christ and by the spirit of Christ in us. That the good in us was made strong and able to overcome evil—and this is our redemption—Christ came to show forth the perfection of his Father—to show us what we ought to be—and his power works in us to effect a change in our lives. Truth surely must mean an understanding and a realizing of these truths and a living by them.

Strauss had put it thus: "According to Kant, also, it ought not to be made a condition of salvation to believe that there was once a man who by his holiness and merit gave satisfaction for himself and for all others; for of this the reason tells us nothing; but it *is* the duty of men universally to elevate themselves to the ideal of moral perfection deposited in the reason, and to obtain moral strength by the contemplation of this ideal. Such moral faith alone man is bound to exercise, and not historical faith."[26] "I do not fully understand this doctrine," Anne wrote simply. "I did in some measure when we were speaking together, but I could not grasp it intelligibly to carry it away with me and upon the whole I feel puzzled and uncertain . . . I cannot speak as I used to do to the children [in her classes] . . . I did not manage the children well at all."

It is, however, possible that Clough had absorbed some of his more radical religious ideas from the reading of the *Life of Blanco White,* which he described as "strong meat" and a "very striking production" which had "almost . . . persuaded [him] to turn Unitarian."[27] White's history, which caused a considerable stir at the time of its publication, must have seemed "strong meat" to Clough not only in its revelations about the still-surviving Spanish Inquisition, but also because it showed how a sincerely religious man, adhering to conscience, could be led step by step further and further from orthodox Christianity.[28] Bred up a Roman Catholic priest, White had become successively an Anglican and a Unitarian. His *Life* was a kind of *Apologia* in reverse, the story of a spiritual pilgrimage whose grail had been the unity of Reason, Faith and Conscience. "I thank God," he wrote, "I never had the gratification of any party in view—my sacrifices have been made to *Truth,* to *Liberty of Conscience,* to the *abolition* of Church Tyranny: else I should exclaim, 'I have washed my hands in vain.' "[29] White had been intimately connected with the Noetics, had been made an honorary member of the Oriel Common Room, and had gone with Whately to Dublin as tutor to his son when Whately became an Archbishop in 1831. He had already given up one promising career in the Spanish Church, but when in 1835 he realized that he could no longer give credence to the Trinity, he left Whately's protection and went as a Unitarian to live on his small pension in Liverpool, where James Martineau, the leading Unitarian minister of his day, had his congregation.[30]

101

Clough spoke highly in 1845 not only of White's *Life* but also of a Dissenting journal known as the *Prospective Review* (then being published by John Chapman, who also published Strauss and various Unitarians, Martineau in particular), saying that he felt "no common attraction for the book and the party [that] brought it out—viz. the high Unitarians."[31] The degree of that attraction is not generally recognized, but the Unitarian connections he began to form at this period played a major role thereafter in his life, for it was through them directly or indirectly that he met his wife, secured the Principalship of University Hall, met Emerson, and emigrated to the United States.[32] Of Martineau himself, who was known for his powerful intellect and was an influential figure among Dissenters during much of the nineteenth century,[33] Clough wrote:

An evening or two [ago] I met Martineau accidentally at a small party chez mon seul ami Unitarien. I liked him greatly. He has a little, I think, of that tendency to use the flattering self-satisfaction or self-consoling unction which one is told is the fault of Sister Martineau, but he talked simply, courteously, and ably, and has a forehead with a good deal of that rough-hewn mountainous strength which one used to look at when at lesson in the library at Rugby, not without trembling. I hope I may not fail to see him and speak with him again. But I am but little at Liverpool.[34]

Yet in spite of this rare though characteristically qualified avowal of attraction, it is evident from some of his unpublished notebook jottings that Clough was saying no more than the truth when in 1849 he told Hawkins that, in spite of having "seen a good deal" of the Unitarians "for some years back . . . I have never entertained any thoughts of joining them."[35]

Clough's objections to the Unitarian doctrines are interesting, for they indicate the influence which transcendentalist, Emersonian objections to Unitarianism had already begun to have upon him. Martineau had discussed in the *Prospective Review* the case of Theodore Parker, the American Transcendentalist who had been virtually excommunicated by orthodox Bostonian Unitarians for preaching that belief in Christ's miracles was not essential to Christian faith, which must rest on man's own, divinely implanted knowledge of God.[36] Martineau (although privately he thought Parker an atheist)[37] avoided condemning him in his article, but felt he had to insist on the uniqueness and centrality of Christianity; therefore he offered a definition of Christianity as being simply "the absolute acceptance of Christ as the Son of man and the Son of God," and held further that the nature of Christ's authority was that of a "divine example," who had "done the work of God himself, and condemned Sin in the flesh."[38] Clough's reaction to this was at once quizzical in tone and transcendental in posture. Jotting down in private notes his comments on Martineau's article, he begins abruptly: "a divinely *ordained* [example of the] conquest over Evil—[in the Temptation and in the Passion]—*effected by divine humanity. —*How far then is that human nature identical with the divine? [The square brackets around "example of" were inserted by Clough.][39] What, in fact, did the Unitarians mean by "divine humanity?" "How far is human nature in us dependent for its divine strength on the acts of this divine humanity? Are they an *actus causatius* [causativus?] to us for anything else? If in either respect we do so depend on it can it be no more divine than ourselves? And apart from these questions remains another, viz. How does human Nature conquer Evil—in its own strength or in God's strength?"

Clough took the transcendentalist position, enunciated by Emerson, that if human nature were divine then Christ had no *historic* value: "God is, not was," as Emerson put it.[40] Biography was morally invalid. Martineau's veneration of Him and of all Biblical history must be misplaced: Adam and Christ could be seen as a mere "Time-Effiguration of the Untemporal truth." "Is there anything in the notion of a Fall and a Redemption which is not conveyed in the common philos. expressions? So Atonement and Grace." Perhaps the historical element in Christianity (which Emerson rejected) was irrelevant: "And secondly, if so [if Atonement and Grace could be reduced merely to philosophical concepts] is it essential to connect these truths of human nature [its capacity to conquer evil] with the historical phenomena of Christ and his life? May not Adam and Christ . . . be but a Time-Effiguration of the Untemporal truth?" If, however, Unitarians justified their adherence to historical Christianity by saying that there might be "a special benefit for us in seeking divine aid through Christianity—in consciously uniting ourselves to him distinct even from any benefit which he may have done us [i.e. distinct from salvation through the Atonement] . . . if so don't we get the Ch[urch] System?"[41] If, in despite of reason, that is, the Unitarians clung to the supposed historical basis of Christianity because they sensed that some support to faith might be derived from it, while disliking the literal interpretation of the Atonement, how did they logically differ from the position of the Church from which they stood apart, but which would have been valuable to them?

In short, the doctrines of Unitarianism appeared to Clough to satisfy neither his reason nor his faith, and it is evident that after his researches in 1845 he was never again drawn to it. Socially, too, he thought it occupied an anomalous position that benefited nobody. His better acquaintance with the Unitarian businessmen who were his employers at University Hall between 1849 and 1850 confirmed this opinion, and he was clearly hostile to some of them for reasons that were not entirely religious.[42] Yet it was not until he was in Cambridge, Massachusetts, among the American Unitarians that Clough committed to paper his considered opinion:

I do not doubt that the Protestant has excluded himself (necessary perhaps it was that he should so do) from [the] large religious experience which the Roman Catholic preserves. I am convinced again that the Unitarian is morally and religiously only half educated compared with the Episcopalian. Modern Unitarianism is, I conceive, unfortunate on the one hand in refusing to allow its legitimate force to the exercise of reason and criticism; on the other hand, in having by its past exercise of reason and criticism thrown aside because of their dogmatic exterior treasures of pure religious tradition.[43]

Far more deep and lasting an influence on Clough than White or Strauss, however, was Ralph Waldo Emerson, a man whom Clough and his friends had been reading for years and to whom the young poet made the unique avowal that he had "largely learnt" from him.[44] First introduced to the English public by Carlyle in 1841,[45] the American's work had gained a considerable and enthusiastic readership, especially among the younger generation, and Clough must have been familiar with both Emerson's first and second series of essays by 1845, when Anne, whose reading Clough

guided, was studying the second series.[46] Late in 1847, Clough wrote
Emerson, inviting him to be his guest at Oxford:

Oxford perhaps may have some interest for you. Our University has
not perhaps a very large influence in the world of letters and learning,
but it has even now I think a good deal to do with the thinkings
and doings of our Upper Classes: and at any rate has a good deal
of character of its own . . . Your name is not a thing unknown to
us—I do not say it would be a passport in a society fenced about
by Church Articles. But amongst the juniors there are many that have
read and studied your books, and not a few that have largely learnt
from them, and would gladly welcome their author.[47]

What Emerson meant to Clough's contemporaries is a large topic,
some aspects of which have been well studied.[48] With one exception,
however, it is difficult to learn what Emerson meant in particular
to Clough.[49] Part of this is due, of course, to the fact that Emerson
was not well known at first hand by most of the older English scholars, and the tradition which has come down is roughly that those
portions of his thought which are not Carlyle's are mysticism and
"quietism." The other, perhaps more basic, reason is that there is
an innate paradox in the relationship: the man who is most profoundly and genuinely affected by Emerson's teachings would be
precisely the man least likely to lend himself easily to a study of
influence. When one "has it all within" one, to use Clough's phrase
about facts, one does not give footnotes. But there is abundant biographical evidence pointing to a warm friendship and correspondence between the two; there is at least one open avowal of influence; there are other overt gestures which suggest the same; the
source of one of Clough's poems, *Natura Naturans,* has been found
by Veyriras in Emerson's essay, "History";[50] and some may see a
quality emanating from a period in Clough's life and thought which
is "Emersonian." The evidence warrants more sustained attention
and interpretation than it has hitherto received, and it may yield
further insight into a turbulent period in Clough's life and writings.
Townsend Scudder has written of Emerson's influence on some of
the young men in his audiences that they "turned their faces towards
him as thought he were a Messiah."[51] Depressed or straitjacketed
financially, politically, and religiously, the more emotional portion

of Emerson's followers found that "his words aroused ideas and emotions so compelling as to hinder them from sleep . . . He gave them the strength to believe in themselves. Worshipfully they followed him, repeating his phrases as though they were revelations sent from the skies . . . conservative . . . magazines . . . began to speak reprovingly and fearfully of an Emerson cult."[52]

Like Strauss, Emerson had been shaken by recognizing the fallibility of miracles as proofs of religion and at Clough's age had resigned from his Unitarian ministry when he felt unable any longer to administer holy communion.[53] Unlike some contemporaries and the eighteenth-century rationalists, however, Emerson preserved a sense of the immanence of God, and when he insisted that man himself was divine and that therefore "God is, not was" and found His presence first in Nature and, later, more and more in the "Over-Soul" of which all men partook, his audience felt that they had heard not a destructive, negative voice, like Strauss's,[54] but one expressing a faith that rested on eternal and not merely "sensual" things.[55] His doctrine put immense stress on the self and self-reliance, for his idea of the soul stretched to its utmost the Protestant emphasis on the individual and made of every man an atom of moral responsibility. He advocated the rejection by each man of the claims of society and convention, for the all-important fact of man's divinity was to be made real only by acts of individual assertion. Emerson spoke for a kind of permanent revolution of the spirit, in which a "received opinion" should be regarded as a potential bond, "vulgar society" should be merely that "whose poetry is not yet written," and where "only in our easy, simple, spontaneous action are we strong."[56] There was implicit in his words a sort of moral egalitarianism which suggested that acts and actors must judge themselves: "All things are moral," he wrote,[57] and shocked a Scottish audience by saying that man is " 'always on his way upwards,' " even from the gallows or brothel.[58] He dismissed Biblical history, although valuing history itself highly, and called the story of Christ's life mere "biography"—edifying, but less important than the individual soul and "the immense possibilities of man."[59] God could be known only through the soul, and that existed for each man only within himself and through his self-defined actions. Only by living, Emerson held, could man experience religion or obtain the answers to the questions his soul "lusted" to ask: "Work and live, work and live . . . Do not require a description of the countries towards which you sail . . . These questions which we lust to ask about the future are a confession of sin. God has no answer for them."[60] Prefiguring some modern thinkers, he preached rebellion against society as a principle: "Whoso would be a man must be a nonconformist" is central to his thought, for to conform to dead usages is to blinker the self in a game of blindman's buff.[61]

Indeed, were it not for Emerson's charm, tact, and preference for what he called "the positive degree"—and perhaps for his genius—it would be one of the mysteries of nineteenth-century studies how Emerson could have escaped the bitter hostility that met men like Strauss.[62] Instead, he won for himself a wide audience on four continents. He preferred to emphasize what man could and should do, rather than to criticize Christianity per se, but unless we understand the extent of his heresy, his unequivocal paganism as Clough saw it, we will fail to understand either his influence, or Clough's interest in him.

Emerson was especially persuasive in making men feel that they had a duty and a glorious opportunity to *act* on their intuitive, perhaps subversive impulses, to conquer what he called "That divided and rebel mind, that distrust of a sentiment because our arithmetic has computed the strength . . . opposed to our purpose."[63] And Froude, who followed Clough's lead and gave up his fellowship a year later on grounds of conscience, told the visiting American that his wish to do so was partly Emerson's responsibility and asked for his advice about giving up his profession—advice Emerson withheld.[64] Clough might have said the same thing if he had not been too proud—and perhaps too Emersonian as well—to place responsibility for his actions on another man. A young man named Crawshay told Emerson that he had refused to take the religious tests—and therefore his degree—at Cambridge because of Emerson's teachings.[65]

Another such figure was M. D. Conway, a young Southerner who later became Emerson's disciple and biographer. The first interchange between them is preserved in two moving letters. Conway, who had begun to question the strict Methodism in which he had been raised, wrote to Emerson in 1851: "About a year ago I commenced reading your writings. I have read them all and studied them . . . I have shed many burning tears over them; because you gain my assent to Laws which, when I see how they would act on the affairs of life, I have not courage to practise. . . I sometimes feel as if you made for me a second Fall from which there is no redemption by any atonement." Emerson replied, not attempting to minimize Conway's struggle, but holding out to him the values that made it worthwhile, and using words that lodge themselves in the memory:

What interests both you and me most of all things . . . is the morals of intellect; in other words, that no man is worth his room in the world who is not commanded by a legitimate object of thought . . . A true soul will disdain to be moved except by what natively commands it, though it should go sad and solitary in search of its master a thousand years. The few superior persons in each community are so by their steadiness to reality and their neglect of appearances . . . Its full rewards are slow but sure; and yet I think it has its reward on the instant, inasmuch as simplicity and grandeur are always better than dapperness.[66]

Emerson's attraction for these young men did not fundamentally rest on his being an original thinker. He had learned much from Coleridge and Carlyle, and Wellek has shown that Emerson's knowledge of German philosophy was not "technical" and was frequently secondhand: others such as Pochmann have modified this view somewhat, but in general Emerson's philosophical, like his political thought, was not in any profound sense either original or radical.[67] But he did not claim originality for himself, and that was not the basis of his appeal. Part of it undoubtedly lay in the force of his personality; the "considerable sarcastic strength" Froude saw in Emerson's face was mingled with a manner that seemed to embody simplicity to the point of austerity, honesty, high-mindedness, and special reserves of kindness and insight.[68] But part of Emerson's significance for men like Clough rested also in his personal history: in resigning his ministry and in cutting himself adrift from his livelihood and much of established society, Emerson at twenty-eight, their own present age, had done what some of them wished to be able to do themselves. He had acted with grace and style as a "committed man," and had on his own terms thriven, exerting ultimately not less but more influence and widening his personal and intellectual horizons. When he said therefore that "whoso would be a man must be a nonconformist" his audience could feel that he himself embodied the latent promise of his words, and when he urged "Be it how it will, do right now"[69] his followers could have seen in him—for all his rejection of the role—a leader and a hero. Emerson could speak of the "morals of intellect" because his life suggested to his audience that he knew what the words meant and that he had, in searching so consistently and with uncompromising integrity to comprehend, express, and communicate fully his own innate moral knowledge, indeed been commanded by a "legitimate object of thought." "Sad and solitary" he had not hesitated to go, but in contact with others he seemed to make that solitude shine like a spiritual adventure.

Clough and Emerson became close friends; indeed the poet probably did not have a closer friend among his older mentors, as the tone of their correspondence demonstrates. Their intimacy appears to have extended even to a willingness to share their personal journals, for Emerson wrote in 1849 that he had "looked into [Clough's] journals" on their Paris trip and later invited Clough to help edit his own English ones.[70] And Clough's references to Emerson are free of the ambivalence shown in his remarks about virtually every other figure influential upon him. But Clough made it a characteristic—one in keeping with the American's teachings—not to be in the usual sense any man's disciple: he might acknowledge guidance, but the more deeply he was moved by another's teachings the less likely he was to discuss it casually and the more likely, on principle, to make it his own by living it out. Emerson's example may be reckoned as one of the forces which operated on Clough when he was determining to leave his fellowship; this may even seem likely, but we should be doing a disservice to Clough's independence of mind if we attributed that act solely to Emerson's influence or made of Clough his disciple. Indeed they were friends perhaps precisely because Clough no longer needed to be such a disciple.

Neither Emerson's mystical strain nor the pantheism of his "Nature" (which, however, was already being superseded in his thought by the late 'forties) appealed to Clough's mentality, but the American's idealism and his stress on intuition as a mode of (or substitute for) epistemology found fertile soil.[71] Only one short sentence survives from a speech that Clough made at the Decade on the question whether "the study of philosophy is more important for the formation of opinion than that of history," but it bears the clear impress of Emerson's attitudes.[72] The assumption of the question under debate was that character could be profoundly formed by external influences: a doctrine opposite to all Emerson taught. Clough perceived the assumption, and refuted it in Emersonian terms. "What is it to me," he asked, "to know the fact of the battle of Marathon, or the fact of the existence of Cromwell? I have it all within me." It was not, he explained, that the battle or men themselves were of no importance, but "it is of no importance that I should know it."[73] What mattered, as Emerson's "History" suggests, was man's knowledge of the meaning of moral courage in defiance of the many: only by his innate knowledge did those facts about Cromwell or Athens assume importance, and unless he had "it all within [him]" the facts were worth nothing. "The mind is One, and nature its correlative," Emerson had written to explain his intuitional approach to history, ". . . there is properly no history, only biography."[74] Facts loomed too large in most men's minds, encumbering and tyrannizing over them; to understand them rightly, man must look inward and assert the "immense possibilities" within the self: "if the man is true to his better instincts . . . and refuses the dominion of facts, as one that comes of a higher race . . . then the facts fall aptly and supple into their places." It was a valuable approach, for it freed him to look without prejudice on other cultures, and other values: "How easily these old worships of Moses, of Zoroaster, of Menu, of Socrates, domesticate themselves in the mind. I cannot find any antiquity in them. They are mine as much as theirs."[75] Within a few years Clough was to call just such a roll of names as these to indicate the multiplicity of religious truth: if both Arnold and Schlegel had failed to make historical facts true teachers, Emerson, at least, had shown Clough how to make himself their master.

The Gentleman was another topic which Clough discussed at the Decade, and Emerson's essay on "Manners" may have helped form the intuitional approach of the younger man's argument. Accurately to estimate the originality and courage of the young poet's words, J. C. Shairp wrote, it would be necessary to understand the "peculiar mental atmosphere" of the Oxford of the day, and to know how overrated "pleasant manners and a good exterior" were.[76] Clough addressed his words to an audience whose Oriel members knew that their notoriously snobbish Provost was said to give "two fingers to a commoner, and a whole hand to a tuft" (nobleman or gentleman commoner),[77] and whose Christ Church undergraduates were accustomed to dining, if they were noblemen, before the dons had been served and at high table (their teachers sat below), waited on by a band of poor fellow students known as "servitors" who were let into the hall to eat the "broken meats" only when everyone else had finished.[78] Shairp described how Clough "went into the origin of the ideal" of the gentleman, "tracing from medieval times . . . the notion of a 'gentle knight' " down to its "deterioration into the modern Brummagem pattern which gets the name. These truly gentlemen of old had invented for themselves a whole economy of manners . . . These manners, true in them, became false when . . . copied from without by modern men."[79] Emerson had written precisely the same thing: "What fact more conspicuous in modern history than the creation of the gentleman? Chivalry is that, and loyalty is that, and . . . half the drama and all the novels paint this figure. The word *gentleman* . . . is a homage to personal and incommunicable properties. Frivolous and fantastic additions have got associated with the name."[80] Clough wrote:

When the same qualities are in the hearts of men now, as truly as in the best of old time, they will fashion for themselves a new expression, a new economy of manners . . . But many men now, wholly devoid of the inward reality, yet catching at the reputation of it, adopt these old traditional ways . . . of bearing themselves, though they express nothing that is really in them.[81]

Emerson repudiated formal social status as an index of true gentility: "I may go into a cottage," he wrote, "and find a farmer who feels

that he is the man I have come to see, and fronts me accordingly."
Similarly "a natural gentleman finds his way in . . . The chiefs
of savage tribes have distinguished themselves in London and Paris
by the purity of their tournure."[82] Again, Clough repeats his message: "I have known peasant men and women in the humblest
places, in whom dwelt these qualities as truly as they ever did in
the best of lords and ladies, and who had invented for themselves
a whole economy of manners to express them, who were very 'poets
of courtesy.' "[83] It would be a mistake, of course, to suppose that
neither Emerson nor Clough had read Rousseau, but the similarity
of the way in which the two contemporaries develop their arguments,
and the very ring of phrases like "economy of manners," suggest
that, at the very least, Rousseau had been reinforced for Clough
by the American.

Rousseau and Emerson alike faded somewhat into the background
in 1846 as Clough plunged further and further into the "terrestrial
world" of social reform, letters to *The Balance,* and "college tutorism"—with a continued success that made Hawkins appoint him
sub-dean in 1847—but his "old scruple" did indeed prove a Felix
who could not long be put off, and in 1847 the dialogue between
himself and his conscience reached a climax. The idea that he might
eventually have to give up his tutorship as a matter of conscience
had been present in Clough's mind, as we have seen, since the time
he undertook it, although then his only really specific objection to
the Thirty-Nine Articles had been what he called his "Puseyitic
position."[84] (He was not a Puseyite, but held a Puseyitic position,
he had written. He meant by this that without accepting the emphasis on church authority and doctrine, he objected, like Pusey, to
the state of anarchy within the Church of England that let her
give over the administration of church discipline to men who were
appointed by the government as bishops and archbishops and whose
attitudes would be questionably secular.)[85] In 1845 Clough had
tried for a professorship at one of the proposed new Irish colleges,
no doubt feeling that service in one of these secular bodies would
be more honest than continued residence in Oxford.[86] Nothing came
of these colleges at the time, however, and in 1846 Clough turned
his attention to political economy, beginning at the end of the year

to gather the material for the *Retrenchment* pamphlet. This pamphlet strongly expressed his dissatisfaction with Oxford; looking at Clough's activities in 1847 as a whole, one cannot escape the impression that each of his acts was designed to express the same thing. Unconsciously he was beginning to push himself by stages away from the city he knew he loved too well. At any rate, soon after publishing his pamphlet Clough for the first time began to show that his doubts were now more than questions. Belief in the ethical teachings of Christianity—the Commandments and God's justice and love—survived, but the doubts he had formed earlier about the authenticity of Scripture and origin of religious authority remained and had now been joined by more profound questions. Clough now was aware that he did not understand to his own satisfaction the meaning of Grace, Free Will, or " 'Atonement by a crucified savior.' "

. . . the Evangelicals gabble it, as the Papists do their Ave Mary's—and yet say they know; while Newman falls down and worships *because* he does not know and knows he does not know.

I think others are more right, who say boldly, We don't understand it, and therefore we *won't* fall down and worship it . . . Until I know, I will wait; and if I am not born with the power to discover, I will . . . trust to God's justice; and neither pretend to know, nor without knowing, pretend to embrace.[87]

"God has no answer for them," Emerson had written, "work and live, work and live." The present, he said, is infinite, the future, finite.[88] Clough was approaching that view, and his subsequent statements on religion must all be understood to have been made on the basis of this agnosticism.

The issues of religion and university reform were perforce closely related in the minds of young Oxford liberals after 1845. "Convinced that there was virtue in the times," as Ward writes, they began more and more to bend their efforts to realizing that faith by reforming outmoded elements of the university system which had grown up for two centuries without rationalization under the constraint of the seventeenth-century Laudian statutes.[89] A fragmentary petition among Clough's MSS which probably dates from around this period is not substantial enough to merit discussion here, but its existence underscores his participation in these matters.[90] More to the point are the two letters to *The Spectator* written late in 1847 in which he replies to an attack made on the old universities by Frank Newman, John Henry Newman's free-thinking younger brother.[91] Newman, a former Balliol fellow who had resigned rather than subscribe to the Articles, had become a professor at London University. He opened the academic year of 1847 there with a speech reported at length in *The Times,* attacking the old universities not only for requiring subscription but for following wrong principles in assuming that morality could be taught by coerced observance, "public instruction," and "precept."[92] An anonymous correspondent named F. who gave his address as Lincoln's Inn (perhaps F. D. Maurice, who had been made chaplain there in 1846) applauded Newman's address and defended him against the attacks of *The Times.*[93] Another letter-writer named M. then attacked both F. and Newman, and the following week Clough entered the fray under the pseudonym of Alpha.[94]

It had long been clear to Clough, as his sardonic comments about the Tractarians' view of Milton had shown in 1839, that a man's thought, writings, and morality could not be severed.[95] But the university must leave men free to follow their consciences, must cease to be almost entirely in the hands of the clergy; and the structure of the great educational institutions had to change, so that academic careers could be planned and carried out with some hope for future standing and stability. (The weakness at the professorial level was one of the major issues for the reformers.) De facto, education was more and more secular, and in a well-turned phrase, he pointed out that religious tests and "all our orthodox etceteras" hung on the universities "as loosely as did the folds of the surplice on Sterne or Sidney Smith."[96] The last paragraph of this letter is a cry from the heart so descriptive of his own frame of mind—his fear "in conformity to lose [him]self" mixed with the knowledge that he could still say "Oxford, with all thy Articles, I love thee still"—that it is worth quoting at some length:

. . . to many observers it is a fact . . . that subscription, combined with the exclusively clerical tenure of a . . . large proportion of fellowships, is killing one at least of the universities by sheer atrophy. Many,

114

who, after proceeding through the confessedly unmeaning signature of matriculation to that of the Bachelor's degree, feel doubtful in that most doubting time of life between twenty-two and twenty-six, whether that which they believe and desire to be acting on is precisely a moral counterpart of the pure intellectual entity contained in the Thirty-Nine Articles . . . many who but for this doubt would stay, would study, would teach—depart, and are lost to the university . . . perhaps to the nation.

And that, of course, was precisely what Clough was preparing to do; his best poetry, to be sure, was yet to come, but in terms of his practical career the usefulness to the nation of this exceptionally intelligent and highly trained man was about to end.

For a man must live, though it be by common-law practice, or penny-a-lining. Many again, yet worse, swallow with compunction, for bread's sake, and literature's; and conforming ever [sic] to ordination, in their conformity lose themselves . . . the University persists in excluding this "foreign gold" of the scrupulous and thoughtful, and in debasing the limited currency which she suffers to circulate. Most true it is that those who know the place cannot but say, be it in the bitterness of exclusion, or be it in the discontent of conformity, "Oxford, with all thy Articles, I love thee still." Yet without thy Articles, I think they would love thee quite as well, and serve thee a good deal better.

His second letter was much briefer, but it too is interesting, for it eloquently sums up the humanistic value of a secular, "liberal" education. Francis Newman wanted to divorce moral training from university instruction. Was this really possible, Clough asked: "Can a course of general instruction be other than a moral proceeding? Can art and science ignore their relation to human life? Can I talk to the mind without being overheard by the spirit? And can I speak to my pupils of free-will and justice, and allow them un-admonished to be slaves of passion and selfishness?"[97]

"Can I talk to the mind without being overheard by the spirit? Can a course of general instruction be other than a moral proceed-ing? Can art and science ignore their relation to human life?" These are the words of a man to whom teaching was a true vocation. It was one of the ironic tragedies of his age that, as Clough himself saw, the more scrupulous and thoughtful a man was, the more likely he was to be caught in the meshes of outdated laws and rendered unable to fulfill his function.

One feels often with Clough that conscious recognition of his deepest feelings came only at the time of their expression in words, but from that moment of recognition, as from a gauntlet thrown down, there was no thought of retreat. Within a week of writing his final letter on Newman's speech, Clough invited Emerson to Oxford, and within the month he took the occasion of some chance words of the Provost to resign his tutorship. "You spoke of a Tutor as a Teacher of the 39 Articles," he wrote Hawkins. "For such an office I fear I can hardly consider myself qualified." The idea that he must teach the Articles, as well as give them "the ordinary negative acquiescence of a layman," was "new to him." For the last year his lectures had been exclusively classical or mathematical and the issue had not seemed unequivocal; now that it was, he placed the order of his going entirely in the Provost's hands: "In any case my pleasure in looking back to my tutorial days is not likely to be marred."[98]

Hawkins now quoted an apparently little-known college statute which required a tutor to instruct his students not only morally but specifically, indeed most of all, in religion and the articles: *"maxime in rudimentis religionis et doctrinae Articulis in synode Londini anno 1562 editis."* The only question remaining was how far Clough's doubts went. Hawkins did not wish to hurry Clough into declaring himself beyond the pale—quite the contrary, he hoped to retain so successful and hard working a Sub-Dean. But he believed that no man should hold the privileges and functions of a position won by subscription if he did not still assent to its doctrines.[99] Clough neither hurried nor retreated. His resignation as tutor was effective as of the end of March 1848. In May he joined Emerson in Paris; during the summer he returned to England, continued his intercourse with Emerson, and wrote what some have considered his farewell to Oxford, *The Bothie*. In the fall he gave up his fellowship also. "I do not feel my position tenable in any way," he wrote the Provost in October. "I can have nothing whatever to do with a subscription to the XXXIX articles—and deeply repent of having ever submitted to one. I cannot consent to receive any further pecuniary benefit in consideration of such conformity."[100]

A few months later, Hawkins, feeling free now to ask his former

Sub-Dean as "a favor" to explain to him the nature of his difficulties, wrote asking Clough what was perplexing "young men at present."[101] Clough's reply was couched in terms that sum up the basic rationalistic arguments: ". . . Miracles are poor proofs. The doctrine must prove them, not they the doctrine. Can we be sure that anything is really a miracle? . . . Again books like Strauss's life of Jesus have disturbed the historical foundations of Christianity. And people ask further what has History to do with Religion?" Precisely as he had learned to do from Emerson, he dismisses the historical claims of the Bible, asserting that true religious knowledge can be validated only intuitively: "what has History to do with Religion? The worth of such a doctrine as that of the Holy Ghost as the Lord and Giver of Spiritual life is intelligible: but what is the value of biographical facts?—External Evidence is slighted: but I think the great query is rather as to the *internal* Evidence."[102] Following Schlegel ten years before, he had concluded that pre-Christian religions, intermixed with the "slime" of idolatry, were to be rejected. Since then, however, Emerson had shown him how to "domesticate" "these old worships . . . of Zoroaster, of Menu [a Persian sage and law-giver], of Socrates,"[103] and now Clough asked: "Is Xtianity really so much better than Mohometanism, Buddhism (a more extensive faith) or the old heathen philosophy? Are those virtues and graces, which are our religious and moral tradition, really altogether Christian? Is there not a good deal of Homer and Virgil in them? Nay, if the loftiest of them belong to Christianity, are they exclusively Christian in matter of fact, or necessarily Christian in matter of philosophy?"[104] In a day when, as Jowett wrote, merely to believe that God had revealed his truth in any form but that of Christian revelation was proof of heresy in the eyes of the orthodox, these words of Clough were enough for Hawkins to place him beyond the pale. They had no further correspondence, except for the occasion in December 1851 when the Provost refused to recommend Clough for a position as Principal at the entirely secular University of Sydney because it appeared to him "that no one ought to be appointed to such a situation who is at all in a state of doubt and difficulty as to his own religious beliefs."[105]

Clough did not expect the rebuff, for he had evidently given

Hawkins's name as a reference without first asking his permission. No doubt the Provost's support had formerly been a matter of course, and Clough had supposed that he could still turn to him without formality for a recommendation. Clough replied to Hawkins's letter briefly, asserting in his flattest style his assurance of his rights both to offer himself for the job and to expect Hawkins's support "not as absolute recommendation, but in particular testimony of this or that qualification."[106] But that support had been withdrawn, and was gone forever. Clough might get testimonials from friends, but not the crucial one from his superior at Oriel, the only man living who had been, as it were, Clough's master. Dr. Arnold was dead and Clough and University Hall were parting company at the Hall's wish. Without Hawkins's help, and with the explanations its absence would entail, Clough was unemployable, even, apparently, where education was theoretically separate from religion. He had already acknowledged to Tom Arnold that he had "jumped over a ditch, for the fun of the experiment and would not be disinclined to be once again in a highway with [his] brethren and companions."[107] Now the extent of his separation was made clear. A possible position at Aberdeen was also closed to him on religious grounds. So was Rugby. Its Headmastership was vacant and but for Clough's resignation, he might have been a desirable choice. ("We might have had you," as Shairp had said sadly.)[108] Other institutions would follow suit. Religion ruled the schools, and it did not want a heretic as a teacher. Clough could no more teach in an English university than an avowed Communist could teach in the United States in the 1950's. The system closed itself against him on principle, and if Clough's career were destroyed the schools and their representatives, like Hawkins, could justifiably reply that it was better that one should perish than that many should go astray.

In the meantime, the author of at least some of Clough's perplexities had come to Oxford, spending two days there at the end of March and being lionized. He refused to "roar," to discourse to large audiences, or to enter into polemics, and so, as Clough wrote, "as the orthodox had mostly never heard of him, they did not suspect him," and "everybody liked him." To Clough, Emerson gave the impression of "perfect intellectual cultivation," and had a pleasing look and voice, Yankee though they were, which in his lectures grew in authority until he seemed "prophetic at times." He was, Clough reported laconically, "unequivocally Pagan, but dislikes controversy." He reminded people of Newman, though Clough found his manner "much simpler."[109] Emerson was much drawn to both Clough and Froude, whom he also got to know. "Truly I became fond of these monks of Oxford" he wrote Lidian Emerson,[110] paying them the traveller's highest compliment of finding in them the essential lineaments of what was best in his own countrymen, and even giving thought to a joint undertaking of a new transatlantic journal.[111] Emerson's words, the quickly emotional Froude wrote him a month or so later, had been as seeds in the wind, and he hoped that "in a few years . . . even here in Oxford you will see whole acres yellow with the corn of your sowing."[112] But Emerson summed up his reaction to the university as an institution with the phrase, "At Oxford you may hold what opinion you please so that you hold your tongue," and reflected in his journal: "One sees readily, in the embittered acuteness of the Oxonian reviewer in snuffing heresy from far, how hapless an unbeliever he is, and why he inveighs so angrily against that which he vainly resists in his own bosom."[113]

After a month in London, he went on to Paris, then in the grip of the revolution of 1848, and there Clough joined him. Clough not only spent May with Emerson in Paris, but also as much time as he could in London, hearing him lecture there in June, and later in Liverpool where he saw him off on the boat to America. Drawn to each other by their writings even before they had met, the more they saw of each other the deeper their friendship grew; Emerson finding Clough "the best *pièce de résistance* and tough adherence that one could desire."[114] A year before, Emerson had written in his journal of his life in Boston, "Ah! Who has society?— people to talk to?—people who stimulate? Boston has 120,000 and I cannot now find one: and elsewhere in the world I dare not tell you how poor I am, how few they are."[115] With Clough he had "society." Together they spent most of their afternoons and evenings,[116] attending the public meetings of the new women's clubs, devoted to the cause of women's equal rights, and watching the revolution in and out of the Chambre des Députés.[117] Most of all, they talked. Such talk, such friendship with "this genius of Clough," Emerson later concluded was, "the most real benefit" he had got from his visit to England.[118] A discussion of their social views will be deferred to a later chapter; here it is sufficient to point out the degree of personal affinity that was established between them on the basis of their shared attitudes, so that Emerson was to think of Clough, oddly enough, as "the best American," and Clough found no American to compare with Emerson for profundity and solidity of intellect.[119] The quality of Clough's own response, given to understatement as he was in his letters, is perhaps best summed up by the interchange that passed between them as they walked together on the decks of the steamer that was to take Emerson, in mid July, back to America from Liverpool. "What shall we do without you?" Clough, as Emerson told E. E. Hale, said to the older man. "Carlyle has led us all out into the desert and he has left us there!" Emerson, telling the story, said, "I put my hand upon his head as we walked, and I said, 'Clough, I consecrate you Bishop of all England. It shall be your part to go up and down through the desert to find out these wanderers and to lead them into the promised land.' "[120]

That bishopric, however, was a cross in a society "fenced about," as Clough had warned Emerson on inviting him to Oxford, "with Church Articles." His occupation, and even, for a time, his sense of identity were gone. "We might have had you," Shairp wrote to Clough in 1849 when Rugby was looking for a new Head; "might have been" would from now on be a recurring echo in Clough's life.

CHAPTER IV

The World's Arena

During the last period covered by this study, the five and a half years from 1848 through part of 1853, Clough underwent a crisis that involved him on all fronts—intellectual, emotional, economic, and professional. He emerged from it in many ways, as he was fully aware, a changed man, "wiser" now, as he put it and, we may infer, sadder. Out of this crisis grew the insight and energy which equipped him to write his greatest poetry, but it was a time of great difficulty for him, for in it many of the convictions that had moved him to act were tried and found wanting. During this period, the radical don, the free agent, the Sub-Dean and promising academician whom no material consideration could restrain when it was time, as Emerson said, to speak with éclat, gradually dissolved under the pressure of a new life.

In these years Clough took three important trips abroad: to France in '48 during its revolution, to Italy in '49 during a similar crisis, and to America in '52, where a revolution had already established republicanism and all its fruits. On one level Clough wanted in those trips to discover whether the fruits of republicanism were bitter or sweet; he was not to be pleased with his findings. But he was also searching for something else: really, for himself. He found that new identity eventually, but the process was gradual and painful; his London years were largely those in which the old mold was broken and a new one not yet shaped.

Clough's response to the revolutions in Franch and Italy began with feelings of elation. Italy was already in turmoil when the French uprising began on February 22, 1848. The end of the winter usually found Clough in a relatively low state, as he wrote Blanche in later years, but in March of 1848 he rejoiced that "all these blessed revolutions" were keeping him from sinking into "hopeless lethargy."[1] The revolutions were "blessed" to Clough because they seemed, to reformers of the day, to hail what Fejtö has called the "opening of an era," the triumph of liberal ideas on every front over the old, repressive policies of conservatism as it had worked in the Holy Alliance of European monarchies and the Church.[2] Orthodoxy was being challenged everywhere. Strauss had been heard attentively by the European revolutionaries, who were often pantheists.[3] The "people" were waking up and wanted "rights"—the right to vote, the right to work and to be paid a living wage. Women wanted the right to own property and to divorce. The movement was international. In France, the combination of increasingly repressive governmental policies with economic depression and foreign revolutions led finally in '48 to explosion. Guizot, the learned, rigidly Protestant, but politically unscrupulous President of the Council of Louis Philippe told the middle class to "Get rich," and said "There is no need for statesmen, barriers will do." Another of his aphorisms was "You need two things to govern a country; Right and Might."[4] We hear in such phrases echoes of M. Lieuvain of *Madame Bovary,* speaking contrapuntally with Rodolphe and the cows. But the country did not get rich. There was no work to be had; goods stayed in the shops.

A number of ephemeral reforms were begun by the Provisional Government early in 1848, and Socialists pointed to the independent cooperatives run by artisans and workers which had flourished in Paris for some time as examples of how labor could be organized, overlooking the fact that these usually involved highly skilled and relatively sophisticated men.[5] When a national government actually created a system of National Workshops Clough must have rejoiced. Yet instead of being cooperatives and ending sweated labor and unemployment, they resembled, rather, the English Workhouse system. In return for a pittance, able-bodied men did make-work, and they grew angry. On April 16th, incited by Louis Blanc, they made a great march through Paris. The government put it down.[6]

A Constituent Assembly elected April 23 soon set up a Provisional Executive Committee which promptly repudiated even the theoretical reforms instituted in the preceding months. The Socialists were out, successive uprisings were systematically crushed, and Louis Napoleon, soon to be Emperor, gained power until in December he was elected President of the Council. A year later, in 1849, the French Government helped destroy the Roman revolution of Garibaldi and Mazzini, a bitter scene which Clough also witnessed. The French revolution of 1848 ended, as Bourgin writes, in a triple fiasco: social, political, and international,[7] or, as Clough commented in 1849: "God be praised for the downfall of Louis Philippe. This with a faint feeble echo of that loud last year's scream of *à bas Guizot* seems to be the sum total. Or are we to salute the rising sun with *Vive l'Empereur* and the green liveries?"[8] (Throughout his reportage from Paris, Clough tended, consciously or not, to rely on the symbolic meaning of clothing in a rather Carlylean manner.)

At the beginning of his stay in Paris, Clough "walked about Jerusalem and told the towers thereof with wonderful delight," as he wrote.[9] With Emerson he attended the public meetings of the newly formed clubs which had become almost a traditional accompaniment to French revolutions. At one of those dedicated to women's rights the rudeness of the Frenchmen, "greedily seizing and creating double entendres . . . disgusted" Clough, but he was impressed by the chairwoman, a Mme. Niboyer, who showed "considerable power and patience" and was perhaps a novelty to the men who now saw "a woman face them . . . *not* for purposes of flirtation."[10]

He investigated, too, the identities of some of the editors of the almost innumerable, anonymously written new journals, for such knowledge was an essential preliminary to grasping the revolutionary political structure.[11] And until the failure of the revolution became evident when the government put down a popular uprising on May 15, Clough was in high spirits. He wandered around Paris *"pour savourer la république"* in the midst of the riots, unconcerned about his own skin, avid for news beneath his mask of languid indifference, delighted with sights that showed there was some justice after all for the poor, and at the same time very amused by the French and all the absurdities attendant on the great moment.[12] The *garde mobile* was a new militia, democratic in being open to all classes, full of youths, and regarded as a reform.[13] Clough rejoiced in it: "I contemplate with infinite thankfulness the blue blouses, garnished with red, of the garde mobile; and emit a perpetual incense of devout rejoicing for the purified state of the Tuileries, into which I find it impossible, meantime, to gain admittance."[14] It was not all exactly as it should be, even so: "I growl occasionally at the sight of aristocratic equipages which begin to peep out again, and trust that the National Assembly will in its wisdom forbid the use of livery servants. But there is not very much to complain of. Generally one can not better express the state of Paris in this respect than by the statement that one finds it rather pointed to be seen in the streets with gloves on."[15] The last observation is typical of Clough's sensibility. Like the legs of the dead man, seen through the crowd in *Amours de Voyage*,[16] the essence of the experience, the thing beyond the "scenery after which you always go awhoring" (as Clough wrote when Shairp objected to *Amours*[17]) has been caught in these words.

Clough saw the failure and crushing of the workers' uprising of May 15 and knew it was all over. He uses mock Carlylese to take the edge off his expression of disillusion: "Ichabod, Ichabod, the glory is departed. Liberty Equality and Fraternity, driven back by shopkeeping bayonet, hides her red cap in dingiest St. Antoine . . . the tale of bricks will be doubled, and Moses and Aaron of Socialism can at the best only pray for plagues—which perhaps will come—paving stones for vivats and émeutes in all their quarters."[18] The *garde mobile* had "dropped its dear blouse and red trimmings for a bourgeoisie-praetorian uniform with distinctive green hired-soldier epaulettes. The voice of clubs is silenced."[19] In a tone in which indignation, disappointment, and an indestructible instinct for observation are catalyzed temporarily by the language of burlesque, he proclaimed: "Wherefore—Bring forth, ye millionaires, the three-months-hidden carriages . . . ride forth, ye cavalier-escorted amazons, in unfearing flirtation, to your Bois de Boulogne: the world begins once more to move on its axis and draw on its kid gloves . . . The golden age of the Republic displays itself now, you see, as a very vulgar parcel-gilt era."[20] The tone of the burlesque was in fact only a mask designed to conceal from himself as much as from his readers the depth of his disappointment and frustration at this end to the affair. He accepted it superficially with humor and contempt, but ultimately, when its meaning, the basic impermeability of society to attack, became clear in the following year, it became a lesson that was to influence him more and more as time went on.

A few days later the government held a national *fête*. Up the street came a great chariot full of *jeunes filles* in classical garb, the "tricolor streaming from the left shoulder and (artificial) oak wreaths in their hair . . . they were de-classicized by their use of parasols."[21] Later, "It was funny in the afternoon to see the classical virgins walking about with their papas and mamas, people of the under-shoe-making and backstreet-shopkeeping class."[22]

Before the work of the revolution had been completely undone, Clough was grateful for what he hoped would be its results. But later, Clough reflected that the best part had been the first fortnight, when he had seen "the real nation" in its shirtsleeves.[23] Himself inclined to accept bad tailoring without complaint, he shows throughout his writing particular sensitivity to the symbolic meaning of dress. With a sort of tenderness he recalled "The sentry posts occupied by men in blouse, of the national or mobile or republican guard—and Tuileries gardens and all public places full of the same blue blouse, while the Palace itself showed occasionally on its balcony some convalescent *blessé de Fevrier* [a wounded veteran of the first revolt] helped along, as he took the air, by wife and child. All things quite decently and in order without any visible repressive external force."[24] Decency, order, unpretending self-respect and freedom— they meant a great deal to Clough, and their fleeting existence cast a glow over his memory of the whole. "France's prospects," he wrote in July, "are dubious and dismal enough, and one is almost inclined to think that the outbreak was premature; with their ideas so far from ripe the French had better, if possible, have endured a little longer the immorality of L. Philip's government. But yet on the whole one accepts the whole thing with gratitude. It will, I think, on the whole accelerate change in England; and perhaps, my dear

125

Tom, you may yet live to see some kind of palingenesy effected for your repudiated country."[25]

The hope against hope of this letter was all the optimism that he could muster for the revolutions of this era. Never again did Clough feel in any society that he was walking about Jerusalem and telling the towers thereof: the coaches, the gloves, and the parcel-gilt would certainly be there, waiting for their day in the sun. With this experience he began to realize that quick solutions to social problems might yield worse results.

Clough's trip in 1849 to Italy, although longer than his stay in France, was less significant to his thought, for he had learned enough already about failed revolutions. The experience was highly relevant to him as a poet, and *Amours de Voyage* transmutes what he saw, both in himself and in the world around him, during those hot summer months of the siege of Rome. But his letters from this period are remarkable for the growing languor and even cynicism of tone which the bitter events he saw around himself inspired. He began hoping to see "heroic deeds" in the Italian struggle, but on the whole the disillusion about reform which Clough had begun to experience the year before was confirmed.[26]

He went primarily because he was in sympathy with the aims of Mazzini and Garibaldi. The Italian liberals wanted "Independence, Unity and Liberty": national unity, freedom from the Pope, and the civil liberties that England and even France took for granted. The Papal States around and northeast of Rome had remained until 1846 in nearly feudal darkness. Until his death in 1846 Pope Gregory XVI had prohibited both the railroad and telegraph from entering the vital area containing Bologna and Rome. There were no political parties, and no opposition of any sort was tolerated. The country was administered by the cardinals, whose instruments were the police, and who did not scruple to use torture, the Inquisition, and elaborate spy systems. (These well-known conditions should be borne in mind in considering Clough's evident anti-Jesuitical feelings.) The confessional was not inviolate, education was frowned upon, study of Dante as well as of the Copernican system was suspect, and political economy was a "forbidden subject." An illustrative letter that even Stendhal might have hesitated to invent, written by the Cardinal Legate of Bologna to Cardinal Lambruschini, warned of a certain citizen that "If one may judge from appearances, he would appear strange to political intrigues . . . Nevertheless, as some imagine that he may belong to the class called 'Thinkers' I consider it my duty to acquaint your Eminence with it, in order that he may be prudently watched."[27] It may sound like comic opera, but the jails were real and so in 1849 was the revolution.

Clough met Mazzini several times in Rome. He brought with him a letter of introduction from Carlyle,[28] whom he had recently got to know and who, with his wife especially, had been a good friend of Mazzini while the latter was an exile in London. A letter of April 23rd, 1849, to Clough's friend F. T. Palgrave described his first visit to the idealistic revolutionary whom the conservative press was vilifying: "Yesterday afternoon I . . . paid my visit to Mazzini. A French envoy or agent was with him and I had to acknowledge the triumviral dignity by waiting almost an hour in the antechamber. However, on the envoy's retiring he discoursed with me for half an hour. He is a less fanatical fixed-idea sort of man than I had expected. He appeared shifty and practical enough. He seemed in excellent spirits, and generally confident and at ease."[29] In spite of the careful distance of his tone in speaking of Mazzini, Clough clearly was moved by the man and his aims. "The feeling everywhere is, he says, simply political or National—Communism or Socialism are things undreamt of. Social changes are not needed. There are no manufacturing masses, and in the lands a métayer system."[30]

Clough responded to Mazzini's idealism. But it had been clear almost from the beginning that the newly proclaimed Republic of Rome could not long stand. The Pope, Pio Nono, had fled to Naples and from there he had issued appeals for help. Both Austria and France had responded, France intending to protect the Pope, thus conciliating the domestic, Catholic-French vote; rout the Austrians, and, of course, crush the rebellion. Mazzini's was a lost cause, and he knew it, but he chose to fight in Rome for the glory and the symbolic worth of the gesture. "Since we were destined to fall," Mazzini wrote later, "it was our duty, in view of the future, to proffer our *morituri te salutant* to Italy from Rome."[31] He told

Clough at the time the same thing: "he expects foreign intervention in the end—and of course thinks it likely enough that the Romana Republica will fall, but he is convinced that the separation of the Temporal and Spiritual Power is a thing to be, and that to restore the Pope as before will merely breed perpetual disquiet."[32] For all his irony, Clough was persuaded. "Tell Blackett," he wrote, "he really must defend S.P.Q.R. It is a most *respectable* republic. It really (*ipse dixit*) thought of getting itself a monarch, but couldn't find one to suit."[33]

It was not long before he had thoroughly identified himself with the republican cause. "You will have heard of our driving back the French," he wrote. It was "our little republic," and "these black-guard French." In a frequently quoted passage, the English poet wrote after the siege had ended that "Last night I had the pleasure of abandoning a café on the entrance of the French. The Italians expect you to do so.—It was quite composedly done—no bravado or hurry."[34] The experience was used for *Amours de Voyage,* which he was composing at this time. He walked about the streets and sat in the cafes, reading, writing, and absorbing the ambience. He saw as much of the treasures of Roman art as he could, using a special permit given him by Mazzini, and he worked his own visits to the Pantheon, as well as a contemporary slander about Mazzini's selling it to the Protestants, into the texture of his new poem.[35] And he saw a "good deal" of Margaret Fuller, who was helping in the Roman hospitals.[36] But it is difficult nevertheless to explain Clough's lingering on in Rome even after the siege was lifted on July 4th. He offered various excuses—he wanted to see the art, it was difficult to get through the French and Neapolitan lines, shipping was uncertain—and these were certainly true. He could, however, have left either early in the campaign, or immediately after the siege. That he did not, but in fact stayed another fortnight or so, and this in the hottest part of an unsanitary Roman summer, is probably related to what the Roman experience meant to him as a whole. "Perhaps it will amuse you hereafter" he wrote to Anne, "to have a letter commenced while guns are firing and, I suppose, men falling, dead and wounded. Such is the case on the other side the Tiber while I peacefully write in my distant chamber with only the sound in my ears."[37]

It probably would not have amused Anne, with her unwavering, devoted earnestness, but it may have done Clough, who was experiencing a sense of dissociation. "I wish it were over, for one can do nothing meantime. I went up to the Pincian Hill and saw the smoke and heard the occasional big cannon and the sharp succession of skirmishers' volleys bang, bang, bang . . . A special house has been appointed for the English to retire to . . . But it is rather a waste of time."[38] What interested Clough was no longer the formal issues, from whose resolution so little could be expected, but life, the actual life of a city under siege and its relation to his own dissociated state of feeling. What he kept coming back to in his letters was really one thing: the divorce between feeling and fact, between official attitudes and real ones, between postures and practice. Where was the truth? What were his "real feelings?" They shifted continually. He admired Mazzini, and hoped the Romans would win—but Mazzini was "shifty and practical" enough, and of course the republic would fall. Eternal Rome was in a state of siege, and he was anxious that its art not be destroyed, but "it is funny to see how much like any other city a besieged city looks.—Unto this has come our grand Lib, Eq and Frat revolution!" "Rome in general might be called a *rubbishy* place; the Roman antiquities *in general* seem to me only interesting as antiquities—not for any beauty," but "I wish England could intervene if it were but the monuments, which . . . I fear are but too likely to receive irreparable damage."[39] Again and again one senses in his writing that he is watching himself watching, at times unable or unwilling to make moral judgments, at other times quickly roused to passionate feeling, out of touch with the reasons for feeling: "It is curious," he repeated, for the observation clearly had gone deep, "how much like any other city a city under bombardment looks.—One goes to the Ara Celi, or the Palatine to look at the firing; one hears places named where shells have fallen; one sees perhaps a man carrying a bit of one."[40] Again he wrote, with the same very personal mixture of tones: "It is hopeless.—I am doomed to see the burning of Rome, I suppose:—the World perhaps in the same day will lose the Vatican and me!—However, these blackguards won't get in yet, I guess.—My love to all good Xtians."[41]

A few years later in February 1852, at the bottom of his fortunes

and spirits, he tried to explain himself to his fiancée, who was at
least as puzzled by his sudden shifts of mood and conviction as
Mary Trevellyn was by Claude and perhaps more so. He desperately
wrote Blanche:

To a certain extent it seems to me that the whole world is apt to
wear a mere pictorial aspect, that it must be by an effort that I accept
anything as fact. This is the meaning of what I have often told you
that I 'believe in you'—I do not think that I can say the same to
anyone else, though I can with less effort or with no effort talk and
get on with old familiars . . . but if I am to make a choice, to
act . . . I cannot turn, I think, except to you. There has never been
in my whole life I may say *any act* of mine, sealing either friendship
or love, up to this time. It has seemed to me a great thing (a thing
that at times I doubt the truth of myself) to have done this at all.[42]

This must be, in the whole of that often startling correspondence,
one of Clough's most remarkable letters. It is also, I think, one
of the "truest," in the sense of being the true voice of feeling. It
is Clough's greatest achievement as a poet that he was the first
of our poets to recognize and use as the matter for modern poetry
the state of mind that is symptomatic of our time and informs the
greatest art of the twentieth century, from Picasso and Giacometti
to Joyce and Eliot and Pinter. In expressing this conscious hopeless-
ness, in becoming aware of his loss of a sense of his own reality
and of the significance of the world about him, in expressing, in
short, his alienation, he was making himself one of the first English
poets to discover and seriously explore a theme that has become
basic to the art and philosophy of our age.

But the depression and frustration which Clough was able to transcend and make use of in his art found expression in his prose too.
Sometimes he could transmute it here also; sometimes it remained
unleavened as the limitations of his new life became gradually more
and more clear to him.

In October 1849, after returning from Italy, Clough took up
his duties as Principal of University Hall. The position had been
offered him a year before, some months before he had quitted Oxford for good, and with this in the offing he must have felt free

after so many years of intensive work to take his extended holiday.[43]

The tone of irritation and frustration that makes itself heard in Clough's religious writings between his leaving Oxford and composing "Notes on the Religious Tradition" around 1852 or 1853 is audible also in other works from the period 1849–1851. They were bad years for him, and he knew it, writing in 1851 to Tom Arnold "Nothing is very good, I am afraid, anywhere. *I* could have gone cracked at times last year with one thing or another, I think—but the wheel comes round."[44] There were realistic reasons for his depression. The first of these was the nature of his employment as Principal of University Hall, a new Dissenting establishment affiliated with the university Clough had once called "Stinkomalee."[45] Short of both funds and students and run by Unitarian businessmen for whom Clough clearly felt disdain, the Hall had hired him largely because they felt they needed someone from the Establishment, and thought, as Henry Crabb Robinson put it, that Clough would be a "feather in our cap . . . bring us . . . éclat" and help keep them from feeling so "excommunicate."[46] But his work as Principal of eleven students kept him busy only some two hours a day, and the trustees were capable of questioning the servants behind his back, and of objecting to his leniency with a student who played cards and drank what seemed to them too much beer.[47] And he was very much alone. *The Bothie,* as James L. Osborne said, was clearly written by a young man who wanted very much to get married.[48] But he found himself in the fall of 1849, and for the next year or two, not only unable to marry but, at the age of thirty, having to start more or less from scratch. He knew few people in London, apart from the Carlyles. His income had suddenly shrunk from around £800 to something like £150. He had formerly been Tutor and Sub-Dean of one of Oxford's leading colleges, governing a large number of undergraduates and holding a prominent position among the most intelligent and best-educated men at the country's leading university. He had helped elect Gladstone for the university; he had been a public speaker whose words were for years remembered by his hearers; he had found his voice and begun to publish in the press and in pamphlet form. He had been, as he wrote to Blanche later, "in very great force."[49] Now, in place of the numerous easy friendships he had enjoyed in Oxford, where he had lived all his adult life, he lived in two rooms in Gordon Square, isolated by day and required to await the few invitations that initially came his way for company in the evening. Not given to complaining, he nevertheless wrote in January, 1850 to Shairp that "London generally speaking is lonely, for evil at any rate and partly for good. A loneliness relieved by evening parties is not delightful—but I get on well enough in general, looking forward always to the Long Vacation."[50]

The worst blow of all was that with the "stigma of the abjured XXXIX Articles" upon him, he could not get other work. He might perhaps become a tutor in a private family if the people were radical enough, but he could hope for no more promising a connection than the one he had formed with University Hall.[51] Tom Arnold, who in his despair at England's condition and disappointed in a love affair had gone out to New Zealand, wanted to come home (he too, as it turned out, had more or less ruined his career, though in his case the matter was complicated by a late conversion to Catholicism),[52] but Clough advised this dearest of his friends against it: "As for your coming home, I incline to think it would be a very great hazard. I, like you, have jumped over a ditch, for the fun of the experiment and would not be disinclined to be once again in a highway with my brethren and companions. My situation here under a set of mercantile Unitarians is no way charming."[53] But he could not get back on the highway. He was soon to find that some of his former acquaintances, like Hawkins, would not even let him take another road. He was stuck, quite possibly for life, in an insignificant, ill paid, and unpleasant position in which his talents were hardly used. He did not, however, give up. He set himself to learn what he could from it, and to turn inward the fires from which he hoped to go on producing his work.[54] He compared his "over provocable" self, now repressed, to the coal which burnt more intensely in proportion to its "grimy period" of suppression. And during this period he was to write his most ambitious and most successful poems, *Amours de Voyage* and *Dipsychus*. But the struggle to preserve and indeed remake himself left its mark on him. Just after he had accepted the post at University Hall,

Clough wrote Tom: "Whether London will take my hopefulness out of me as it did yours, remains to be seen. Peut-être."[55] In fact, it did, and Clough became slowly aware of the fact. In part, he realized that he was simply waking up to the realities of life from which the comfortable, supportive life at the university had shielded him. Often, he was grateful for what he was learning—"ignorance" he wrote, "is a poor kind of innocence"—and glad that he had got out into real life. In a mellow, end-of-term mood when his first year was almost over he wrote:

Actual life is unknown to an Oxford student, even though he is not a mere Puseyite and goes on jolly reading parties.—Enter the arena of your brethren and go not to your grave without knowing what common merchants and sollicitors, much more sailors and coal-heavers, are well acquainted with. Ignorance is a poor kind of innocence. The World is wiser than the wise and as innocent as the innocent: and it has long ago been found out what is the best way of taking things. "The Earth," said the great traveller, "is much the same wherever we go": and the changes of position which women and students tremble and shilly shally before, leave things much as they found them.[56]

But the recognition that "the World is wiser than the wise and as innocent as the innocent" went very deep, for it was an affirmative way of expressing his recognition that his unconventional gesture of what had appeared pure idealism might have been wrong in more than the merely practical sense. He had come to question the purity and superior moral wisdom shown by himself two years before, and "the best way of taking things," instinctively known by most other people, was probably not, he realized now, the way he had taken them. Not by cutting himself off from his fellows and taking a "higher line" was he going to improve them or himself.[57]

It was probably around this date or between 1850 and 1851 that he wrote what has been called the "Review of Mr. Newman's *The Soul*."[58] I shall deal with it and his other writings on religion together in this section, for although his expressions and opinions become more clear during this period, neither the "Paper on Religion" nor "Notes on the Religious Tradition"[59] show any change in his basic attitudes after 1848. Dogmatic Christianity was impossible for him. "Miracles," as he wrote Hawkins in early 1849, were "poor proofs," and he did not believe in the literal truth of crucial Biblical accounts. He doubted even the literal fact of the crucifixion: in a passage from "Notes on the Religious Tradition" he writes "Whether Christ died upon the cross I cannot tell; yet I am prepared to find some spiritual truth in the doctrine of the Atonement." The "virtues and graces, which are our religious and moral tradition," were not "really altogether Christian"; other older, "more extensive faiths" had also perceived religious truth. Until he knew he would be silent, and he adjured silence on others. He continued to believe in some sort of life after death, but he never discussed this, nor does he seem to have tried to find an intellectual justification for his departure from pure reason. He admitted it to others, in fact, only at moments of bereavement.[60] These are the essential points of his position, and have been discussed in a previous chapter.

Three impulses and convictions moved him in greater or lesser degree in writing these pieces. The first was the conviction of the impossibility of finding answers to the questions "the soul lusts to ask" as Emerson put it. The second was annoyance at those who presumed to have found such answers. And the third was the deliberate adoption, in the face of the frustration he felt, of a posture that would be sufficient to contain within himself that very longing for answers: a posture which would transcend that annoyance and be stoic, anti-Romantic and to some extent anti-heroic. His tone might be serene, bathetic, or disillusioned, as the mood took him, but never, from now on, enthusiastic.

It was Frank Newman's enthusiasm indeed, more than anything else, that Clough objected to. He approved the freethinker's rejection of all dogma in favor of "the human heart and conscience"[61] and he applauded also Newman's rejection of the inculcation of a sense of guilt and shame as a means of moral teaching. He is critical now of Arnold's exploitation of his own youthful moral enthusiasm and takes the occasion, in a much-quoted passage, to attack the Rugby method:

Is it perhaps that in our times the conscience has been over-irritated? . . . Be strict, if you please, be severe, be inflexible. If a rule is made, it must and shall be observed! . . . But meddle not rashly, O

pedogogue, with the conscience . . . The child has done wrong;
doubtless, and must suffer for it; but do not therefore talk of guilt,
repentance, and redemption . . . Yea, though he seem incorrigible
do not think him, for God's sake do not call him a reprobate. Give
a dog a bad name and hang him; give a boy a bad name, and he
will hang himself.[62]

This anticipates the attack on Arnold in *Dipsychus*, and naming
the Headmaster he writes: "There are men, such was Arnold, too
intensely, fervidly practical to be literally, accurately, consistently
theoretical; too eager to be observant, too royal to be philosophical;
too fit to head armies and to rule kingdoms to succeed in weighing
words and analysing emotion; born to do, they know not what they
do.[63] But the largest portion of his essay is in fact an attack on the
book, motivated by disgust at Newman's emotional "Methodism"
and his attempt to have his cake and eat it too. Newman purported
in this work entitled *The Soul: Her Sorrows and Her Aspirations*
to offer a universal explanation of the religious impulse that would
make belief possible to the rationalist, by developing, as Clough
put it, a "religious Ontology."[64]

Among other things, Clough did not like Newman's style, which
heightens drastically, for example, as he describes the soul's conviction of its state of grace: "On getting a clear perception that it
[the Soul] is asking that which He delights to bestow, it believes
that its prayer is answered . . . and pledges itself to Him . . . 'Not
now, only, Oh my Lord,' it exclaims, 'but henceforth and always,
Thou art mine and I am thine.' "[65] Some unenthusiastic souls might
think this is affectation and fancy, but the "pure" soul knows better,
for it has wedded God. Clough's comments are fair but his tone
occasionally contemptuous. He objects both to Newman's assertion
of a sense of his being in a personal relationship to God, and to
his stress on what Clough calls "devotionality." The exclamations,
enthusiasm, and "deep inward fire" which, to be sure, Newman
had said ought to be kept private, dismay Clough.[66] "Let no man,"
writes Clough, "desire to analyze . . . the overflowings of the grateful heart," but on the other hand let "these effluxes be limited."
"If you cannot contain yourself, go, like Joseph to your inner chamber for a moment; but be speedy: O wash your face, and come

forth quickly to speak calmly and reasonably with your brethren."[67]
"You have found out God, have you?" he asks in like vein in the
"Paper on Religion." "You have found out God, have you? Why
who can it be that made all these contrivances for our comfortable
existence here; who put things together for us: who built the house
that we live in, and the mill that we work in, and made the tools
that we use; who keeps the clock in order, and rings the bell for
us, and lights the fire, and cooks the victual and lays the table
for us? Don't we find it laid every day? Was it nobody, think you,
that put salt in the sea for us?"[68]

But it was "superstitious for a Protestant devotee" like Newman
to "recognize the sensuous presence of the Son,"[69] and rather than
worship God because life had been made pleasant for him Clough
would turn pantheist.[70] Rejecting Butler and his positive arguments
for religion by analogy to the natural world, Clough turns to the
astronomical metaphor he is soon to use tellingly again to express
the sense of chaos and meaninglessness the world now has for him.
Gravitation and Newton have replaced Ptolemy: "Which explains
all! And the world has not done congratulating itself on moving
in an ascertained ellipse around an established center of all, when
lo, the center is no center, there is another somewhere; a center
of centers; it is not the sun now, but in the constellation Hercules
or something or other."[71]

For this bewilderment prayer is no answer: there is only work
and silence. Men rise from their knees wondering still "what shall
I do." He gives the Carlylean answer. "We are here," he insists,
"to do something . . . to live according to Nature, to serve
God . . . Not by saying 'I go, Sir,' shall he do work in the Vine-
yard, nor by exclaiming, 'Lord, Lord!' enter into the kingdom of
Heaven."[72] "Ah my friends," he urges, in the face of confusion,
"Let us be—*Silent*."[73]

Perhaps he sounds like Carlyle; his words, he notes with deliberate
bathos, may seem "noise" beside the "great Carlylean trumpet."
Perhaps the world, he implies, needs such anti-heroic figures as himself, "poor trumpeters" who will give their attention to the foot
soldiers and the "somewhat dirty earth" they tread upon.[74]

What endures, then, of religion, he writes in the somewhat later

and more serene "Notes on the Religious Tradition," endures in
no dogma or sect but everywhere: "Where then shall we seek for
the Religious tradition? Everywhere; but above all in our own work:
in life, in action, in submission, so far as action goes in service, in
experience, in patience, and in confidence. I would scarcely have
any man dare to say that he has found it, till that moment when
death removes his power of telling it."[75] It is not accurate to say
of Clough's religious position that it amounted to nothing but "quietism,"[76] unless one is willing to tar Emerson and Carlyle and other
more recent thinkers with the same brush. Like Emerson, he would
go seeking for guidance in Hume as well as in Bishop Butler,
in the past and the present, in discarded precepts and in the fashionable ones, in the Bhagavad Gita and the laws of the Persian, Menu,
in the Koran and Homer, in Lucretius and Socrates: "Every rule
of conduct, every maxim, every usage of life and society must be
admitted, like Ecclesiastes of old in the Old Testament, so in each
new Age to each new Age's Bible."[77] But ultimately, man will never
find *the* truth: "When we have tried all things, what we hold fast
is not the entire truth; when we have seen all we can there is still
more that we cannot do."[78]

Writing to his fiancée Blanche Smith, probably at roughly the
same period that he wrote this essay, he summed up in very simple
words the position which indeed transcended the frustrations which
uncertainty had formerly caused: "about being religious—the only
way to become really religious is to enter into those relations and
those actualities of life which demand and create religion. So have
good hope."[79] To be of good hope was, after all, the only possible
answer.

That same new recognition of the world's impenetrable mixture
of wisdom and innocence permeates the tone of a puzzling but interesting little cycle of fables Clough wrote around 1851, which were
titled "Conversations Between the Sun and the Moon" by Mrs.
A. H. Clough, Jr. when she arranged the manuscripts.[80] In fact,
the pieces are primarily monologues by the Earth to the almost
wordless Sun and the Moon, his "sweet companion," who occasionally interpolates a comment. A better name would perhaps be "Conversations of the Earth with the Universe." Printed for the first

time in Appendix B, these enigmatic little tales, which in some ways show Clough's prose at its best, quite escape classification, and this may explain why they have so long remained unknown. Not really Christian in outlook, lacking in plot, circular in form, with the most carefully controlled tone whose flatness reverberates like a thin sheet of metal in the wind, the "Conversations" are in essence a statement of the metaphysical dilemma of modern man as he seeks but is unable to communicate with the world around him. The failure of these pieces to see the light of day epitomizes the inability of his own period (not to say our own) and even of his own wife to sympathize with what was most unique in Clough.

The pieces vary in length from a few lines to long paragraphs. The first two are marked A and B, and the last three X, Y, and Z, but the intermediate sketches are separated only by dots or a wide space, and sometimes merely by a new paragraph. Clough may originally have intended to write a complete cycle of twenty-six fables but this seems unlikely; the significance of the few letters he has given rests in their implication that this is a sort of primer, a reduction to its primary elements of the endless cycle of questions man asks of the universe and of human relationships. The effect of simplicity, even of flatness in the tone is, of course, delusive; behind that effect, as in some of his poetry, is a sophistication so self-aware that it has turned, partly for relief and partly for the assurance of touching reality, to expression in short words and simple sentences.

The basic metaphor in this cycle is astronomical: it is in fact the same as the one Clough used in his "Paper on Religion." The inevitable overtones of Dante and Milton writ small are deliberate, for its point of departure is an ironic vision of the world's self-congratulation as it defines itself anew through science. As the fable develops the humor of the vision ebbs, for science's answers become more and more unsatisfactory and man's teleological dilemma stands naked once again. Neither love nor God have anything to say to him: their language is not his, their awareness of his existence is in some sense in doubt. The Earth in these metaphysical, psychological little scenes is clearly man, and partly Clough. The Moon is woman, and bears a certain resemblance to the Eve of "The Mystery of the Fall"; she also sounds very like the letters of Blanche Smith, to whom Clough had just become engaged and with whom his relations were frequently stormy, for Clough's was a more complicated consciousness than she was used to, and she knew it. ("I do not know that I know you—I could not explain you to anybody else," Blanche wrote at about this time, "but I feel you.")[81] Beautiful to the Earth because she turns only on herself, the moon in her narcissism is much more content with life than Earth. The Sun is God, or the Power that governs the universe, or the "supreme existences."[82] He exists in the sketches more as a resounding silence than as an active participant, and it is one of the achievements of the work that we accept him and the Earth's sense of awe about him. Like the fool who worships God in the "Paper on Religion" because He supplies him with "contrivances" for "our comfortable existence here," so the Earth complacently begins by finding the Sun circling round him "good and attentive to me."

Questioning, isolated, longing for knowledge, the Earth feels misunderstood by the Moon, who "looks bright" but has "little stirring" on her. She thinks he is stupid not to shine more. He is unable to communicate with her, but intensely introspective: as soon as he has the truth about himself he will "*change*," but in fact truth eludes him. He doesn't know who set him going—and the Sun won't answer, when looked to, except to say "That is hardly the question." The Earth is jealous of the Sun: he wants to be the center of things and be moved around at the same time that, in a defensive moment, he supposes "it is no such great matter." He himself is dissatisfied with his circular course. A straight line would be better. Finally, he begins to think about himself and the other planets and the Sun. He learns by trying that he cannot will his course. He misunderstands the Sun, thinking it revolves around himself, and is baffled by Saturn's rings. He discovers at last that he is affected by everything in the sky. Halley's comet calls him dull: he replies that, from his point of view, there is very little difference between them. In the end the Earth apologizes to the Supreme Existences for his "fanciful conjecturing" about them; these were his attempt to "realize" them.

A selection *en bloc* from these "Conversations" will give better

139

and more briefly the flavor of these writings than any paraphrase could:

"I wonder," said the Earth to itself very quietly one day, "whether my sweet companion here, the Moon, has all these thoughts and considerings and calculatings and conjecturings that I have. She looks at times very blank, I think, and unintelligent. However, very likely, she is none the worse if she hasn't."

"I don't understand about Apihelion and Peligee and all that," meantime was the Moon saying; "and to look at the surface of me, I am afraid there seems to be mighty little stirring. However, I get on somehow; and look bright, they say—and see something of the rest of the world. That must do, I suppose."

. . .

"I revolve in my orbit, my ellipse, my unvarying determined track around my Sun," said the Earth. (For the Earth after many mistakes had at last made out to its satisfacton that the Sun did not, as it had supposed, go around it, but it around the Sun.) "I," said the Earth, "upon my course and ye, other planets, upon yours—alone, irrespective, independent of each other, each around the Center for itself." So the Earth thought it did so, and intended to be doing so, but the law which is its Will did not suffer it; and at last the Earth found it was not doing so and made a motion as it were to correct itself and was surprised and disappointed to learn that though it would yet it could not.

Only quotation in full of this 2000-word cycle could do justice to it, for Clough deliberately understates the points he is making in it and, because of the simplicity of the diction, the value of a phrase depends more than is common on its relation to the whole: "and at last the Earth found it was not doing so and made a motion as it were to correct itself and was surprised and disappointed to learn that though it would yet it could not." So Clough on the Will. The words are simple to the point of repetition, and the MS, which is evidently a first draft, shows that Clough was most careful to achieve that tone: the "him" for the Earth is changed to "it," a stray "but" not absolutely necessary is removed, "discover" gives place to the shorter "learn," and the heavier "a considerable time" to the flatter "all the while." Change that "it" to "he," as the earlier readings have it often, and sentimentality threatens; let it stand, and it begins, with the work as a whole, to suggest the universal nature of this dilemma, as the earth and the stars themselves become as powerless as man to will the course of their orbits.

"Does it matter that the Earth has just found me out," said that which men call Neptune. "I existed all the same before."

"To worship is not permitted: it is more than I dare do to conceive of you seriously as more than what I see you."

"O Supreme Existences," said the Earth one day after a deal of fanciful conjecturing. "Be it forgiven me, be it no sin in your eyes, if in the half playful effort to realize you, I have spoken of you as with levity."

Not "with levity": "as with levity"—the difference is significant. He is not playing at metaphysics, but pretending to play, and behind these fables lie the years of seeking for answers he now no longer expects to find. "To worship is not permitted" because it is a response which derogates Mystery in the very act of apprehending it; implicit in the act of worship are ontological assumptions which Clough is loath to make. Written in a unique form which he shaped to fit a voice that would be more recognizable today than it was in his own period, these "Conversations" are paradoxically a statement of the near impossibility of achieving true converse with the world.

The pervasive uncertainty, the sense that "lo, the center is no center, there is another somewhere, a center of centers" in some still unknown constellation, which colored Clough's religious views during these years also found expression, of course, in his political writings. Of these two survive, one the misnamed "Address on Socialism,"[83] and the other an unpublished little fable, "The Young Cur,"[84] which bears the same relation to his "Letter" that the "Conversations" do to his writings on religion.

Clough was uncomfortably aware during this period of his new political dyspepsia. One of the unpublished letters written to his fiancée around this time is full of self-contempt and what he himself called "transcendently cynical" contempt for others, particularly for a "hopeful radical" whom he had met at

a plunge into mid-Belgravia . . . a pretty little dinner party to be sure, the ladies so full of *information* and French novels—how charming!

141

But of all things to be seen, or heard you, I think, would most have admired *My* transcendently cynical remarks—my sneer, my sarcasm . . . Oh what a pity you lost all that. Had you not . . . a sort of sympathetic impression about 10 o'clock last night . . . of my being then engaged in a contemptuously triumphant putting down of a hopeful radical (le nommé Congreve) who still would hold to his belief in progress, democracy, and that sort of thing.[85]

His "Letter to the *Christian Socialist*," as it would be better to call it, is only a little more temperate in tone than this, and is clearly motivated at least partly by a reaction to the views of his *Retrenchment* pamphlet of some three or more years earlier. Christian Socialism was a movement which had sprung up in 1848, literally on the night of the last Chartist riot, the "fiasco of Kennington Common," when two Anglican clergymen, F. D. Maurice and Charles Kingsley, and J. M. Ludlow, an Englishman educated in France, had decided that something must be done to Christianize and ameliorate the brutal conditions in which the workers lived.[86] Shortly afterward Tom Hughes, who had been at Rugby while Clough was there (though three years younger) also joined the group.[87] Well meaning and serious, but limited by its upper class background, Christian Socialism gained more practical effectiveness after its founders were joined in 1849 by a French émigré named Lechevalier who persuaded them to espouse the cause of workmen's cooperatives. These shops, run by skilled artisans who shared the profits among themselves, had been tried with some success in France before and during the revolution as a means of combating the worst effects of laisser-faire capitalism. An exposé in December 1849 by Henry Mayhew in the *Morning Chronicle* of the iniquitous "slop system" by which clothing was produced in London (piecework was awarded to the lowest bidding subcontractors, thus driving wages to starvation levels and encouraging, as it were institutionalizing, prostitution among the seamstresses) gave the Christian Socialists the impetus to start a Working Tailors' Association in January 1850.[88] Successful, it soon had many imitators, and a general Society for the Promotion of Working Men's Associations was established. On November 2, 1850 the first issue of *The Christian Socialist: A Journal of Asso-*

ciation was published in London by Ludlow and the others further to publicize and support this cooperative movement.[89]

Clough's so-called "Address," or rather "Letter,"[90] was a response to the front-page editorial of the first issue of this journal, as a comparison of the two shows. (The relation of his writing to the publication has been obscured by the treatment of the MS, however, for it was not published during his life—not indeed until 1964—and his wife omitted any reference to it from her edition of his works. Later his daughter-in-law, Mrs. Arthur Hugh Clough, Jr., who informally arranged the MSS, slipped a sheet of paper around it on which she penciled the title "Address on Socialism," perhaps because the letter begins "Gentlemen," and it has been known by that misnomer ever since.)

The journal's basic premise, and the one to which Clough objected most, was that Socialism and Christianity were essentially identical. Socialism was in fact simply Christianity in practice, and could not, indeed, survive without its moral virtues. Christianity and Socialism alike stood against the idea of self-interest—or profit—and under neither could rivalry—competition—be sanctioned. Cooperation—association—meant merely the "practical application of Christianity to the purposes of trade and industry." And because of the identical nature of Christianity and Socialism even those socialists who thought themselves atheists were essentially Christian. "Christianity," the editorial proclaimed, "however feeble and torpid it may seem . . . is truly but as an eagle at moult, shedding its worn-out plumage; . . . Socialism but its livery of the nineteenth century (as Protestantism was its livery of the sixteenth), which it is even now putting on, to spread ere long its mighty wings for a broader and heavenlier flight."[91] They looked with eagerness to the new order that might be established:

If it be given to us to vindicate for Christianity its true authority over the realms of industry and trade; for Socialism its true character as the great Christian revolution of the nineteenth century, so that the title of "socialist" shall be only a bugbear to the idle and to the wicked, and society, from the highest rank to the lowest, shall avowedly regulate itself upon the principle of cooperation, and not

143

drift rudderless upon the sea of competition, as our let-alone political economists would have it do.[92]

Clough found these statements highly questionable. In his letter he announced himself a "fixed customer" of the Working Tailors' and Working Shoemakers' associations; their work was not very good, but he was "more of a student than a man of the world . . . Indeed, I have sometimes thought my old West-end tailor, cognizant of this, didn't always quite do his best for me."[93] Still, their "new establishments appear[ed to him] so valuable as experiments" that he would put up with their disadvantages willingly. But he questioned their basic reasoning, and in particular "this assumed identity of Socialism and Christianity" evident in their "new periodical, *The Christian Socialist*." It might be comforting to think they were based on the same ideas, but it was not true. "I did not feel much edified," he wrote, "when a distinguished evangelical divine cut *ex cathedra* your Gordian knot of social inequalities and social miseries by the calm enunciation on the text that the poor shall be always in the land. Yet I must allow that it does seem the Christian view of things, that the poor always *will* be there."[94]

They might argue that England was a Christian nation and that they might expect the English to cast out "the evil spirits of Selfishness, Oppression, Greediness, Tyranny, and the like," but in fact England was "baptised, mostly, but very doubtfully regenerate." English society was not truly Christian and they ought not to "go about to establish a social system, proceeding on an hypothesis of as yet unattained and it may be unattainable success." The literal sharing of goods in common might be "truly Christian," but so long as Christian Socialists remained in this society, they would not achieve their aims—and Clough was no longer sure he shared them.[95]

The young man who had once called himself the "Apostle of anti-*laissez-faire*," who had insisted that honesty and fairness, not competition, ought to be the basis on which wages were set, and who had ridiculed the idea that "Capitalism, who keeps his carriage, will never be able to build mills unless Labor, who barely keeps himself, saves money to help him,"[96] now held that the world could not go on without the spur of competition, and that it was a good thing for the man beaten in the race to learn "in any case another time to look out sharper."[97] The reversal of attitude is striking: *caveat emptor,* he is saying, I am not my brother's keeper:

I agree with the Psalmist, who tells us that no man can save his brother, and that it is very well if he can save himself . . . I think we are each first of all intended to look after his [. . . ?] own self. It is not my business to see that my chance companion in the railway carriage takes care of his ticket, and his umbrella; and wraps up his throat sufficiently against the cold . . . I do not go to my new next-door neighbor to tell him who ought to be his butcher; and in the pit of the theater if I detect the best place and the man beside me doesn't I do not obtrude on him a philanthropic request to anticipate me.[98]

Self-abnegation and busybody charity were not Clough's line. "Each man" he repeated, "is to look out for himself: and if he doesn't, must learn to do so. Competition is not naturally wrong: it is merely one way, and the most efficient yet known . . . for teaching men this great law of a sadly uncelestial world."[99]

With a grim self-mocking pleasure and an irony that hisses in all directions at once, he goes on to detail some of the regrettable but unavoidable inequities of life, his sense of alienation and impotence finding its vent in the language he chooses and personae he invents. "You" are healthy and strong (the casting of these roles is not, one suspects, unrelated to his present state of mind) but "I poor devil"—who, to be sure, can write a better magazine article—have only two fingers on one hand, and am half-blind and rheumatic. The imagery of castration is carried further and he becomes the amputated beggar on his board, a beggar who ought not to suppose that "because Lord Verysoft in his cab is a fool therefore I on my board am a wise man." Moreover, the "Upper Classes" may "know a thing or two . . . which you and I don't."[100]

"I have used a little gall of satire" to "blacken the ink," Clough remarked in closing.[101] Certainly he had, and the most satirical of all was the last stroke of his signature, "Your obedient Servant / Citoyen," the nickname he had flaunted proudly some years before. The "mutilation" that Symonds sensed as having occurred in Clough's life is nowhere more evident than in the writings of this period. He may well have been on the way, as he wrote in 1852, to being "wiser" but London—and his own grounds for being there—had indeed taken, as he had feared, some of the "hopefulness" out of him.

"The Young Cur," which has never been published, presents roughly the same view of social change as the "Letter" just discussed, but like "Conversations of the Earth with the Universe" it is a better piece of writing than its essayistic counterpart. Only some 200 words long, its language is tight, heightened, and almost cryptic; it stands midway between prose and verse, and midway, both chronologically and in content, between the "Letter to the *Christian Socialist*" and the "Epilogue" to *Dipsychus*. It is interesting, not only for its stylistic impact and economy, but for the quiet finality with which Clough's mind appears to dispose of the notion, basic to radical thought, of man's perfectibility. It is cast, like the "Epilogue" just mentioned, in the form of a dialogue between an uncle and his nephew: I quote it here in its entirety:

> The young cur observed one day to the elderly sheep dog his uncle, "It is clear to me that in themselves, and in the idea, all dogs are equal."
> "Nay, thank God," replied the other, "that there are some neither as ugly as me nor as silly as you."
> Some time afterwards the young cur in a more thoughtful temper resumed. "Circumstances, it is obvious, exercise a most powerful influence. Early habits and associations; locality; education; good or bad company; what one sees and what one has to do. It cannot of course be expected that I who live with the lower orders and go running after sheep should be what I should, of myself, be—under more favoring circumstances. From circumstances come great distinctions, but originally and in themselves I have no doubt that all dogs are equal."
> "In the same way it would seem to me an obvious conclusion," replied the other, "that originally and in themselves all circumstances are equal. It is a good thing to be cleanly, and yet at the same time how pleasant dirt is."
> The young cur did not see the cogency of this.[102]

Equality is a chimera. Moral judgment cannot be abrogated. Dirt and republican ideas are, by inference, equated. Social inequality is to republican ideas as cleanliness is to dirt: harder and better. As a piece of writing, condensed, elliptical, and suave, the fable is very effective. The avuncular sheep dog seems to have earned his mellow cynicism and is a likeable fellow; his earnest nephew, struggling through his string of clichés and lingering, self-conscious, half-ashamed sense of social superiority, will, we suppose, outgrow his folly. Clough is writing well here: the distance afforded by his satiric stance gives him a control of the issues and of the tone which the "Letter" lacks. He has attained for his piece that enigmatic tone essential for a fable which suggests it is a parable worthy of exegesis. But the distance had been paid for in hope and was dearly purchased.

CHAPTER V

The Hopeful Country

At the end of 1851, Clough lost his job at University Hall, and he was faced with the prospect of having to find work where there was none. His application for the Principalship of the new University in Sydney came to nothing.[1] He was engaged to Blanche Smith, the daughter of a wealthy and prominent Unitarian, Samuel Smith, and cousin of Florence Nightingale, but after the disappointment of his Australian hopes he felt that even that connection had to be severed.[2] He applied for various other positions connected with education, but again and again these proved to require one kind of religious orthodoxy or another, and he realized afresh how entirely he had ruined his career. There was nothing left, if he stayed in London, but "unmarried poverty" and unspecified "literary work," but he was not publishing anything he had written. In May he wrote to Blanche, undoubtedly feeling more despair than he admitted: "We shall be parted my dear Blanche; it is no use, I think, and I do not like concealing from you what is on my mind day after day (not that I am so particularly depressed . . .) but—I shall have to say that I see no prospect or hope of anything . . . You see that really with Education for my profession I have so far less chance than others in their professions or in this—because of the stigma of the abjured XXXIX articles."[3]

Finally, he wrote to Emerson to inquire if he thought there were any prospects for him as a teacher of Latin, Greek, or English in America. He was now reluctant to leave London's society, and said "I am half-loth now after nearly three years' apprenticeship to quit this great town; it is almost like beginning to go down from a high

148

mountain which it has taken long hours to get to."[4] He had made a success out of his "plunge into Belgravia," and his friends and acquaintances included, for example, Lord and Lady Ashburton. Clough was aware of how much London had to give him, and he "hated," after once being uprooted, to have to endure it again. Emerson, however, wrote him most encouragingly. Clough's heresies would apparently be irrelevant in the United States. There were plenty of opportunities through teaching to marry on a modest but comfortable income. Clough might live with him, Emerson, for some months, help him to edit his journals of 1848, and get acquainted with "all the atrocities of republicanism . . . Do not doubt our industry to employ yours," he wrote. He had doubts about how well Clough would like America: "I think it takes a long enuring or wonting to make a genuine Englishman tolerate our modes," and he would not advise him positively to come when there was in the balance "such a splendid contingency as an English first-rate literary reputation," but he thought that with his "names and titles, real powers and excellent prestige," Clough held a "very safe" card, "safe for a permanence though one may easily meet some trying delays at the outset." Clough determined to go, and by the middle of November 1852, he was in Boston.[5]

He stayed in America seven and a half months—rather too short a time perhaps, but a crucial and, while it lasted, a highly productive period in his life; the day of June 1853 when he rather precipitately sailed back to England was both literally and figuratively a turning point in his life. The question of why he returned to England has been much discussed, for it is difficult to disentangle the web of conflicting hopes, financial rewards, personalities, and opportunities that surrounded the act.[6] One of the significant facts that emerges from this study, however, is that Clough's stay in America, for all its drawbacks, many of which would have disappeared with time, was one of his most intellectually productive periods; it is clear also that the country had both a much needed stabilizing effect on his attitudes and opinions, and a stimulating effect on his self-confidence and thought. He knew this, writing an American friend just after he returned to England, "I like America best."[7] He did not, certainly, like all things American, and especially in moments of loneliness he complained, sometimes peckishly. Harvard was an "old-woman" sort of place, even the stone of its buildings lacking substance, and Emerson "the only profound man in the country."[8] He had met the society in which Thoreau and Alcott mixed, and he recognized early what has since been called the isolation of the intellectual in American life, perceiving in "pokey" Concord that the "Diogenes tub philosophy," what Carlyle called "Gymnosophism," was as naturally encouraged by democracy in America as in Athens.[9] By contrast with the ancient, stone-built cities he was used to, Cambridge with its wooden architecture and new institutions seemed not quite real, like its houses, "all tidy, and all insubstantial." They were like the "tall Gothic Church . . . altogether a make-belief, being wooden in material and Unitarian in doctrine."[10] He sometimes felt annoyed and alienated by such orthodoxy as prevailed among the orthodox Unitarians (which made Blanche nervous), but he found their prayer book "very funny," describing how a fashionable Episcopal Church in Boston had turned Unitarian en masse, "cut off the tails of the prayers and pruned things here and there—and lo, they have a very handsome Common Prayer book quite as good as any Genuine One, and nothing disagreeable in it."[11] But for all these qualifications America, he soon realized, called out from him his voice, and he became aware that he was needed, that there was work he could do and do well, and that, above all, there was for him in Cambridge a stimulation and climate that rewakened his energies and feelings of hope. In London he had felt, and was to feel again, nearly "helpless to effect anything." Here it was "an immense thing to feel that you really are . . . wanted." His old "habits of doubting" which Blanche had disliked were diminished, he explained, because "this country is so much more hopeful *for me*." His sense of himself as a free agent grew, and he wanted to concentrate on the kind of writing and teaching that would be "work to some purpose." And although he called his feeling a "vain confidence" he could now assert that "there was something in me to be done beyond mere subsistence."[12]

That new confidence was not vain. Cambridge and Harvard might be provincial in comparison with London and Oxford, but in contrast to the prose writings of his London years, which were not lengthy and remained largely unpublished during his lifetime, the copious material he wrote in America (with the exception of a few pieces meant to be kept private) saw print almost immediately. Indeed, within a four-month span, the *North American Review* published essays by him totaling more than 25,000 words; when his first contribution had been accepted by this, the most intellectual journal of the day, the editor had "beg[ged him] to write another . . . on anything [he] liked."[13] During the seven and one-half months he spent in the United States Clough's formal writings included the six "Letters of Parepidemus" (a name derived from the Greek for "sojourner"),[14] three review-articles,[15] translations from *The Iliad* which he planned to use for a lecture, a large portion of his five-volume revised edition of *Plutarch's Lives*,[16] and the incomplete "Review of a Book on Progress."[17] In addition, he composed another lecture (or gave an old one) on an unknown topic.[18] To this material we should add his essay on Charles Eliot Norton's *Considerations on Some Recent Social Theories,* for this piece, written shortly after his return to England about a book by one of his best American friends, summarizes the position he had consolidated during his stay in America.[19] We know a good deal about him during this period, moreover, because his letters to Blanche form almost a diary.

The opinions he expressed in the writings do not, of course, being Clough's, fit neatly under any party label. He was not likely to take on wholesale the opinions of any group he might join, and the old issues by which he had defined his views in England were suddenly no longer live ones. Socialism and association, for example, are hardly referred to; there was no "Condition of America" question. The vital issues were Abolition and American expansionism, the "Manifest Destiny" that was embroiling her frequently with smaller Latin American countries. These gradually came to the fore in Clough's consciousness, and the latter called forth some of his most vigorous—one might say happiest—invective. But the basic and most obvious challenge to a foreigner, and in some ways the hardest to accept, was America's primary assumptions about political and social egalitarianism.

Clough came to grips with these assumptions, at least overtly, almost immediately and with a positive response. He began the "Letters of Parepidemus" while still on shipboard, and although some of them were published, some are more like journal entries than essays and are among the least formal and most personally revealing of his writings from this period. In the second of the "Letters," still unpublished, he averred his sense of "reimpatriation" and his readiness to like egalitarian ways: "Twenty-five years ago . . . though but a child [I believe I] carried away with me a good deal of ineradicable republican sentiment—I return to the habits and feelings of your country (mine I am not legally entitled to call it) with something beyond all question very like a sense of reimpatriation."[20] In language that is most unqualified for Clough he went on to defend American notions of equality. It was only a libel when a "countryman of mine once asserted in my hearing that [the] great American syllogism was All men are equal: therefore I am your superior. 'Tis false, my dear sir. The prevailing, and, I persuade myself, almost universal feeling which comforts and rejoices the souls of your countrymen, is on the contrary All men are equal: I am no man's inferior." He felt with "moral and spiritual emancipation . . . Thank God I am no longer any man's superior!" Perhaps men weren't really equal; still one must act as if they were: "Equality—By all means; it is far the most agreeable and comfortable hypothesis—Even if we are not, O too introspective and rigidly philosophical European—if we are not, let us suppose we are. Let us suppose at any rate . . . that we are not politically or socially other people's superiors." Clough reported with English amusement that a missing shop clerk had been referred to by another as a "gentleman." He was astonished to find that the daughter of his landlady, Mrs. Julia Ward Howe, who opened the door for him and did the dishes, turned up later in the afternoon as another guest at a tea. At the Emersons' (Mrs. Emerson was, it is true, a bad housekeeper) two Irish maids washed up the breakfast things in a bucket in the corner of the dining room. All the servants were Irish, and service was universally bad, slow, and resentful. The Irish servants were "slovenly-ish," but quick to learn the "I'm as good as you are" attitude. "Mostly there is the feeling that there is nobody to do things for you" and if only they could afford it Blanche should bring an English maid with her when she joined him.[21]

Yet although in his social manners Clough could be reserved to the point of seeming shyness, basically he was at ease with New England manners and with America's relative lack of pretentiousness in social relations. It was the "simplicity" of life in America that he had liked most, he told R. H. Hutton in later years,[22] and the "agreeable and comfortable hypothesis" he had early perceived that Americans held—"I am no man's inferior"—made easier not only personal relationships but a way of life less showy and wasteful, and more natural than the one he had left behind.

As the months went by, Clough became initiated into American politics and his opinions began to mold themselves into what was to be their characteristic shape: essentially liberal in aims, he now opposed methods that were revolutionary, and solutions that were quick and easy, or that would have to be reached by forcibly altering the structure of property. The era was a turbulent one in this decade before the Civil War, and New England of course was a center of resistance both to slavery, which had been a rankling issue for generations, and to the policies of expansion of Presidents Polk and Pierce. These were intimately connected with Abolition, for in spite of the Missouri Compromise, each new accession of territory reopened the old question of whether it should join the union as a free or slave-holding state.[23] Clough said he knew nothing about the details of American politics, but in fact he was an apt student who quickly engaged himself with what was going on, wrote Blanche or journalized about it, and then tried to reassume a mask of indifference, sometimes without success. "Ticknor, Prescott and Co. . . . high Whigs, which means Tories and quite aristocratic" belonged to "a rather exclusive tip-top conservative set"[24] and were, he explained, Old Hunkers.[25] Emerson "st[ank] in the nostrils," Clough discovered, of most of the Boston Brahmins who were serving as Clough's sponsors in his academic endeavors. "And Dr. Howe," he added of his landlord, "is rather, or indeed a great deal worse than Emerson. Theodore Parker would be the worst of all."[26]

On Abolition Clough was no firebrand. The Fugitive Slave Act had recently been tightened, and the enraged Abolitionists had responded by increasing the activities of the Underground Railway. The house Clough lived in was a center for the movement that helped "prevent the return of slaves to the South," for his landlord

153

was Dr. Samuel Howe, who with his wife (author of the "Battle Hymn of the Republic") edited the abolitionist paper *The Commonwealth*. Clough seems to have been unaware of the extent of their activities, for he wrote Blanche in mock horror that "Mrs. Howe is a great Free Soiler, and I almost fear, *worse*. I have seen a most dreadful abolitionist paper lying about."[27] It may well have been the Howes' own production. (Mrs. Howe seems to have been full of surprises for Clough. Not only did she do her own housework and hold political opinions, but she "dressed so low I'm always in terror lest she should come up bodily out of it, like a pencil out of a case."[28] In later years she published a book of verse called *Passion Flowers*.)

Clough despised the Fugitive Slave Act as a "piece of truckling to the South," but he wrote Blanche that if he were an American he would be a Free Soiler, and would be willing to compensate the South for its slaves if it gave them up.[29] The significance of property was much more evident in Clough's eyes now than it had been in the mid-40's when he had attacked great landholders and their unqualified defense of the rights of property; in the intervening years he had seen too much of the destructive reaction that could follow on such attacks.

But the same principle that led Clough to defend reparation for the South and coolly stand off from the Abolitionists, made him a strong, even violent opponent of America's policies of aggression, as he saw them, towards her smaller neighbors to the South. Two of the "Letters of Parepidemus" take up this issue in increasingly hot terms. The Mexican War, by which the United States had gained immense new territories through superior force of arms, had recently ended. Now there was an active war party that was calling for the "liberation" of Cuba from the crumbling Spanish empire. "Manifest Destiny" was the aggressive slogan of the Democratic Party. In 1848 President Polk had hinted he might annex the Mexican province of Yucatan, which Great Britain or Spain might also wish to take, and shortly afterwards he tried to buy Cuba from Spain. He was rebuffed with the statement that the old country would sooner see her island possession "sunk in the ocean." President Pierce, inaugurated later in 1848, followed similar policies. The expansionist forces, who were largely Southerners interested in acquiring new subtropical lands for slave-holding, took this as encouragement for their piratical efforts, called "filibusters."[30] These were spontaneous, private raids of "liberation" which had gone on for years and had caused some international scandal.[31] The world was discovering, as Schlesinger has said, that the United States did not regard the Monroe Doctrine as "a self-denying ordinance."[32] Clough himself had a young and wayward student whom he thought would probably end up either over the Rocky Mountains, "filibustering in Cuba, or sowing other wild oats à la jeune Américaine."[33] That there was some sotto voce encouragement for the attitude, however, was made startlingly evident in 1854 when three American ministers announced in Ostend that if Spain would *not* sell Cuba to the United States the latter, "by every law, human and divine," would be justified in taking it by force.[34]

Clough's response to such policies was intensely hostile, and in one of his later "Letters of Parepidemus" he discussed his somewhat ambivalent feelings toward the American ideal of equality and America's own evidently ambivalent feelings on the topic. The Americans, in his view, seemed to feel themselves very much more equal than the Cubans and Hondurans. On two recent occasions, he wrote, he had heard Americans say that Might was Right: once in regard to copyright law and once on the topic of "annexing" Honduras.[35] America, who saw herself as the hope of the world, was adopting the worst of Europe's cast-off doctrines. Might was not right; to preach it was to welcome the "refuse" of European thought and revert to barbarism. He had "carried away in early life" an idea to which he still clung: "a sense, I mean, of natural equity between man and man, and a reluctance to take more than my fair share."[36] Now he was "astounded" to hear "most respectable and worthy citizens, in a most unfilibustering part of your republic" uttering the "to me extremely strange, and even in Europe I thought long ago exploded sentiment that might is right." Angry now, his rhetoric took on the Swiftian tone of the manuscript piece "An Ill World." "Is it really true, Sir," he asked, "that this doctrine . . . is beginning to be prevalent on this side of the Ocean? Do not the vast intervening expanses of salt waters over which the winds blow to you from the unhappy despotic East defecate them ere they touch your shores of these impurities—are you so hospitable or so careless as to offer a gracious welcome, as to the hapless refugees of the ancient kingdoms, so also to the very refuse of their speculations? I had hoped it had been otherwise."[37]

Clough must have been one of the first English literary figures to take English imperialism as a matter for serious concern if not thoroughgoing stricture. To the question of how to justify "legitimate aspirations and honorable ambitions after progress, extension, development and what not,"[38] Clough suggested that that man who "can for the common good make the best and most serviceable use of God's gifts to man is, for the sake of the common good, entitled to do so." In life, "the strongest has a right to do the hardest service; he that can endure most pain has a right to claim it—the spade to the digger and the hoe to the hoer." And land, therefore, should belong to him who "for the common good, can turn it to the best account." This would justify some acts of imperialism—the French presence in "the haunts of the Algerian pirates," the English possession "for the protection of trade of the world" of sentry or police bases in Aden or Singapore.[39] But England had not the right to "lordship" over the East Indies, India, and China, or to force a "poisonous drug" onto the Chinese market against Chinese wishes— and America had not the right to take another nation by force.[40] America which "maintain[ed] the doctrine that all men are equal" certainly had no right, either legally or morally, to take territory because another nation mismanaged it.[41] If America adopted the "exploded" doctrine as her own, her vitality and essential nature as a democracy would die; once let "Might is Right" find its way into the political creed and "It will bring with it the seed of downfall to your whole commonwealth; it is the one deadly antagonist, as I conceive, of all true Democracies."[42]

The following "Letter of Parepidemus" is frankly a tirade launched at the "Anglo-Cannibal."[43] It exhibits Clough's invective at its richest, and bits of Latin, Italian, and French float on the surface of a style that abandonedly and inventively mixes fable and excellent name-calling with Biblical allusion and deliberate bathos, while using as its terms of reference everything from the *Inferno*

156

to London cabdrivers. The total effect is strangely unified: the wild
vitality of the allusive coloring simply strengthens one's sense of a
mind bringing all its consciousness and overwhelming moral indignation to bear on an issue and expressing it through the overriding
imagery of voracious and gluttonous eating. "What a fool I was
to write that last letter," he begins, "Enough, enough!—Do manus.
I surrender, I retract, Cuba shall be yours, O Philibuster . . . The
Spaniard is unquestionably and in all senses our inferior; we *are*
the race of the World—the Anglo-Savage for ever—He shall eat
his fellow man through the whole world." He slips into the language
of allegory to describe bitingly America's visions of her Manifest
Destiny, which he characterizes as Providence: " 'More, more,' said
the rude little child at dessert to its good and kind friend, Providence.
'Say, "if you please" my dear,' said Providence. 'If you please, Providence,'—'Presently, then, my dear,' said wise Providence, 'not quite
so fast.' " (Unfortunately, in the other printed text of this passage,
the irony is obscured by an unfortunate misreading of "Providence"
as "Prudence.")

Manifest Destiny, Clough is saying, is cannibalism. He travesties
the notion that it is the "obvious will of Providence" for Anglo-Saxon
America to annex its Latin neighbors of inferior blood:

Sooner or later, however, according to the obvious will of Providence,
the Anglo-cannibal shall devour his brother. O happy Anglo-Cannibal.
May he never disagree with thee. Nevertheless, since it is a divine
law in one sense or other . . . that "whoso sheddeth man's blood,
by man shall his blood be shed" and "Whoso eateth a man, by a
man shall he be eaten," be prepared O Anglo-Cannibal with a calm
heroic resignation to natural destiny—Eat, O Eater that shalt one day
be eaten . . . Eat me, O Eater, and may I not prove very indigestible
to you.

He offers as a parable the information that the Hindus think that
when a tiger has killed a man, its spirit then guides the tiger in
pursuit of "new blood guiltiness." Perhaps, Clough suggests, with
deliberate bathos, the next transmigration of the souls is—(that is,
ought to be)—service in a London cab, "or, in the form of an
[ass?] [that] for the hire of kicks and thistles draws an everlasting
dung cart." "Such polluted human-tiger-souls" as these, he says,

must Dante have met in Hell and looked upon with "austere satisfaction" when he wrote that "Caina [the deepest circle of Hell] awaits him who . . . wishes to extinguish life."[44]

It is curious but characteristic of Clough that at approximately the same time that he was releasing these violent expressions he was able to write to Blanche about one of Pierce's speeches: "Gen. Pierce's speech—O, it isn't really at all aggressive I believe—he was forced to say something for his party, but he was kept within the lines pretty well . . . they say Mexico must be dropping in soon and then there'll be all the old question of Extension of Slave Area over again—However I don't listen much to things—except very occasionally."[45] Did Clough really think he didn't "listen much" to politics? Or was he assuming indifference for Blanche's peace of mind (she feared and discouraged his nonconformity)? At any rate, knowing himself to be "over provocable," he probably needed his assumed indifference to public events to maintain a moderately steady course.

But this kind of outburst was now no longer Clough's general tone. The "new body" he had foreseen he would have to make for himself "all over again" in America did indeed begin to appear, and was a far more dispassionate figure for the most part than he had once been, and perhaps a more effective one. Privately he was still emotionally volatile, but in his public writings he actively sought to achieve the most persuasive tone. Getting "the right tone was *the extreme* difficulty" in composing his first article for the *North American Review* on the *Oxford University Commission Report,* but the effort was worth it if it would "do some good."[46] He had written before on education. But neither the "Petition on University Reform"[47] nor his letter of evidence to this very Commission, now printed in its *Report,*[48] had been proper places to formulate broad and philosophic positions on education, as he wished to do in this new and growing country. Now he took the opportunity, after describing the history of the *Report* and how the university worked, or failed to work, to address himself to the basic aims of a university education, considering not how to make the existing machinery more efficient, but rather the basic questions of what and how a man should study to become educated. In effect, he outlined in broad terms what the American system has become: a program in which students study general courses for one or two years and a specialty for the next two, while taking continual, minor examinations. At present, he pointed out, for three years the Oxford undergraduate dragged his heels until, towards the end, he spent some hurried months getting up his Greek and Latin texts. Clough suggested that the curriculum be widened, not merely by the insufficient reform of allowing the "suffering pilgrim . . . to lay down a portion of his classical burden at the feet of the examiners at the end of the second year," but beyond that by encouraging him to spend the third year working in one of some four departments of study. Instead of allowing everything to depend on a single final examination, after which some would foolishly be declared "the cleverest men in Oxford," Clough advocated holding more frequent but less individually significant examinations which would encourage not personal competition but "the strictly plain and severely true ascertainment not of whom he has beat, but of what he has done." Perhaps recalling his own derelictions under the present system, Clough pointed out that the only real compulsion to study was fear of failure; the ability to cram was developed, but not "a real inward taste, and liking, and passion . . . for study and the subjects themselves of study."[49]

Clough ended this review with a passage that has unfortunately been omitted from the *Selected Prose,* for it contains a statement of what was probably his final position on the idea of a university education and of his hopes for higher education in America. One cannot but feel that, as Clough hoped it would, it struck an answering chord in the Americans who read it. Its tone, to which he had given such attention, is both simple and noble. "A University," wrote this man, who had as much right to speak on the topic as any of his contemporaries,

is not necessarily a finishing school for the sons of richer people; it may be a finishing school for those, whatever their parentage or private means, who are worth the pains and expense of a finished and complete education. If this country, in *her* public schools, possesses a means for discovering in all parts and places the most promising boys, is it not all the more incumbent upon her to give these chosen individuals that which, in other places is offered at random to a class or section of society—a really high culture, an education worthy of the name?[50]

In effect, Clough was advocating the sort of system which has gradually evolved, both in England and America, of making college freely available, through either governmental or private scholarships, to the country's best students. Pick out, not the richest, Clough urged, his vision soaring in a perhaps American way, but "the fittest" and give them "this benefit in its fullest measure."

The American Republic does not appear to be wholly unfitted for the existence of institutions aiming at the highest ends, and using all the means, of the wealthiest and most learned European Universities. Might not a University exist upon this side of the Atlantic, which should combine, with the freedom and openness of the French and German institutions the strict requirements and thorough-going discipline and the munificent aids and rewards which are found in those of England, or are, at any rate, aspired to in the Report of the Oxford Commission?[51]

One feels that one is hearing a man who knows what education is and ought to be, and who knows how to make others believe the truth of what he had said. It was America's loss that he did not stay to help make real, in the country where such visions were turning into fact, the dream he evidently had.

But he could not stay. His father-in-law-to-be had offered to subvent his daughter's marriage in the amount of £500 a year if they lived in England. Mr. Smith later extended this offer to cover an American household also, but his real wishes were clear. Clough could guarantee no income in the United States and he had so far made only enough to keep himself. He did not much want to begin a school, but he would have been willing as a last resort to do the obvious thing and begin by taking pupils in his house if he had a wife. He suggested it, among other alternatives, several times and Blanche agreed, but clearly had misgivings.[52] Her life as a member of wealthy English Unitarian society had been extremely sheltered, and she would, Clough knew, deeply miss not only her family and friends but all the upper-middle class amenities she took for granted. Even the austere Clough found some American social customs peculiar: Blanche, no pioneer, would have been de-

cidedly uncomfortable as a schoolmaster's wife. Of course Clough
could have insisted that she join him to live for the first few years
essentially on her father's money, knowing all the while her reluctance to do so (Clough and the Smiths had hoped, it would appear,
that a professorship would materialize at Harvard) but such a course
would have required a degree of egotism he did not possess. When
the offer of a £300 a year job (little better than a clerk's, at least
initially) came to him through the offices of Carlyle and the Ash-
burtons, he returned to England at once and soon took the position.
His gain was not merely domestic and financial. To return to England was to return to the center of things. He thought of London
before he left it in 1852 as a mountain which he had succeeded
in climbing, and sometimes of America, while he was there, as culturally "barren" and intellectually a "desert" in which only Emerson
was lifegiving.[53] Its insufficiency he summed up as "Knowledge,"
"the precious intellectual aliment" which one breathed in the very
air of Europe and in European tradition and experience. But, as
he admitted in closing this "Fragment on America," "for a man
to act—there [were] no places so hopeless, so unnerving" as
those European capitals, while in America, as he acknowledges in
a different prose piece, "each individual human being . . . may
feel that his worth as such is recognized."[54] The notes of hope and
a sense of his own potential usefulness in society are not ones we
hear again in his prose; he had rather, as his wife wrote, a "sense
of being constantly at variance with the ordinary sentiments of those
who surrounded him."[55]

Nevertheless it is apparent that with the end of his American
period his views had achieved a certain hard-won serenity. It is
a realistic, perhaps even somewhat grim attitude but more stable,
as he himself implies, than his enthusiasms of the 40's. He expresses
his ultimate position in his July 1853 review of Charles Eliot Norton's anonymous book, *Considerations on Some Recent Social Theories*[56] and the roughly contemporary, unpublished "Review of a
Book on Progress."[57]

Norton, only twenty-six when he produced this collection of six
essays, was in the eyes of his friend Clough a "noble youth." A
Boston Brahmin, son of one of the "aristocratic" members of the

Whig party who was also a leader of the orthodox Boston Unitarians, Norton was largely a Tocquevillean conservative. Like those of many of this caste, his ideas resemble in more than one way those of the middle class English Dissenters and were decidedly to the right of Jacksonian democracy.[58] His essays express his fear of the tyranny of the majority and look for the control of a somewhat frightening national liberty through religious teaching.[59] On the other hand, he wanted to see the masses educated, and he thought that the inequalities of property which arise from the "injustice of human institutions" should be remedied. More significant from Clough's point of view, however, was Norton's adoption of the utilitarian view that "the object of each man's life is to attain happiness," and that the object of a govenment is to attain for its subjects "progress."[60]

On the whole, although Clough agreed with what his friend had written, most of the essay is given over to the expression of his own revised views on liberty and necessity. Timko considers this passage on liberty, to be discussed below, as central to Clough's thought; and this is true from this period onwards.[61] But it is important in grasping the development of Clough's ideas to recognize that this very limited concept of liberty, which rejects spontaneity and equates it rather with service, is a late stage of his intellectual growth—late, hard-won, and grim. The word "liberty" in fact is of no particular significance in Clough's prose before this date, and he seems to have articulated it prominently only when rejecting some of its connotations. Part of the reason for this may be that it was too closely associated with what Clough sardonically called the "Grand Lib, Eq and Frat" revolutions to be used seriously by one who avoided mottoes and party labels on principle. To put it positively, one might say that Clough's concern for the integrity of the individual, his development, his well-being, and his freedom of conscience was constant in his thought. But the means by which those goals could best be achieved were variables, and necessity became more and more a welcome spur to this development as spontaneity and the unconstrained search for happiness ceased to seem socially promising or useful.

With Norton, therefore, he rejected "the high doctrine proclaimed by the fervid Italian leader of the supreme 'authority of the People as the collective, perpetual interpreter of the will of God.' "[62] *Vox populi* was not *vox dei*. It is interesting to read this, even though we have seen it adumbrated in the "Letter on Christian Socialism," for we see that the wheel has come full circle. While still under Arnold's influence, Clough had debated and denied this adage in an undergraduate essay written in 1840.[63] In the years of his "very great force" when his reforming zeal had been at its height, he had not precisely supported it but he had championed the laborer's rights much as if he did believe it. Now, a "wiser" man, saddened by the lessons of the French and Italian revolutions and taught by experience not to expect too much steadiness or precision of thought from the uneducated masses, saddened perhaps too by his experience of his own fallibility of purpose and strength, he went out of his way to renounce whatever faith he may ever have had in pure democracy and in the leadership of the man he had called "noble Mazzini." "We cannot," Clough wrote, "any more than our author, soar to the high modern Mazzinian acceptation of the ancient maxim [of *vox populi, vox dei*] . . . A people can be the slave of cupidity and resentment; a people can be pusillanimous, dastardly, and base; a people can be also fiendishly inhuman; the fears and passions of a people, when once excited, are more hopelessly irrational . . . more appallingly terrible, than those of councils and kings."[64] On some occasions, "the common impulses and plain feelings of the people may be . . . honest and good." But for fairness, honor, delicacy, or administrative efficiency, they could not be trusted.[65]

In like manner, his fragmentary "Review of a Book on Progress" rejects men like Mazzini and Châteaubriand who put more faith in glorious acts than in ordinary honesty and hard work, and who "aspiring in a pure enthusiasm to liberate Nations, to overthrow despots, to die in a 'Cause,' nevertheless are not prepared on all occasions to tell the truth, to control base appetites, nor indeed to face danger. There are men who will charge in battle who will sleep in the sentry box."[66]

The love of spontaneity which had caused him to cherish the "dear blouse" of the Revolution, and which had inspired *The Bothie,* he now explicitly renounced. Already in a letter to Blanche he had said that *"service"* and not love was "All."[67] Now he departed even further and more explicitly from the Rousseauistic position of *The Bothie*. He writes well and with a decidedly valedictory note, as if saying farewell to ideas he had once loved, of "the dream . . . of ardent and generous spirits of our time" that men might without constraint "be good, and without trouble, happy." "Disappointed a thousand times, they still persist in their exalted creed that there must . . . be here on earth . . . a state of social arrangements in which the spontaneous action and free development of each individual . . . member will . . . form 'a vast and solemn harmony,' the ultimate perfect movement of collective humanity." In this utopian moment "beautiful thoughts will distil as the dew, and fair actions spring up as the green herb; there, without constraint, we shall all be good, and without trouble, happy; there, what in its imperfect form is vice, shall gently and naturally flower out into virtue; there contention and contest, control and commandment, will be the obsolete terms of a dead language, with no modern equivalents to explain them."[68] Such hopes were understandable; Virgil, writing of the Golden Age, had also entertained them, but such a world never had existed, nor would exist.

Writing in a way that suggests he spoke from his own experience, Clough upheld, as he had done to Shairp a few years before, the salutary influence of necessity, of having to do what one did not like: "There are many, surely, who looking back into their past lives, feel most thankful for those acts which came least from their own mere natural volition—can see that what did them most good was what they themselves would least have chosen, that things which, in fact, they were forced to were . . . the best things that ever happened to them."[69] He who at twenty-one had written that duty meant "the blind non-recognition / Either of goodness, truth or beauty,"[70] now urged the value of adversity, and looked in his "mature free will . . . with some little regret, but also with no little scorn, upon the bygone puerile spontaneities of the time when he did as he liked."[71]

He disagreed, therefore, with Norton when the latter held up happiness as the proper goal of man. Not happiness, said Clough, but service was man's reason for being. This statement led him to another, perhaps the most significant of all his reversals of opinion, for in it he seemed to reject almost entirely the value of material progress: "The crying evil, as it appears to us, of the present system of unrestricted competition is not so much the distress of the workmen as the extreme slovenliness and badness of their work."[72] In 1846 he had written that he "rated very low the intelligence of any man" who was not aware that "physical well-being . . . must be the basis of national morality."[73] In writing that, he had put himself squarely among the Liberals, whom Newman later attacked and defined, in part, by their adherence to this belief.[74] Now, however, he had abandoned this basic tenet and seemed to embrace almost the opposite point of view. In a sense, his idealism inevitably led in this direction. Not only manufactures, the poet held, but also art, and even morality and religion, had been "infected" by the "miserable truckling to the bad taste of the multitude." The "quiet undoubting confidence" in a material progress embodied in rising literacy rates and new ease in transportation he rejected in the "Review of a Book on Progress."[75] Similarly, writing on Norton's work he insisted that "the object of human society is not . . . one of securing equal apportionments of meat and drink to all its members. Men combine for some higher object; and to that higher object it is, in their social capacity, the *privilege* and real happiness of individuals to sacrifice themselves. The highest political watchword is not Liberty, Equality, Fraternity, nor yet Solidarity, but *Service*."[76] "Unto this," he had written Tom Arnold in 1849, as he watched the erstwhile French revolutionaries pour into the dying Roman republic they had successfully besieged, "has come our grand Lib, Eq and Frat revolution."[77] Yet if Clough could not have one kind of goal for his moral devotion, he would find another. No sense of cynicism or world-weariness could detain him long. "Service" might be hard, unattractive, and charmless, like the man who wished to know of the universe "*if* things are bad, that they are so,"[78] but this ideal was the essence of those "actualities of life" into which man must plunge if he hoped to become religious.[79]

When Clough was sailing towards America in 1852 he considered the meaning of his progress on this quest. "How disagreeable," he wrote, "to go somewhere else and have [to] pass through all this process over again; be unborn, and have to make oneself . . . a new body all over again."[80] The unmaking and remaking of that new body was precisely what Clough achieved on that journey, and no student of Clough's prose writings from the period immediately preceding that trip can be sorry he took it. It is only natural, too, in view of the stimulation he found in this country, to regret that he did not stay. But such a wish would perhaps be a trifle presumptuous. Clough was not alone in finding life in the United States limited, as the great stream of expatriate American intellectuals and others attested. Clough stayed in England not only for domestic and financial reasons. He stayed because, as he said, he found there "in the very atmosphere . . . some precious intellectual aliment." His intellect informs every line of his poetry, and we should not, I think, cavil that he knew what sort of sustenance he must have.

CHAPTER VI

The Battle by Night

Shortly after *The Bothie* was published in 1848, Matthew Arnold, himself about to publish his first volume of poems, wrote to Clough:

I have been at Oxford the last two days, and hearing Sellar and the rest of that clique who know neither life nor themselves rave about your poem gave me a strong, almost bitter feeling with respect to them, the age, the poem, even you. Yes, I said, to myself, something tells me I can, if need be, at last dispense with them all, even with him: better that, than be sucked for an hour even into the Time Stream in which they and he plunge and bellow. I became calm in spirit, but uncompromising, almost stern. More English than European, I said finally, more American than English: and took up Obermann, and refuged myself with him in his forest against your Zeit Geist.[1]

This is a puzzling, even tantalizing statement. What in *The Bothie* was so provoking to Arnold? Why does he lump together "the age, the poem," the time spirit, America, "even" Clough himself into a complex of forces he must resist? Why does he oppose Obermann to them, and see his own necessary posture as one of flight to and seclusion in nature? Different hypotheses have been advanced. One scholar thinks Arnold was repelled by Philip's youthful fickleness and found the story too frivolous, too distant from "the grand style."[2] Another, approaching the question more broadly but relying too exclusively on Arnold's own writings, concludes that the *zeitgeist* the poet resisted meant "the current fashionable opinion, especially as opposed to ascertainable critical absolutes."[3] Neither interpretation is fully satisfactory, however, for Arnold was not given to breaking butterflies on the wheel, or to reacting violently to mere jeux d'esprit, if that were all *The Bothie* meant to him, or to using a word like zeitgeist merely as a careless synonym for "fashionable thought." It was not merely a "fashionable" critical opinion that Arnold derided—more, felt threatened by—so violently when he picturesquely portrayed Clough and his "set" as plunging and bellowing in the Time Stream, nor is the urgency of Arnold's response to be explained by the sense of rivalry which existed between the two friends, although no doubt this exacerbated the situation.[4] What Arnold objected to was something deeper. He disliked in *The Bothie* what he must have perceived as a central self-delusion about the world and the possibilities for effective rebellion in it. For fundamental to the poem is the faith that a gesture of rebellion against, and alienation from, society and a high culture can if sincere be successful in a basic sense. When Philip leaves England literally for the other side of the world with a peasant bride, an iron bedstead, and a box of tools, Clough is asserting not merely the material but the moral possibilities of the nonconformist who seeks in a "world elsewhere" if not a new Eden at least a new dispensation for life. The hope that Clough had long felt for what was "being carried on by [his] generation," and the certainty that "the basis of national morality" was in significant measure dependent on the "physical well being" of its citizens—that the spiritual is not wholly separable from the material life, and not separable at all if the material world is one of misery—are both implicit here.[5] This was an essential element of the zeitgeist shared by those of whom Ward says that they were "all convinced that there was virtue in the times."[6] Their sense of social hopefulness, their belief that social reforms, if judiciously and thoughtfully undertaken, could be meaningful and shape lives spiritually as well as formally for the better; their conviction that this was the area to work at first, the proper field of battle: it was from all these assumptions that Arnold recoiled. *The Bothie* was "more American than English" because America was further gone in such misguided thought than England. To Arnold, nothing serious could be accomplished by putting faith in anything so temporal and pragmatic as physical labor and a new environment: so to teach was crude and dangerous doctrine. He refuged himself with Obermann in his forest because like Sénancour—and indeed, like

Clough—he was profoundly dissatisfied with modern society, but he preferred Sénancour to Clough because Sénancour "felt to the uttermost the bare and bleak spiritual atmosphere into which he was born" and did not attempt to conceal its hollowness.[7] "Bleak frankness" such as the Romantic's, Arnold felt, in telling "naked truths" was better than envisaging the reform of the primary, spiritual ills of society by secondary, pragmatic methods.[8] Van Wyck Brooks regards Arnold's reverence for *Obermann* as reflecting the "limitation of [his] very great personal nobility of mind [by] his distrust of human nature" and his stress on "the order of the mind rather than of the heart."[9] Trilling, in almost opposite terms, sees Arnold's interest in *Obermann* and rejection of *The Bothie* as his reaction against modern man's schizophrenia, against the modern preference for world betterment and system-making over true poetry.[10] Arnold himself saw as requisite for the artist the attainment of a superior, Goethean vision of human life and human nature, a vision which Clough's dangerously naive involvement with pragmatic social issues prevented him from achieving.[11] Yet Arnold knew that he had not achieved that breadth of vision and unity of spirit. "The true reason," he admitted in a well-known letter to his sister Kay, that his poems did not "square in all their parts is that my poems are fragments—i.e., that I am fragments . . . the whole effect of my poems is quite vague and indeterminate."[12] His search for wholeness in the authority of tradition and the heritage of the past was not entirely satisfactory, but as Trilling himself has pointed out, Arnold rejected the attempt of poets to deal with the nineteenth century out of his fear of being "split into segments" by the "critical intellect" and of losing his own poetic powers. "What Arnold feared in all his friends, and especially in Clough as the most intimate, was a thing that he feared in himself . . . the driving restless movement of the critical intellect trying to solve the problems of the nineteenth century." The age was "deeply unpoetical" and it was better for poets to look elsewhere.[13]

In E. D. H. Johnson's view, most Victorian poets suffered from a sense of alienation from their culture not unlike Arnold's. Alienated from their age—and therefore, inevitably, from themselves as well—they impoverished themselves, Johnson points out, through their hostility to "the progress of industrial culture." Keeping aloof from that new society, they ceased to be able to speak naturally to it. Arnold's protagonists "suffer in all innocence for their superiority to the Time Spirit," while Tennyson's are haunted on the unconscious level by "dreams, madness, and visionary incitements to unearthly quests." A "unified, imaginative vision," in Johnson's words, was beyond their powers—for they were "fragments."[14]

No such description could with justice be made of Clough. His vision was not alien to his age: his diction is a product of it: his life was a testament to his involvement with it. Unconsciously, Arnold had identified not Clough's weakness but his strength in describing him plunging and bellowing in the time stream. Clough neither sought his audience nor wrote down to it: the uncompromisingly difficult and un-English titles of his major poems perhaps epitomize the demands he made both upon his audience and upon himself. Arnold complained that Clough's work showed a deficiency in a sense of the beautiful; but it was not beauty which Clough took as his subject or by which he wished to define his style, but life.[15]

We can accept, therefore, Arnold's description of Clough's plunging in the time stream, recognizing further, however, that in so doing Clough was open to vital experience as well as buffeting. One result of this study is that we are enabled to see better into the age and understand better the frighteningly powerful sanctions the Established Church could still exercise. Economic alternatives for the man without capital were few. In a world without an open civil service, large corporations, non-sectarian education, modern sophisticated communications media, or almost any of the other economic apparatus by which our own largely unreligious intelligentsia now supports itself, a man with Clough's record was nearly unemployable. Society was closed and immobile, and the sanctions it enforced against those who threatened its order were harsh. Businesses were closely held family affairs, for the most part, and men were trained into them from childhood. Almost no one could support himself and a family on literary work: a "literary man" was almost inevitably one with a private income or rich wife. A man who left his profession to make a career of literary hack work might find himself barely able to survive even as a scribe, like David Masson's acquaintance, John Christie.[16] Yet "literary work" is what unknowing commentators have suggested that Clough might have turned to had he "really" wanted to "do" something. Unconsciously, we have been filling in the blank spaces on the Victorian social and economic map with our own experience. To do so, however, is not only to be inaccurate in our judgments but unfair. In that static and rigid society, religion and the social order were still closely intertwined: the apostate who threatened religion by rebellion might threaten all order, and this surely was part of Provost Hawkins's rationale in refusing Clough his testimonial.

Facing the end not merely of a promising career in the Establishment at Oxford, but of hopes for any career at all, Clough went through a period of disillusion. He is commonly said to have been impelled to this reaction by the disappointment of his revolutionary hopes. No doubt this disappointment was a contributing factor. But it was not the major factor, although the notion that it was is the sort of misconception that has made Clough appear a weak or unconsequential man. It was not a general sense of pathos and *weltschmerz* about things in Italy and France that made Clough go "cracked at times" in his worst year, but rather the belated realization by this intensely proud man—the more proud because he kept his pride inward—that he had himself ruined his career, that his mistaken hopes had reflected some serious lack of insight in his makeup, that he wanted to but could not get back into the highway again with his fellows, that he had been a fool not to foresee the present results.[17] Gestures of commitment would not reform hypocrisy or earn him a living, he had learned; and he was not more clever than his friends for having thought so, but only more naive.

The "transcendentally cynical" attitude he said he once adopted was not, however, dyed very dark.[18] The position he ultimately came to politically was that of a rigidly impartial liberalism. Progress, undoubtedly, he urged, but not progress that condoned individual vice, violence, or murder, or national schemes of oppression and aggression which justified the means by the ends.[19] Clough does often, as Timko has suggested, display a quality—"positive naturalism" as he calls it—"which enabled him to accept man and his actions for what they are rather than what . . . they ought to be," but the tone is not a constant, and such acceptance may be tinged with tragic knowledge.[20] Earlier than almost any other English poet, in *Dipsychus* he sees that the machine was a symbol of man's dehumanization and alienation in the modern world. He does not ask man to throw his body upon it; seeing deeper, he points out that the danger was that man might now *want* to throw his body upon it, that for the man whose only job was "fiddling with a piston or a valve" it might become impossible to answer "which is worst, / To be the curser, or the curst, / The victim, or the murderer?" Although he had been himself the "committed man" Emerson had described, who "cumbers himself never about consequences" but acts with "*éclat* . . . watched by the sympathy or the hatred of hundreds," he resisted the idea of moral solipsism or anarchy.[21] He had learned much and in some ways profited greatly from his experiences: out of that crisis, indeed, came almost all his important poetry. But he saw eventually where he had misjudged; only a very idealistic and very naive man would have done as he had: he was "wiser" now.[22] Words such as these with their tone of recognition and acceptance are significant as closing notes in the drama of Clough's career. The attitude of more than one of the contributors to the "Memoir" seems, like Mrs. Clough's, to apologize for that career's lack of success. But success meant something different for Clough, and perhaps we should rather measure his achievement by the goals he strove for and the standard of personal growth he adopted than by other, secondary ones. Ultimately that measurement must rest heavily on our understanding of his poetic achievement, and some of the answer will certainly lie in the relationship between Clough's poetry and the ideas and the prose studied here. To enter on that subject fully would be a lengthy task. The scope of this study has been limited to establishing what in fact Clough's major ideas were, and what it meant that he should have held them. But it may be useful to suggest, very briefly, some of the ways in which these researches may illuminate the study of Clough's poetry.

The very violence with which Clough's later memorialist, John Shairp, had to reject *Amours de Voyage,* crying "No I would cast it behind me, and the spirit from which it emanates and to higher, more healthful, hopeful things purely aspire," is emblematic of the malaise of the era, a malaise of spirit widely recognized and not requiring recapitulation here. In a succeeding period Yeats wrote, "Things fall apart, the centre cannot hold." One might sum up some of the differences between the Victorian and the modern periods by saying that although Yeats's words applied to that age also, it would not have understood them: most of the best minds were bending every effort to *make* the center hold. The poet's vatic role was conceived by most as affirmative, for, seeing that danger more deeply, theirs was the responsibility for suppressing what more than one may have felt as their fragmentation.

Clough did not accept this role, perhaps for personal, perhaps for intellectual reasons. He had had to learn very early to accept unhappy facts and make something of his life in spite of them. Clough's particular experiences made him almost a prototype of the deracinated man, for he suffered from the experience of being uprooted many times, intellectually, emotionally, socially, and religiously. Cut off from his family, his family's love, and from his country (however alien he had been in America it was all he knew) at the age of ten, from faith at twenty, from effective power in politics by circumstances and history, from ancestral ties and from the upper and business classes alike by training and education, and finally by his own acts from the present—Oxford—and the future—his career—he serves as a kind of paradigm of the man who has experienced alienation. It is the triumph of his best poetry that it speaks of that condition, rather than hides from it. In making it his subject, Clough made himself its master.

That Clough did not use the term "alienation" is of course irrelevant: what matters is that the posture of his heroes is fully and consciously a cry against that "huge machine" in which "No individual soul has loftier leave / Than fiddling with a piston or a valve," in which morality has departed, "Terror bring[s a] secret bliss," the victim welcomes his murderer, and the death of God, not publicly proclaimed, one thought, till Nietzsche, is celebrated with the absurdity of "Dong / Dong, there is no God; Dong."[23]

His three major works treat the topic in varying ways. In *The Bothie,* the earliest of the three, the alienation is least complex and is primarily experienced externally: Philip Hewson, the Radical, having withdrawn to the only half-civilized world of the Highland

173

glens, thrice steps out of even that society and ultimately steps off the visible world altogether into the Antipodes. The reasons behind Philip's alienation are clearly definable in external, logical causes which are primarily social and political. He is uncomfortable in his society on principle, because it denies equality and subjugates man to man and woman to man. He is uncomfortable also because it is impossible, or nearly impossible, to live up to its sexual standards, and the sacrifice it demands is too high to be borne for long.[24]

Amours de Voyage is about a different kind of alienation, alienation from the self. Written in 1849–1850, the period when Clough said he "could have gone cracked at times," the title of this poem is ironic, for love is something—like all feelings—that the hero cannot experience. The poem may well be Clough's masterpiece on account of the perfect harmony that subsists between what might be called the objective correlative—the complicated civil and foreign war being waged in the streets of Rome, and the war, equally futile, doomed, and piecemeal—like the man whom Clough saw incongruously carrying a cannon ball through placid streets—going on inside Claude. The hero, like Rome, is waiting, latent, hoping to erupt into decisive feeling but unable and unwilling to do so at the right time. Clough, who refused, as he told Shairp, to go "awhoring" after scenery, used the Italian revolution not for its political or touristic implications but for its essence; far more than in *The Bothie,* place and politics are not his subject but analogues of it.[25]

"Politics, Art and Love," Clough said in a rejected line of *Amours de Voyage,* are what matter in life.[26] In *Dipsychus,* written a year or two later, none of the three has any direct significance at all. Here the hero is more isolated than ever. Those external forces which were rejected in *The Bothie* as the corruption of society, and in *Amours de Voyage* rejected—though ambiguously, for Clough's tone is frequently critical of Claude—for being bourgeois are here scarcely even considered. Philip, that is, had been successful in resisting the lures of sex and high society. His alienation was deliberate, and justified morally and intellectually. (It is significant that he received the blessing of Adam—tutor and father-figure—on leaving the Old World.) Claude's alienation from society, on the other hand, had been rewarded not by love but only by a frustrating fiasco and loneliness. His deracination was both internal and external: he was as isolated from the war—about which he could not even speak to his acquaintances:

> Passing away from the place with Murray under my arm, and
> Stooping, I saw through the legs of the people the legs of a body.
> You are the first, do you know, to whom I have mentioned the matter.
> Whom should I tell it to, else?—these girls?—the Heavens forbid it!—
> Quidnuncs at Monaldini's?—idlers upon the Pincian?[27]

as he was from his feelings for Mary Trevellyn.

In *Dipsychus*, the relationships of *The Bothie* have drastically altered. In the latter all the threats were external to the hero: in *Dipsychus* the source of evil is not exterior at all; it may be internal, a sort of perverted, devilish Inner Voice. It may even, in fact, not be evil at all but only the way of the world, or common sense, or the universal libido—aggressive, grasping, selfish, sexual, sensible—which Clough had belatedly discovered in himself and the world at large. As Clough was careful to point out in the Epilogue, "the beauty of the poem" is that "perhaps he wasn't a devil after all—nobody can say."[28] Yet what the Spirit has advocated is directly contrary to most professed morality; and what we see in this dramatic poem is Clough's perception that the nature of morality itself is changing.

In a passage that prefigures Nietzsche, Clough wrote:

> I am rebuked by a sense of the incomplete,
> Of a completion over-soon assumed,
> Of adding up too soon. What we call sin,
> I could believe a painful opening out
> Of paths for ampler virtue.[29]

Did sin exist? Had morality any basis—either in theory or in fact? In *Dipsychus* the hero, in a dream shot through by the mockery of bells, asks these questions in a sort of ectasy of despair:

> Ring, ting; to bow before the strong,
> There is a rapture too in this;
> Speak, outraged maiden, in thy wrong
> Did terror bring no secret bliss?
> Were boys' shy lips worth half a song
> Compared to the hot soldier's kiss?

175

> Work for thy master, work, thou slave
> He is not merciful, but brave.
> Be't joy to serve, who free and proud
> Scorns thee and all the ignoble crowd;
> Take that, 'tis all thou art allowed,
> Except the snaky hope that they
> May some time serve, who rule to-day,
> When, by hell-demons, shan't they pay?
> O wickedness, O shame and grief,
> And heavy load, and no relief!
> O God, O God! and which is worst,
> To be the curser or the curst,
> The victim or the murderer? Dong
> Dong, there is no God; dong![30]

Today, few serious artists approach morality as a settled question. Sartre and Gênet, Pinter, Robbe-Grillet, Kurosawa, and Antonioni all recognize and deal with the question Clough put—"And which is worst, / To be the curser or the curst, / The victim or the murderer?" In the premises of that question Christian morality and its doctrine of self-abnegation stand rejected. The escape from this dilemma into sensuality, which also forms so great a theme of our art today, is adumbrated in the same song of Clough:

> O Rosalie, my lovely maid,
> I think thou thinkest love is true;
> And on thy faithful bosom laid
> I almost could believe it too.
> The villainies, the wrongs, the alarms
> Forget we in each other's arms.
> No justice here, no God above;
> But where we are, is there not love?
> What? what? thou also go'st? For how
> Should dead truth live in lover's vow?
> What, thou? Thou also lost? Dong
> Dong, there is no God; dong![31]

In all three poems, the settings are analogues of the poet's state of mind, and not merely scenery. Just as Rome was an analogue of Claude's strife-torn but curiously unresponsive spirit, so Venice in *Dipsychus* functions symbolically to represent corruption, ease, and luxury. The seductively pleasant motion of the gondola by which the hero is enthralled is an image of the sensuality to which he ultimately also succumbs. Comparing this to the earliest of his three long poems, one might say that *The Bothie* is about the soul in the shelter of the wilderness, while *Dipsychus,* for all its Venetian setting, describes the discovery of the wilderness in the soul.[32] Clough wrote *Dipsychus* under the impulse of the shocks his intellect and emotions had been receiving, and in this poem there is nothing to fight for except perhaps the very self. The poet himself cannot interpret last year's cry of agony: "Interpret it I cannot: I but wrote it."[33] The horizons of life have shrunk: the question that agitates life is basically sensual. The body has become more important, for everything else has lost significance. Alienation it would seem cannot go much further.

Yet Clough's treatment of alienation in this poem is complex and subtle, for the hero really is wrong from the beginning, and the Spirit is very largely right. He is more evil in the beginning than at the end of the poem; when he is pleading with Dipsychus to act, he is almost entirely sympathetic. Dipsychus is not really pure, as he comes to realize, and his downfall—or regeneration, as you choose to regard it—is the result of his realization that his flashes of insight and honesty do not constitute living, and that to accede to the world's ways in some things is not necessarily to damage himself forever. The Spirit asserts towards the end of the poem and Clough's tone indicates his approval, that he has his own sort of morality, although one he does not speak of.

Throughout *Dipsychus,* indeed, ordinary morality itself is called into question. What we see the hero learn is that morality, in the conventional sense, scarcely exists: sex is not a moral issue in the poem, although the protagonist thinks it is, and neither is pleasure or self-satisfaction. The protagonist does sin, and profoundly, but he is not led to it by the Spirit. The true moral issue and the cause of his death is his guilt at having denied not money to the woman he took up, but *himself.*[34] Sin exists, and the protagonist has committed it, *Dipsychus Continued* makes clear, but it has less to do with carnal pleasure or expedient, worldly compromise than with his alienation from, his lack of commitment to, another human being. Those who see in *Dipsychus* only another *Faust* have not looked deep enough. Indeed, the implicit criticism here of Faust's willingness to learn at the expense of another human spirit is both clear and profoundly important.

Clough plunged, as Arnold said, into the time spirit, but he emerged from it "wiser" and still a whole man. The disappointment of his political hopes and his moral idealism was a waste of spirit only on the practical level. He gave up his hope for immediate political reform, but instead of turning his back on former ideas, of casting it all behind him, like Shairp, and "to higher, more healthful, hopeful things" purely aspiring, he examined the essence of his experiences and made of that confrontation the subject of his poetry.

I say the "essence of his experiences" because Clough clearly also used the surface of his life for his three great verse stories, or poetic dramas. In one sense, to be sure, he appears to offer "poetry of information" to use Kenneth Burke's pejorative term: poetry that tells how things are, that reports but does not presume to judge, that keeps a distance between itself and the event described, and which, to Burke's mind, lacks eloquence, tenderness and tragedy.[35] This may be true, but there is little of that in any poetry, as Burke acknowledges, from this period onward. Clough instead gave us honesty: honesty, if need be, about dishonesty, sordidness, and the very fact that eloquence, tenderness, and tragedy have vanished from our lives. Long before Eliot's Prufrock acknowledged, "No I am not Prince Hamlet, nor was meant to be," and before his lovelorn lady had put another record on the gramophone, solacing herself in a mutual relationship with a machine, Clough's Dipsychus had cried,

> Ah, if I had a course like a full stream,
> If life were as the field of chase! No, No;
> The age of instinct has, it seems, gone by,
> And will not be forced back. And to live now
> I must sluice out myself into canals,
> And lose all force in ducts. The modern Hotspur
> Shrills not his trumpet of "To Horse, To Horse!"
> But consults columns in a railway guide;
> A demigod of figures; an Achilles
> Of computation.[36]

Clough's "modernity" has often been remarked on by contemporary critics. But his language sounds new not because he possessed magical foresight into twentieth-century problems, but because he was able to look directly at the problems which already then existed and to respond by creating the new diction and syntax and tone his subject demanded.

One could expand this argument and multiply examples, but perhaps it is sufficient here to have raised the possibility of this interpretation. Certainly, at the least, one may see that these three great poems were written out of Clough's experiences and commitments to political and religious action. Clearly, too, they trace the curve of his ever-deepening understanding of man's relationship to society and, ultimately, to himself and the universe. After beginning, like Clough himself, with a pure gesture of rebellion and commitment to a "higher" morality, Clough's protagonists lose their moral self-assurance and self-righteousness. Ultimately, the moral vision deepens. Conformity is not the greatest crime: industrialism and technology and "the duty of order" are not the greatest villains. Man, *Dipsychus* says, cannot *be* alienated: but he can alienate himself. "Enter the arena of your brethren," Clough wrote around the time when he was composing *Dipsychus*.[37] Between the thought of that poem and *The Bothie* lie all the years of learning and experience it has been our task here to trace.

Clough did not, however, write merely political or religious poetry, any more than he wrote "poetry of doubt." Beside his enormous subject, considered indeed with unendingly patient subtlety and complexity, particular topical issues shrink to irrelevance. Clough wrote poetry which, for want of a better word, we call philosophical. He explored the most profound questions of human morality, and one may without presumption compare his seriousness and steadiness to that of the greatest poets of this mode of discourse. He put his characters into social and moral dilemmas that tested their capacity to act justly and humanely—to be whole men, truly engaged in their actions—in a system which either opposed justice and humanity or, as in *Dipsychus*, did not fully understand what they were. And he saw a world few of his contemporaries could bear to look at steadily or consciously. The hero of *The Bothie* speaks directly of looking for guidance and finding none:

> Where does Circumstance end, and Providence where begins it?
> What are we to resist, and what are we to be friends with?
> If there is battle, 'tis battle by night: I stand in the darkness,
> Here in the mêlée of men, Ionian and Dorian on both sides,

Signal and password known; which is friend and which is foeman?
Is it a friend? I doubt, though he speak with the voice of a brother.
Still you are right, I suppose; you always are and will be;
Though I mistrust the Field-Marshal, I bow to the duty of order.
Yet is my feeling rather to ask, where *is* the battle?
Yet, I could find in my heart to cry, notwithstanding my Elspie,
O that the armies indeed were arrayed! O joy of the onset!
Sound, thou Trumpet of God, come forth, Great Cause, to array us,
King and leader appear, thy soldiers sorrowing seek thee.
Would that the armies indeed were arrayed, O where is the battle!
Neither battle I see, nor arraying, nor King in Israel,
Only infinite jumble and mess and dislocation,
Backed by a solemn appeal, "For God's sake do not stir, there!"[38]

Only Clough among the Victorians could have written these words, and only he could have said in *Dipsychus*:

I am rebuked by a sense of the incomplete,
Of a completion over-soon assumed,
Of adding up too soon. What we call sin,
I could believe a painful opening out
Of paths for ampler virtue.[39]

"A painful opening out": those words might stand as an epigram for much of the art of the last hundred years. It was possible at once to see what the age—"the vast machine"—was about, and to speak of it and to it. In spite of the Field-Marshal, he stirred.

"A compliment," Clough once wrote, "is the next thing to an impertinence."[40] Emerson had said that the greatest compliment one man may offer another is that of sincerity. The compliment of sincerity was perhaps the only one Clough offered other men, but he made it consistently, and not to his friends only, but to the world at large. Behind sincerity lies respect, and the poet showed it not by catering to his audience or ignoring its faults, but by speaking to and of it directly, by communicating his ideas, his hopes, his fears, and all the threads of thought that made up the fabric of his moral vision. He suffered for his beliefs, for his world was not yet ready to face the truths he put before it, but that respect for his audience, which rested on his respect for himself, is at last being reciprocated, for our own age is realizing that Clough was among the first to see and follow those ampler paths that we—painfully, as he predicted—have been treading after him.

180

Appendices

Bibliography

Notes

Index

APPENDIX A

Clough's Undergraduate English Essays

The following table assigns a number in column one and a date in column two to each essay. Column three gives the titles of the essays and a translation of the Latin or Greek epigrams as well as a reference to their sources. Column four shows the initials or name that appear in a hand not Clough's at the end of the essays. Column five contains Dr. Jenkyns's comments on the essays. He wrote these at the end of each term in the "Balliol College Examination Register" (B.C.E.R.), under the column headed "Exercises."

The unbracketed dates are Clough's. The dates in square brackets are conjectural. They were arrived at by extrapolation from two sources of information:

a. Essays which were dated by Clough. These dates show that the exercises were generally written once a fortnight and were usually presented on a Friday or Saturday.

b. Information in the *Oxford University Calendar* showing when term was kept and when the essays could have been presented.

The essays are contained in three notebooks in the Bodleian Library, MSS. Eng. Misc. d.513–515. The initial work of identifying and translating the epigrams was done by Mr. John Williams, but with his work I have conflated the contributions of Professor Edward Spofford and the previous work of Professor Walter E. Houghton.

183

Appendix A
Clough's Undergraduate Essays

(Bodl. MS Eng. Misc. d. 513) Essay No.	Date	Title	Tutor	Jenkyns's Comments in Balliol College Examination Register (B.C.E.R.)
1	[Oct. 1837]	"On the Effect of Dramatic Representations on the Taste and Morals of a People."	R. J.	
2	[Nov. 1837]	"On Some of the Principal Effects on Literature Resulting from the Invention of Printing."		
3	[Dec. 1837]	"Venice."	R. J.	
4	[Jan. 1838]	"Law of Nations."	R. J.	"Good—but deficient in elegance and neatness of style"
5	[Feb. 1838]	"*Usque adeo magni refert studium . . .*" Lucretius [*De Rerum Natura*, IV, 984–986: "It is always of great importance to consider devotion and pleasure and consider what activities they are associated with; this is important not only when studying men, but for all living creatures"].	R. J.	"Good"
6	May 5 [1838, Sat.]	"*Ego autem satis mirari non queo . . .*" Cicero, *De Finibus*, I, iii [10: "But for my part, I can never cease wondering what	J. Carr	

		can be the origin of that exaggerated contempt for home products that is now fashionable," trans. Loeb Classical Library].		
7	[May 1838]	"Examine the truth of 'νέων δὲ πάντες οἱ μεγάλοι καὶ οἱ πολλοι πόνοι.'" [Plato, *Republic*, VII, 536d: "All the numerous important tasks fall to the young."]	R. J.	
8	[June 1838]	"On the Advantages and Disadvantages of Contemporary History."	J. Carr	"Good—deficient in polish and elegance"
9	[Oct. 1838]	"*Etenim nescio quo pacto magis in studio . . .*" Pliny [the Younger, *Epistolas*]: "And yet I feel that it is somehow more fitting for men to be reticent in their scholarship than to be self-confident."	R. J.	
10	Nov. 8 [1838, Thurs.]	"———' Ευ γαρ καὶ ὁ πλάτων ἤπόρει τοῦτο καὶ ἐζήτει. πότερον ἀπὸ τῶν ἀπχῶν ἡ ἐπὶ τὰς ἀρχάς ἐστιν ἡ ὁδὸς." Aristotle, *Nichomachean Ethics* [I.iv.5; 1095a, 32: "Plato was rightly worried about this and inquired whether the path of philosophy should be away from first principles or toward them."]		[Essay not written]
11	Nov. 23 [1838, Fri.]	"The Influence of the Progress of Luxury and Refinement on Literature."	A. C. T.	
12	[Dec. 7, 1838, Fri.]	"The History and Influence of the Stoical Philosophy."	R. J.	"Improved in style"

(Bodl. MS Eng. Misc. d. 513) Essay No.	Date	Title	Tutor	Jenkyns's Comments in Balliol College Examination Register (B.C.E.R.)
13	[Jan. 18–25, 1839, Fri.]	"The Philosophy of History."	R. J.	
14	Feb. 8 [1839, Fri.]	"The Prevalence Under Different Circumstances of Different Systems of Philosophy Considered as an Index of the Character of Any Age or Nation."	A. C. T.	
15	[Feb. 22–Mar. 22, 1839]	"Examine How Far Aristotle's View of the Virtues in his 4th Book of Ethics is Deficient."	R. J.	"Latin Good"
(MS d.514)				
16	Apr. 19, 1839 [Fri.]	"The Poetical Character of Sophocles."	R. J.	
17	[May 3, 1839, Fri.]	"The Social Condition of the Greeks and the State of Moral Feeling Prevalent Among Them Illustrated by the Events of the Peloponnesian War."	R. J.	
18	[May 17, 1839, Fri.]	"περὶ δὲ τῆς πρὸς τὴν θάλατταν κοινωνίας πότερον ὠφέλιμος ταῖς εὐνομουμέναις πόλεσιν ἢ βλαβερά, πολλὰ τυγχάνουσιν ἀμφισβητοῦντες." [Aristotle, Politics, VII.v.3: "Whether a communication with the sea is beneficial to a well-ordered people or not is a	A. C. T.	

19	[May 31, 1839, Fri.]	question which has often been asked." trans. Jowett.]	R. J.	"Good—full of thought but sometimes obscure and un-polished in style"
		"᾽τέχνη, τύχην ἐστερξε καὶ τύχη τέχνην.᾽" Aristotle [*Nichomachean Ethics*, VI.iv.4, 1140a,20: 'Art loves chance, and chance loves art']. "The Influence on the Progress of Civilization Exerted by Causes Beyond Human Control."		
20	Oct. 18, 1839 [Sat.]	"On the Differences of the Religious Systems of Greece and Rome."	P. S. H. P.	
21	Nov. 1 [1839, Fri.]	"The Protection Afforded to the Person and Property of a Roman Citizen by the Judicial Tribunals of the Republic."	P. S. H. P.	
22	[Nov.–Dec. 1839]	"The Moral Effect of Works of Satire."	R. J.	
23	[Dec. 1839–Jan. 1840]	"From an Examination of the First Book of Aristotle's Politics Point out the Imperfect View of Society Taken by the Wisest of the Greeks."	R. J.	"Improved and very good"
24	Feb. 1, 1840 [Sat.]	"τῷ δὲ ὑπερβάλλοντι αὐτῶν φθονοῦντες ἤδη καὶ ἀπιστοῦσιν." [Thucydides, *History*, II.35.2:" 'What is beyond their own capacity men at once envy and disbe-lieve.'"]	R. J.	
25	[Feb. 15, Sat.]	"Ὁ δὲ μὴ δυνάμενος κοινωνεῖν ἢ μηθὲν δεόμενος δι᾽ αὐτάρκειαν οὐθὲν μέρος πόλεως, ὥστε ἢ θηρίον ἢ θεός."	P. S. H. P.	

(Bodl. MS Eng. Misc. d. 514) Essay No.	Date	Title	Tutor	Jenkyns's Comments in Balliol College Examination Register (B.C.E.R.)
26	Feb. 29 [1840, Sat.]	Aristotle, *Politics*, I [i.12: "A person who cannot cooperate with others or is so self-sufficient that he feels no need of the community must be either an animal or a god."] "On the System of Education Pursued at Athens under Pericles."	R. J.	
27	Mar. 27 [1840, Fri.]	"A Comparison of the Effects of Conquest and of Commerce on Civilization."	R. J.	"Good"
28	May 15 [1840, Fri.]	"*Capesentibus rempublicam . . .*" Cicero, *De Officiis*, I.xxi.72: "It is as important for men who enter public life as it is for philosophers to cultivate a greatness of soul and a contempt for worldly matters."	R. J.	
(MS d.515)				
29	May 29 [1840, Fri.]	"ἀνδρῶν γὰρ ἐπιφανῶν πᾶσα γῆ τάφος." [Pericles in Thucydides, *History*, II.43.3: "The whole earth is the memorial of famous men."]	R. J.	"Good"

30	[Oct.–Nov., 1840]	"The Advantages which History Receives from Biography."		
31	Nov. 20, 1840 [Fri.]	"*Vox Populi, Vox Dei.*"	R. J.	
32	Dec. 4 [1840, Fri.]	"Rhetoric Has a Just Claim to the Dignity of a Science."	E. C. W.	"Good—in matter"
33	Jan. 30, 1841 [Sat.]	"A Comparison of the French with the Athenian Character."	R. J.	
34	Feb. 13 [1841, Sat.]	"The Effects of the Use of Slave Labor at Rome."	A. C. T.	
35	Feb. 26 [1841, Fri.]	"On the Causes which Contributed to Render the Romans a Great Conquering People."	R. J.	"Good"

APPENDIX B

New Poetry and Prose

This Appendix includes a selection of uncollected poems by Clough found during the course of my researches. Two of them, "Salsette and Elephanta," and "The Judgement of Brutus," have been published in recent journals, but the rest are new to print and none appears in any of the editions of Clough's poems.

The shorter poems selected for publication here are representative of Clough in varying moods. The poet they reveal is a less stiff, more varied and charming figure than the persona generally found in the *Ambarvalia* or the "Shorter Poems" section of the 1951 edition. This Clough can dash off a deliciously and solemnly parodic epithalamium on the marriage of a pompous acquaintance, the astronomer Donkin, comment on a topical issue like Chartism, or in other moods make an incantation of the fairy-tale rhythms of "Four Black Steamers" and conjure up, from his exile in America, the image of his sweetheart in "When at the Glass You Tie Your Hair."

Why these pieces have not previously been published can only be answered by conjecture. Clough himself did not live to see through the press any collection of his poems after the 1850 reissue of *Ambarvalia*, first published in 1849, and several of the pieces here printed were written after that date. As all are short and would not have been especially suitable for individual publication in contemporary journals, the most natural place of publication would have been the posthumous editions of Clough's works brought out by his widow. She evidently did not see fit to include them, perhaps regarding them as trivial, *infra dig*, or too personal. The poet himself may have felt the same way. Clough with his tie loosened, however, is a very appealing figure.

In addition to the poetry, the full text of "Conversations of the Earth with the Universe" is printed here for the first time. Comment on it can be found in Chapter IV. To the two Newdigate poems I have given full discussion elsewhere, and readers are referred to the original articles in which they appeared for commentary upon them (see Bibliography). The spelling and punctuation of these pieces and of the six short poems also appearing here are as Clough left them, even when incorrect, for I wished to provide for future editors of Clough's work a text they could rely on as a full and accurate transcription. I have, however, supplied conjectural dates, given textual variants, and made brief comments where it seemed appropriate.

I could not hope, in the short space of an appendix, to do justice to all Clough's uncollected works or supply the lack of a complete critical edition. I chose those pieces which most interested me and in which Clough's different voices are most clearly heard.

Conversations of the Earth with the Universe

A

How stupid of you, said the Moon one bright morning to the Earth, to look so dull in the daytime & never to brighten up but in the dark. Sometimes I don't so much as see you at all, & can hardly believe you are near me, or even exist. The Earth was a little vexed, but did not find any answer. Only at last when the Moon went on to say, But why don't you look as [fol. 98] bright as the Sun there, he replied a little hotly,[a] My Dear friend,[b] you don't understand the thing.

After a long silence & much consideration the Earth resumed & said, Dear Companion about what you were saying just now—May it not be that when you are dark, I am light & vice versa, I dark when you light. Really, said the Moon, who had rather begun[c] to think about something else, that does not seem at all reasonable. Or rather continued the Earth can you be sure that Either of us is ever altogether dark to the other

. . .

[fol. 99]   B

. . .

[a] angrily   [c] ceased
[b] companion

191

Well, said the Moon, it may be so, though I don't think it can be, but in any case it seems very perverse.

————

When Magellan in his ship had got very nearly round the globe, a sudden qualm came over[d] the Earth, & it said to itself, Really, what if I am a round ball, I don't want everybody to go & talk about it—it is no great concern of theirs after all, & I detest of all things to have gossip[e] going on. So the Savages in the [   ][f] killed Magellan. [fol. 100] But the ship and the other sailors went round: so that[g] it did not make any great difference in the end.

————

"Nay talk & talk & talk," said the Earth about three hundred years after; they will believe before long that they have found out all about me. But if ever they get near to that, I shall *change*."
This however seems hardly probable.

————

Nevertheless the Earth went on to say, very extravagantly as it seems, In fact whenever I do fancy anything about myself, it always appears that from that moment what I think true[h] ceases to be true any longer whatever it might have been before.

————

[fol. 101] Who was it set me going, Said the Earth one day half aloud to itself; & looked up to the Sun—it did not care that the Moon should hear—& beyond the Sun looked away among the Stars. No answer seemed to[i] come. The Moon will be hearing me & that I do not want her to thought[j] the Earth to itself; the Moon & I can talk together well enough; but at that great distance It is very uncertain whether even if I spoke my loudest [fol. 102] & listened my hardest I could be heard; or could hear in return[k]; the Stars & I can only see each other I suppose & that, at such a distance, is strange enough if one thinks about it.

————

So the Earth gave up—asking alike[l] & listening; but after a while, as it was revolving on its way Something quite close to it said—some-

[d] upon
[e] gossip [*Sic*]
[f] Clough's lacuna
[g] after
[h] it
[i] come in
[j] said
[k] so for a

thing; but the only part which the Earth could repeat afterwards was "After all, that is hardly the question."

[fol. 103] I wonder said the Earth to itself very quietly one day, whether my sweet[m] companion here, the Moon, has all these thoughts & considerings & calculatings & conjecturings that I have. She looks at times very blank, I think, & unintelligent. However, very likely, she is none the worse if she hasn't.

I don't understand about Apihelion[n] & Peligee[o], & all that, meantime was the Moon saying; & to look at the [fol. 104] surface of me I am afraid there seems to be mighty little stirring[p]. However I get on somehow; & look bright, they say—& see something of the rest of the world. That must do, I suppose.

[fol. 105] After all if I do move round the Sun, said the Earth, I don't see that that proves the Sun to be better than I. I dare say he hasn't half the thoughts that I have. To have things go round one is no such great matter.

Some little time after the Earth used the opposite argument in a little dispute with the Moon. It never occurred to him at the moment[q], but his conscience was a little rubbed, & a considerable while[r] after he found out why. So he at once begged the Moon's pardon, tho' they had made friends again long before, & humbled himself in his own eyes in respect of the Sun.

Some days later[s] while he was going on his way, he heard a sound of words in his ear [fol. 106] to something of the following effect. What we are[t] or where in the Scale of being we know not; of this however [we] may be assured. That to be luminous is a wonderful thing, to radiate out of oneself light & heat not among the least of endowments. Happy are they that receive; happy also are they that give. But of whom Virtue passes, "is he without Virtue in himself . . . Yet what we are[u] or where in the scale of being we know not.

[fol. 107] Why do you always turn around yourself, said the Moon one day to the Earth; I turn around you, & you only around yourself.

[l] ; but	[q] time
[m] dear	[r] time
[n] Perhelion	[s] after
[o] Apogee	[t] I am
[p] going on here.	[u] I am

Sweet companion, replied the Earth, I never thought of that. But after a while towards nightfall The Earth spoke again & said, Sweet Companion, do not you also do the same? It is that, that makes you so beautiful.

[fol. 108] The Earth has had a great many fancies about itself. For a long time it believed that[v] as the circle was the most perfect of figures, it, of necessity, must move in "Circle." It is only quite late that it has found out which way it does actually move, & even now it is hardly quite satisfied[w] that it ought to move as it does. Sometimes it comes into its head to argue, that going round & round is useless & must surely therefore be wrong: the true duty is to advance[x] on in a straight line. Certainly to be at one[y] & the same time both centripetal & centrifugal is on the face of it[z] a fools inconsistency.

[fol. 109] The Moon was once angry with the Earth because the Earth did not move around it, as I, said It revolve around you. And the Earth tried & thought to do it—but willed to do it in vain, for the[aa] Law, which[bb] was[cc] the inner as it were[dd] Will bore away both the Earth & the Moon revolving around the Earth in a larger more complete[ee] orbit around not each other but the Sun—

[fol. 110] What in the world can Saturn's ring be I wonder, said the Earth and the Moon in their talk to each other one fine Night. Why are Venus & Mercury, away near the Sun there solitary unmated orbs.[ff] Why has Mars again beyond me no satellite, & Jupiter & the rest of them so many. In what odd sort of terms do those other[gg] strange celestials keep together, Juno, Ceres, Pallas & Vesta as they call them. But[hh] what in name of all wonder can[ii] Saturn's ring be for?

[fol. 111] The Earth once said to itself, How good & attentive to me the Sun is, to go round me every day & light me up here and lull me to sleep there, & warm me & when I am tired, let me cool again—in

[v] At one time it came into its head that it might
[w] sure
[x] go
[y] the
[z] appears
[aa] the [sic]

[bb] that
[cc] is
[dd] and truer
[ee] perfect
[ff] planets
[gg] [possible reading, "four"—Ed.]

short wait upon my fancies like the best of servants, round & round me every day without stopping—And the Sun all the while was never [fol. 112] moving at all, or if moving at all moving around some far away Central Orb of which the Earth had never so much as imagined[jj] could exist.

[fol. 113]   *X*

I revolve in my orbit, my ellipse, my unvarying determined track around my Sun, said the Earth. (For the Earth after many mistakes had at last made out to its satisfaction that the Sun did not as it had supposed, go around it, but it around the Sun.) I, said the Earth, upon my course & ye, other planets, upon yours, alone, irrespective [fol. 114] independent of each other, each around the Centre for itself.[kk] So the Earth thought it did so, & intended to be doing so, but the law which is its Will did not suffer it, & at last the Earth found it was not doing so & made a motion as it were to correct itself & was surprised & disappointed to learn[ll] that though it would yet it could not.

Then[mm] at last an articulate word or was it echo of a word began to speak within it, which said, Not around

[fol. 115]   *Y*

the Sun only, o Earth, nor by the rule of his attraction only; around him, but in thy course around him affected, influenced, perturbed by every petty, every remote brother planet, & satellite of planet: which thou seest & which thou seest not in the whole of this (at any rate) that[nn] thou callest thy Solar System.

[fol. 116] Dull work, your ellipses, said the Comet streaming by to the Planet, Go this way, replied the other, thou performest me thyself.

Does it Matter that the Earth has just found me out, said that which men call Neptune. I existed all the Same before.

[fol. 117] To worship is not permitted: it is more than I dare do to conceive of you seriously as more than what I see you.

[hh] And
[ii] is in
[jj] fancied
[kk] him

[ll] discover
[mm] But
[nn] which

195

[fol. 117ᵛ]   Z

O Supreme Existences said the Earth one day after a deal of fanciful
conjecturing. Be it forgiven me, be it no sin in your eyes, if in the
half–playful effort to realize you, I have spoken of you as with levity.

Bodleian MS. Eng. Misc. d. 512, fols. 96–118.

I Wed Not Save the Muse Urania

"I wed not save the muse Urania"
With smile, that, pensive—half alabaster[a] wrought
Around his lips & for a moment caught[b]
His eye, so spake he in a younger day.
This bridal morn, o Lady, shall we say
Urania, here before us, into heaven
One hand uplifting, one to him has given
Supporter on his human heavenly way?
Urania art though, Lady? Or a Muse
Whom sage astronomer may fitly choose,
Astrœa? redux! She on Earth again,
* Her stern majestic look unbends, lays by
Her sword unwifely & unwomanly,
Her scales alone, domestic, will retain

Bodleian MS. Eng. Lett. d. 175. June 26 [1844].

"I have got another sonnet to send you written this day on
the marriage . . . of Donkin the Professor of Astronomy—the statement of the first four lines is literally fact." (Clough's introductory
statement to this poem.) William Fishburn Donkin (1814–1869) was
a contemporary of Clough at Oxford although not, clearly, a friend.
Donkin was regarded by W. G. Ward, Clough's tutor, as being " 'next
to the *great man* [Newman] . . . the most distinguished man in Oxford.' " He was already a well known astronomer by 1844 when he

---

* "She is represented, as a Virgin of a stern majestic countenance, holding a
pair of scales in one hand & a sword in the other." Lempriere. [Clough's note]
[a] [reading uncertain; possibly "in banter"—Ed.]
[b] His lips and with illumination caught

196

married the daughter of a clergyman named John Hawtrey. Whether the couple appeared as ungenial as the nicely ponderous turns of this sonnet suggest can only be conjectured, but the maturity of the comedy is new for Clough's poetry—as is the satire on an object of Ward's respect. (See Wilfrid Ward, p. 432.)

Four Black Steamers

Four black steamers plying on the Thames
These are their names
Printed on the paddleboxes anyone may know
Painted up in white
Morning & evening & Noonday & Night
Crowded with people all[a] the decks about
Putting out & taking in & off again they go
This side, that side, up tide, down tide
These are their names
That are printed up in white
Morning, Evening, Noonday & Night
Four black steamers plying in the Thames

Bodleian MS. Eng. Poet. d. 129, fol. 8

Lie Here My Darling

Lie here my darling; on my breast,
I see you so & love you best
Look at me with your glances mild
And play about me as a child[a]

So say I when each morning's light
Awakes me to my [own] delight
And while the slumbers [fade] away
Could think my love beside me lay.[a]

[a] over
[a]Lie here, my darling, on my breast. [This fifth line, a refrain, was later rejected by Clough—Ed.]
[a] Lie here etc.

197

The empty air I kiss in vain,
Yet kiss the empty air again,
And lift my hand, as were she there
To smooth[b] the parting of her hair.[a]

Some happy morning still to be
Indeed we trust the sight shall see [fol. 2[v]]
And I, while on my breast she lies
Look really in my darling's eyes.[a]

Oh happy Morning far away
Beyond the months of slow delay
Come sure, if slow, to make me blest
And bring my darling to my breast.[c]

Bodleian MS Eng. Poet. d. 141, fol. 2[r-v]

This little poem, one of a series Clough wrote to Blanche during his stay in America, dates from the same period as the other "Songs in Absence" from the notebook inscribed "Tibi"—"to you" (No. 13, 1852-3 B Notebook, *Poems* p. 475).

When at the Glass You Tie Your Hair

When at[a] the glass you tie [yr] hair
Look out my darling I am[b] there
Standing beneath the big oak tree
The morning finger-tips I see.

And when at breakfast next you meet
And by the urn you take your seat
Another holds my wonted chair
And yet, my love, I'm with you there.

All day where'er you[c] move about
Upstairs or down, indoors or out
My steps your motions still attend
Above you at your book I bend. [fol. 9[v]]

[b] touch
[c] Lie here, my darling, on my heart
For so methinks I see thee best
Lie, here my darling on my breast

[a] [two words written over—Ed.]
[b] My child I am not far from
[c] Where'er your feet may

Beside your walk amongst y[r] flowers
And in the quiet evening hours
Can sit & hear each word you say
And look & listen while you play.

And when at last the hour for bed
Upon its pillow lays your head
Swift as a bird that seeks its nest
My spirit comes with you to rest

Sits down its happy watch[d] to keep
And[e] as you lie & sink to sleep
To [   ][f] your dreams to bliss
Prints haply on your cheek a kiss

All thru' the nights it sits[g] & sips
The healthy fancies of your lips
In sleep its [   ][h] you sometimes hear
Or half awaking feel it near.

And when the morning's glances mild
Look in & rouse[i] my slumbring child
My darling—in the higher air
Look up, I've come to meet you there.

Bodleian MS. Eng. Poet. d. 141, fol. 9[r-v]. Dated "Jan. 25" [1853]
by Clough.

Thou Bidd'st Me Mark

Thou bidd'st me mark how swells with rage
The childish cheek, the childish limb,
How strongly lust & passion wage
Their strife in every petty whim;

[d] Its happy watches true
[e] Here
[f] send [An illegible word has been written over "send"]
[g] stays [?]
[h] [the lacuna is Clough's: "breath" or "heart" might be acceptable emendations.]
[i] call

199

Primeval stains from earliest age,
 Thou sayest, our glorious souls bedim;
Yet not though true, thy Wisdom says
Will I love less the childish days.

Thou askest, ask it as thou wilt,
 How thus I dare to praise the State
Of Adam's child, an heir of guilt,
 And sin original, innate;
And why the holy blood was spilt
 If sin at last were not so great:
'Tis true, I own; I cannot tell;
Yet still I cherish childhood well.

Perchance, though born twixt good & ill
 To join in warfare through his life,
His heart is in the garden still
 With Eden thoughts his Spirit rife,   [fol. 10]
And therefore conquering Passions fill
 His struggling heart with fiercer strife:
It may be—doubtful Wisdom says,
And lets me love the childish days.

With sin innate, that still descends
 On Adam's children one & all
Perchance innate remembrance blends
 Of Adam's joys before the Fall;
His sinful heart to us he sends
 And we with him his bliss recall.
And so, a truer Wisdom says
Go cherish still the childish days.

We go our worldly ways, & there
 Our Eden thoughts we lose them quite
Only the quiet evening air
 Or dewy morn, or stormy night
Remind us of the Vision fair
 Or bring it back in living might,
And offer to our tearful gaze
The Paradise of childish days.

Such be the Cause, or be it not,
 Believe, & let the Causes go;
New love may every day be got
 So long as here we dwell below;

Of[a] more the heart is ware, I wot,
Than philosophic systems know;
So heed not what thy Wisdom says
But cherish thou[b] the childish days.

May 1839
Bodleian MS. Eng. Poet. d. 126, fols. 9–10

This very early poem should be read in conjunction with the essays of 1839 and "Salsette & Elephanta." It shows the same optimism as these, the still unshaken orthodoxy, and, despite the competence of its neo-classic form, Clough's essentially Romantic attitudes. We see this especially in his faith in the child and in Nature, which influences the child through a highly Wordsworthian "dual ministry of love and fear," acting through "dewy morn and stormy night." In form it is almost identical with the contemporary "Come back again my olden heart" (*Poems,* p. 9) but this is less a *cri de coeur.*

O'Brien Most Disconsolate of Men

O'Brien, most disconsolate of Men,
Whether thy brave delusions lap thee yet
Or the cold victor's scornful epithet
From thy blank soul come echoed to thee again,
Ah be contented! knowing no loftier rule
Stands in the books of chivalry's high laws
Than this which bids one in the least good cause
Risk being thought or even being a fool.
In a great labyrinth it were not nought
Though but to show that one way error lies;
It should be plainer to thy country's view
Henceforward what she can & cannot do;
Ireland by thy misjudging may be taught
And by thy misadventures become wise.

Yale MS.

Bronterre [James] O'Brien (1805–1864) was "intellectually the ablest of all the Chartist leaders" and a warm and brilliant orator, but throughout most of the 'forties he played a losing role of opposition to the

[a] And   [b] still

"Physical Force" Chartists, led by Feargus O'Connor, who gained control of the party. Elected as a delegate to the convention which planned the 1848 demonstration, O'Brien resigned the night before the "Fiasco of Kennington Common" as part of his repudiation of violence: against the advice of friends, he tried to explain his reasons, but the meeting "howled down" the conciliatory speech he tried to give. The movement, however, broke up following the repression its attitude provoked. The "most disconsolate" of the first line may refer to O'Brien's appearance: he was said to become " 'unprepossessing' " when " 'unpleasant thoughts were agitating his mind.' " (G. D. H. Cole, *Chartist Portraits*, pp. 239–267.) O'Brien's later life was full of other, although less public disappointments, and a date of 1848 for this sonnet would be reasonable but conjectual. The MS is a holograph fair copy on a single sheet in Yale's Beinecke Library, on the verso of which appears a fair copy of "Say Not the Struggle . . ." As the latter dates from 1849, Clough if he wrote "O'Brien . . ." in 1848, must have thought enough of it to preserve it and copy it later with another poem occasioned by a battle of political principle, the Italian Revolution.

Salsette and Elephanta are two islands off the west coast of Bombay, famous for their temple caves. Clough supposes Salsette to have been exclusively Buddhist and identifies Elephanta with Hinduism.

The MS of Clough's first attempt at the Newdigate prize, "Salsette & Elephanta," shows slight tears on folios one and two, and I have suggested the obvious emendations inside square brackets. Otherwise, I have transcribed the text as it appears in both Newdigate poems, keeping Clough's punctuation, capitalization, and spelling, but silently changing his seeming hyphens to the dashes he intended, removing the commas with which he frequently preceded these, and adding apostrophes where necessary. Rejected variants and Clough's notes appear along with the text with alphabetical referents. My own notes are given numerically, and may be found with the other footnotes. Clough's line numbering, which appears in the left margin, presents an interesting inaccuracy for which I have conjectured an explanation.[1] I have given the correct numbering in square brackets in the right margin. The poem was first printed in an article by myself titled " 'Salsette & Elephanta': An Unpublished Poem by Clough," *Review of English Studies*, n.s. XX (Aug. 1969), 284–305.

[fol. 1ʳ]   Salsette & Elephanta

Quis Deus incertum est—habitat Deus[2]

[fol. 1ᵛ]

Ideas suggested by the situation of the Temple Caves of Elephanta
& Salsette & speculations on their possible origin (1 to 71). The local
Nature of the Caves and first of Elephanta, as a Temple of the God
Seeva; secondly of those of Kenneri or Canaria in Salsette, dedicated
to Buddha, & his religion (72 to 130). The wretched Nature of both
Views—possible existence of an original Knowledge of Truth of which
they are subsequent corruptions. Probable progress of such Corruption.
(131 to 210) Final Prevalence of the Worship of Seeva in India:
its tendency to encourage Weakness: a remedy for this discoverable
in England & the character, belonging to its scenery & associations
even in Autumn. (210 to [blank]

[fol. 2ʳ]   *Note*

The facts for this Poem have been chiefly derived from Heeren's
Asiatic Nations Vol. 3:[3] the view of the different Varieties of Indian
Religion from F. Schlegel on the Language & Wisdom of India, his
French translator Mazure,[4] & Douglas on Errors in Religion.[5]

The principal Monuments of Indian Antiquity are in the Poem
supposed to be arranged according to the following order taken from
the above authorities.

I   The Vedas or Indian Scriptures; & perhaps the Laws of Menu.
II   The Temples of Salsette & Elephanta.
III   The Epic Poems—the Ramayana & Mahabharata.
IV   The Temples of Ellora, & Mahavipurana.

The Vedas contain a religion free from all the common Indian Idol-
atries. They speak of one God, of whom the Heavenly Bodies, eg.
are Emanations. Schlegel [regards] it as the earliest deflection from
Original [one or two words torn: Truth or Revelation].

[The Tem]ple at Elephanta is dedicated to Seeva. [Wors]hip
of this God is by Schlegel regarded as [a corrup]tion introduced by
extending the doctrine of [fol. 2ᵛ] emanations to all existing things
united with a disbelief in the impossibility of a return. Seeva is the
power of External Nature.

The Temple of Salsette is dedicated to Buddha, whose doctrines are purely Pantheistic; supposed to have been another corruption from the doctrine of Emanations in the Vedas.

Buddhism & the Worship of Seeva at the time of the erection of these Monuments are supposed to have existed side by side. The former was in some unknown convulsion expelled from India, but it prevails to this day in Thibet, China, Siam & almost every other part of South Eastern Asia.[6]

[fol. 3ʳ]   Mid these vain scenes of toil & ceaseless strife
The lust of Enterprize, the pride of life,
Where the mind heeds not, though the eye behold,
What means this relic from the times of old:
Full in the midst of traffic's eager game
Among the changed & changing still the same?

    Lo, in thy shade the labouring boatmen fly,
The busy trader speeds unconscious by,
These seaward breezes to thy portal bear,
Unwelcome freight, the scent of greedy care,   [10]
And the sharp tones of commerce from the pier
Incessant beat & echo in thine ear.

    By the sea sands, beneath the flowery field,
Like some great Truth, so plain yet so concealed,
What dost thou here? the palm leaf oer thee plays,
The wild birds scream, the forest-creatures graze,
[fol. 4ʳ] Above, the common Earth, the vulgar ground
And the tame Ocean's keel-worn level round.

    Thou too, strange Hill,* within whose secret womb,
A City lies, a city and a tomb,   [20]
Where among scented woods & rocky holds
Lake after Lake the winding Strait unfolds—
Is thy sole task at shadowy hour of Eve
The sinking orb's swift Chariot to receive?
25   And then when Mortal Shows with darkness blend
And the high hills to holier height ascend,
To mingle with the Mountain's brother-band
That North & East in solemn silence stand,
Gigantic Quire, around the puny Mart
And whisper Childhood's wisdom to the heart?   [30]

* Such is the description given of the Temple of Kenneri or Canaria in Salsette: and of the Channel which separates that island from the mainland. British India. Edin. Cab. Lib.—Hall's Fragments—Buckingham.[7]

Say, were ye raised in some far distant age,
The pensive fancy of a royal Sage?
Who felt, though Fortune smiled, & Joy caressed,
Strange hungry cravings haunt his vacant breast,
And rapt in vision of the insatiate grave,
Unto the rocks his Wealth, his labour gave.
So should the workings of a human mind
Be with the Earth's unchanging forms combined;
While days and years of mortal reckoning sped
And race on race was mingled with the dead,   [40]
[fol. 5ʳ] This, as the current foamed & fretted past,
With the great Sun, the Stars, the Sea should last.

Is this the secret of the low-browed door,
The vacant vistas of the rocky floor?
Symbol of idle hopes, exhausted powers,
Vain search for truth, and study's useless hours?
Or mausoleum of departed joys,
Where Manhood's aims are laid with Childhood's toys?
And the sole lesson, that the curious eye
50   Can gather hence that all is Vanity?   [50]

Or shall we deem that 'neath Canaria's shade
His chariot wheel the youthful Bacchus stayed?
What time with all his merry rout around,
Piping & dancing through the Eastern ground,
In pomp & festal mimicry of War
The blooming God came travelling forth afar.
They, round, the Pæan sang, the thyrsus threw,
Him in the midst his smooth-paced tigers drew.
For these waste hills, these solitary vales,
These steamy fens where sickness taints the gales,   [60]
These woods, the serpent's couch, the tiger's lair,
This desert land in all its wildness fair,
Of old, 'tis said, with human life oerflowed,
A people's home, a Deity's abode.

[fol. 6ʳ]   Or was it where the islet as in sleep
Floats on its image in the waveless deep,
In memory of his Cyclad home the God,
With human joy,ᵃ perchance, the terrace trod;
Here ceased his travel—hence with wistful eyes
Watched where the waters blend with Westernᵇ skies   [70]
Here bade the rock's memorial temple rise.

ᵃ P d upo it   ᵇ mingled

Nay, graver thoughts to these dim caves belong
Than dreams of Bacchus & the Bacchad[s] throng,
Here as we pace through Elephanta's hall,
And gaze in wonder on the gazing wall,
75 Where the thick Columns close us in, and day
In few uncertain glimpses finds its way,
Far other Senses through the Members thrill
Work on the mind, and chain the Unconscious Will,
Far other thoughts! for lo, around they stand, [80]
They look, they speak, they threaten, they command,
Almost we sink, we bow the suppliant knee,
With heathen prayers to heathen idols flee.[c]

Then whence mid stillness deep as of the grave
This solemn Utterance from a voiceless Cave?
Whose awful presence in the rock abides
The heavy Air, the thick imprisoning sides?
[fol. 7[r]] Who art thou, Tenant of the Temple-tomb,
Voice of mute thunder from the holy gloom?

Tempest and Flood, and Pestilence & Dearth, [90]
And all the changes of the potent Earth,
Are his—his Word the times & tides obey,
And pain & slaughter rage beneath his sway,
That fatal Power, in whose dread Arms we lie,
Made at his Will, and at his Will to die.

Such Seeva's fane. Far other voices roam
The aisles, the Chamber, and the Vaulted dome,
Where Buddha stretched on massy couch at Ease,
* Lifts the curled head, and folds the giant knees.
100 How peaceful here remote from toil & strife [100]
Flowed the smooth current of the priestly life.
For all was bliss & freedom. Sin & shame,
So feared elsewhere were here an empty Name,
And Duty sometime held of heavenly birth
A Phantom banished from the Wiser Earth.

[c] The following skeletal variant appears on a loose scrap of paper inserted in the
MS.:
Oer a rough hill-side- -
- - - - - oerwilered unda
         undefiled
White poplar uprose [?] oer crowning
* These are the distinguishing marks of his statues.[9]

'Away, with all thy visionary train,
'Fond Folly, fly, nor curse the Earth again.
'Take hence thy slaves, these paralysing fears,
'These fluttering hopes, these penitential tears,
[fol. 8ʳ] 'Vain dreams of Law, & Conscience, empty Voice,   [110]
'That bids us suffer, when we should rejoice,
'Cares for the future, Grief's dark shadows cast,
'From the thick clouds that throng the wasted past.
'Those whispered Words of days when Sin was not,
'Of Pain & toil & death, the sinner's lot.
'Of man's once high Estate, his deeper fall,
'And God, a maker & a judge of all.
'Fond fancies, fly, we know you false as fair,
'Babblers of hope, & ushers to despair!
'Who told these secret Truths, & where is He   [120]
'Of whom they speak, the Lord whose slaves we be?
'Come on green Earth—among the rocks & trees— ⎫
'Neath the blue sky—come dwell we here at Ease, ⎬
'For these are God, and we are God with these!' ⎭

125   Who speaks of rest—and Peace where Peace is none?
Who dreams of heaven on this bad Earth begun?
Shall sinful Man to sinful Man restore
The blissful feelings that were his of yore,
The trust of love, the bosom's fearless sense,
And all 'the princely heart of innocence'?[10]   [130]

Is this then all? is such the symboled truth?
And these your lessons from[11] the Nations' Youth?
[fol. 9ʳ] Was it for this the Graver lent his hand,
And Labour wrought, Imagination planned?
For love like this the Earth, a willing slave,
Her Wealth, Her Wisdom, & her Children gave?

Methought beneath these storied roofs there lay
Dim recollections of a holier day,
Memorials apt to wake repentant tears
Like toys that tell us of our childish Years,   [140]
And strong that genial spirit to impart
The tender Conscience, & the loving heart.
But all is dark: through all the Echoing Caves
'Tis Sloth beguiles, or Superstition raves:
With various feeling, various fashion built,
Yet peers in folly, and alike in guilt,

Ye tell of sins forgotten, unforgiven,
And devious Wanderings, further still from heaven.

And yet, as wilful Children, when they roam,
Turn oft their hesitating glances home,   [150]
As troubled Spirits rove at close of day
150 Round the loved precincts where they dare not stay,
So come with all thine idol-forms combined
Strange conscious hauntings of a purer Mind:
And from afar some rays of glory shine,
And faintly gleams primeval Truth divine.

[fol. 10ʳ]   In the far East it shone, where Gunga pours
His holy Stream betwixt his forest-shores;
There dwelt, perchance, a race to whom was given
Wisdom from high & communings with Heaven,   [160]
Mid evil tongues & days with Error rife,
The Saintly Peace of Patriarchal life.

Full soon, alas! that holier frame decayed,
And the voice ceased whose bidding none obeyed,
Foremost did Sloth enact her double part,
Her half endeavours of a guileful heart,
175 Her slavish toil that works & calls for rest,
That gives, but not the utmost & the best.
With her, her Sister Vice—the curious Eye,
That stops to gaze & seek the reason why,   [170]
The questioning Mind that plies her waxen wings
Full oer the deep abyss, the Mystery of things.

She told of Fate, whose fierce relentless force
Still hurries all on Evil's downward course,
She told of Life, a burden & a curse
Good that was gone, & bad that gendered worse.
Heaven, said her tale, is like the Mountains high
Whose pure white Summits mingle with the Sky;
Through Fate's dread Channel from the Eternal Snows
The Changing Stream of Earthly being flows: [180]

[fol. 11ᵛ]   Bright inᵈ their Spring the infant Waters play,
And leap unconscious on the destined way,
The destined bounds their duty soon begin,
And close the deepening, darkening river in.
Through varied scenes his heedless path he takes
Bursts in the cataracts, lingers in the lakes;

ᵈ at

208

The plantain, fairest of the forest's daughters,
Here coyly bends above his glassing waters,
Here on the ripples of the broad expanse,
The sunny beams in starry chorus dance: [190]
Yet every rock & lake & pictured wood
200 Speaks of a distance widening still from good
And each bright ripple tells the current's force
That bears the waters from their heavenly source.

So spake the Sage: and Sloth enchanted heard,
And timid Weakness blest the balmy Word:
Thence to these caves neath Seeva's dreaded Name
Fate, lord of Earth, thy fearful Worship came,
Till man cast down the God that Man had made
And Buddha taught, and half the East obeyed.   [200]
To Thibet's hills & China's towns it came,
And Tartar tribes caught up the passing flame.
But India forth the Atheist doctrine flung,
And firm in weakness round her Idol clung.

[fol. 12ʳ] We too may feel her sense the Spirit seize,
Feel the pale cheek, the faint & faltering knees,
The coward heart which all it dreads fulfils
The awe that palsies, and 'the fear that kills'.¹²
Now as we pace along the terraced hill
Where Night's still breeze arises damp & chill,   [210]
Hear, from below the billows of the deep,
Stern Sentinels, around, their watches keep,
See, the white Moon across the glimmering plain
Peer like a gazing ghost above the main.

Then let us leave this demon-haunted ground
And turn where Hope & cheering Strength abound.
225 Hail, villaged England, Still where'er we be
The heart's fixed eye rests motionless on thee,
Where active hand & open Conscience blend,
And manly vigour seeks its lawful end: [220]
Hail hopeful Thoughts of home—the busy scene,
The Church, the Hall, the Cottage, & the Green.

Come when the Winter Wind is keen & high
Or Spring comes blooming from the sunny sky,
In Summer's pomp, or even when leaves are sere,
And sad decay completes the changeful year.
[fol. 13ʳ] Come to our glades—the lofty Elm enshrouds
His trunk & naked boughs with golden clouds,

Veiled now by mist, now clad in light appear
The dappled oxen or the fairy deer,   [230]
And brighter on the shaded ground are seen,
Long sunny tracts & lines of glistening green.
Come to our Woods—the Birch^e her season knows
And a red glory on the Chestnut glows,
Through changing beech leaves on the long arcade
Descends a tempered light, a golden shade.
Come to our Rivers—Ash & Aspen there
Hang lightly oer them in the still soft air.
And lo, a stiller air, a softer sheen
Gives back beneath the whole inverted scene.   [240]
Lost no bright leaf above that June could show
250   Nor one unmirrored in the world below.

Though, like the caves, the glade & wood & stream
Say, Man is aye unstable as a dream,
Conscious of good, yet ever prone to ill,
Of judgment feeble, impotent of will;
Yet mist & shade & line of glistening green
Speak happier tidings from a world unseen.
The viewless air around us & above
Brings visitations from a guardian love,   [250]
[fol. 14]   And the still prospect whispers words from heaven
Of loftier strength to human frailty given
Strength that our sorest Stumbles shall repair
And lead us faltering up the heavenly Stair.

Come, Faith & 'Self Devotion, high & pure'[13]
In grief triumphant, & in joy secure
The trusting heart, the Strong Elastic Will,
That bounds & presses onward, onward still
Tho' dark the Path & doubtful—though alone
Must each one strive unknowing & unknown   [260]
Yet shall we see as on the way we go,
Some first faint streaks of dawning's distant glow—
Till Earthly Night far spent already end
And the full orb in cloudless light ascend.

Duff MS.   March–April 1839

————————

In brief, the story in Livy from which this poem derives tells of
Lucius Junius Brutus, who aroused the Roman populace to successful

^e Oak and Asp

revolt against the Tarquins after the rape of Lucretia by Sextus Tarquinius. Later, when Brutus was ruling Rome as joint consul with Collatinus, widower of Lucretia, the slave Vindicius accused Brutus's two sons, Titus and Tiberius, of conspiring to return the exiled Tarquins to power. The accusation being proved true, Brutus pronounced the judgment of death against his children.

Clough's poem, like "Salsette & Elephanta" the previous year, was an unsuccessful entry in the Newdigate competition. For a full critical discussion, see Evelyn Barish Greenberger, "Clough's 'The Judgement of Brutus': A Newly Found Poem," *Victorian Poetry,* VIII (Summer 1970).

The Judgement of Brutus

τέτλαθι δή, κραδίη—[1]

Thou to whose gaze the night is clear as day,
And earthly veils in light dissolve away,
Whose piercing glance the folding clouds can part,
That close in darkness round the human heart,
Come, heavenly Muse:—& let the tale be told
Of Sterness, faith, & fortitude of old
How to slight hope, at Duty's doubtful call
The Roman Father gave his best, his all.

Come—but not thou whose fleeting changeful smile
Doth the light heart with fancy fond beguile: [10]
Nor thou, more holy, who as day departs,
In low sweet tones holdst communing with high hearts,
Who in the depth of some untrodden dell
Sittest & singst where infant waters well
And from the soundings of the far heard rills ⎫
The heavy woods, the glow all heaven that fills ⎬
The broad still lake the mighty moveless hills ⎭
(As in some gush, thy heart could not restrain,
Of tender love) dost oft & oft again
[fol. 2] As from a harp with viewless finger draw   [20]
Strange Music strong to melt to startle & to awe.

With thee in converse to forget the strife,
The fearings, hopings, plans & plots of life,
Care's restless hum in thy sweet strain to lose,
With thee to wander & with thee to muse,
How blest! in thee the beating thoughts to still

And with thy boon the emptied heart refill.
Yet come, O, rather thou, that on the swell
Of the rough World from old hast loved to dwell,
And lettest the changeful Stormy Winds of Time   [30]
Tune on thy chords their Melodies sublime;
Thou, whose strong Voice through Earth in all her
                                  bounds
A low deep call sounds ever & resounds;
Thou to whose blast, when thou thy trump dost take,
Such thousand echoes through the heart awake,
That Will, long-dead, doth hear the peal above
Deep in his tomb, & in his cerements move.
Thou sawst the first & thou the final scene,
Thou[a] through those long & dreamlike hours between,
And when Bereavement took the place of Strife,   [40]
In that half-death, that tranced unearthly life—
While men, most curious, still could nought espy
Save the smooth brow, the fixed unshrinking eye,
And he with thoughts unsignified, unknown
Walked in his grief mid wondering crowds alone—
[fol. 3] Thou in his World with him went there apart,
And knewst each movement of the mighty heart,
The sudden wrench, when all without was rest—
Shudder & start convulsively suppress'd,
50   Anger & love, and every varying mood   [50]
To inexpressive calmness all subdued.

    The tale was told; the Consul's ear had heard,
The father's heart in all its depth was stirred,
"From the vile figment of a lying slave[2]
"His word," he said, "his children well might save,
"If needs he would for freedom, favour, gold,
"Have at full price his precious story sold,
"Go, let him tell it where it best were told;
"Go, let him say—'Ye banished lords of Rome[3]
"The Sons of Brutus bid ye hither home'   [60]
"Go, let him say 'What Marcus wronged ye then,
"Titus, Tiberius will repair again
"The father did, the Children shall undo,
"As he to Freedom faithful, they to you;—
"If they so judged, judge all that this might be
"If Tarquin listened, listen too would he"
[fol. 4] "No, no, so born, so bred, so named as they,

[a] And thou

212

*   "In such a year as this to fall away,
           "So strangely, wildly, recklessly to err,
           "So young, so fair, so noble as they were,   [70]
           "It was not, could not be:—on each young head
           "This hand that oft in blessing had been laid,
           "Was it not this, the dripping blade that bore
           "When "the four Men"[4] their righteous purpose
                                        swore?
           "The tongue whose tone their infant ear had caught,
           "Whose lessons oft their riper youth had taught
           "Was it not this, that one time spoke aloud
           "Lucretia's story to the gathering crowd?
           "From whose uncompromising speech the word
           "Of Freedom first in Roman ears was heard   [80]
           "He who to these had given their life, their name,
           "Was he some other then, and not the same?
           "Some other Brutus, not the tyrant's foe,
           "Fit father for the slavish & the low?—
           "No, it was not—how[b] could it be?" Alas!
           "How could it be?"—and yet, behold, it was!—

           Twas known—twas bandied on the Vulgar tongue,
           The Vulgar Ear upon the tale had hung,
[fol. 5]   And Custom now, that paused a moment then;
           Was all but flowing on its course again: [90]
           His love—his trust;—that first had found relief.
           In angry words of scornful unbelief,
           Like morning's shower at sunny noon forgot,
           Like morning clouds—had been & now were not.
           He once assured, as though to know were all
           And the dread sentence passed without recall
           Went forth unwavering on his usual way,
           Amid the crowd, before the tell tale day.

           O Heart[c] prepared & Strong! as on thee burst
  100   The sudden, clear conviction of the worst,   [100]
           Without one change, one strain of self controul
           Thy purpose on thee came[d] & filled thy[e] soul:
           As who on some broad hill's extended wild
           With turfy heights successive still beguiled,

* Eo potissimum anno etc. Livy [on fol. 3ᵛ opposite asterisk]
[b] it
[c] c t Soul
[d] That only purpose [e] constant

At some swift turn, at once, at last descries
The bold bare Peak—the crowning rocks arise
Thence[f] doth afar a cloudy chart unrolled
Of Steeps on Steeps, and Vale on Vale behold,
And seems no more those meaner tops to know
Now stretched, a tost & tumbling sea, below;—   [110]
[fol. 6] So thou thenceforth mid visions of thine own
Dwellst oer the rest exalted & alone.

    So passed the Eve—and Night & silent Sleep
On the seven hills descended dark & deep:
He too, whose heart had borne that birth today,
Stretched on his Couch in wonted slumber lay.
Call it not sleep—the Eye is closed, 'tis true
But the large tear has forced his passage through
And the closed hand, the arm upraised & bare
The inward workings of the Soul declare: [120]
Yet sleep it is—in hours of sleep alone
Could Resolution tremble on her throne;
Nor blinding love nor subtle doubt else find
One passage open to the stablished mind.
And lo! he wakes. his waking looks disclose
The secret thoughts of that unblest repose—
The wandering wondering eyes, that scarce will own
The World that is not that their dreams have known,
The arm still bent, the brow in frowning set,
As though some visioned combat lasted yet,   [130]
And left from things of immaterial kind
Echo & image hold[g] the waking mind.
[fol. 7] Strange time: the conquered troubles of the day
Have from the Memory passed in flight away,
Tis not the slave, the letters haunt his eyes,
Nor bloody axe nor visioned scourges rise;—
Yet tender feeling, quelled in daylight's hour,
In darkness vaguely claims its ancient power;
And still survives, though changed & dim-concealed
Sense of a struggle, where 'tis death to yield,   [140]
Of some strange guest that must not enter in,
Some foe with whom to parley is to sin;—
This still survives—with it surviving still
Lives the same stern Uncompromising Will,

[f] And   [g] held

Which, be it Earth whose Powers are thronging round
Or some enchanted, superhuman ground,
Still must, as anchored barks the billows ride,
Amid the flux of circumstance abide.

Steadfast to Heaven his eyes the Consul raised,
150   And Heaven's wide doors were opened as he gazed: [150]
As on parched Earth, crisp leaf, & drooping flower
In Summer falls the small & silent shower;
[fol. 8] As nightly travellers sudden oft behold
The driving clouds a starry space unfold;—
So calm descended on the dreamer's breast
And Resignation's fixed unvarying rest
So in his trance he saw a wondrous light
Of Peace, if not of Hope illume his travel's night.

Thus dawned the final Morn—the lictors wait
(Alas, sad mockery) on the Consul's state;   [160]
The fasces, (not, today, for pomp) they bear
The gleamy axe (that shall be dull) is there;
He rose, he followed—lo, in order meet
They lead him forth along the wonted street,
'Tis hidden now—lo, there it moves again,
The steady, slow, irrevocable train:
As the proud river's changeless, ceaseless force
Bears the light shallop on its downward Course,
Yea, rather, as the willing boat obeys
The Stream that bears him on his chosen ways,   [170]
And with stout oar, & rudder strong to guide
When most obeying, governs most the tide
So they and he—amid the gazing throng
Forth to the high tribunal passed along—
So they and he;—the deed is now begun
That is to be—yet is already done.
[fol. 9] They followed too—the throng—with wistful eyes
With gathering purposes & strange surmise   [180]
"How was it Sons of such a Sire sho^d stray
"Stray widely thus from Honour's open way;
"And yet that sons of such a sire should die,
"Were the crime worse, & direr danger nigh,
"Could not, should not have been.—Now all was oer
"Nor plot nor violence vexed the City more;
"Thoughtless they had been—worse—but they were
young,

215

"Be theirs the guilt from whom the error sprung;
"The father's deeds, at worse, a mantle wide,
"Might well the trespass of the Children hide.
"And if (as oh! too plainly might be seen
"In that stilled face & that deliberate mien,   [190]
"Where no half[h] thought, with still disturbing qualm,
"But the first purpose sate, severe & calm)
"If, Judge & Consul, he would not forgive
"Then let the People speak, & bid them live!
"Perish they should not, Brutus! nay twas well,
"Twas even fortunate the chance befell—
"Nay, Heaven, it might be had the occasion sent,
"Heaven in those hearts inspired the wild intent,
"That Tarquin, Latium, Italy might see
200   "The love Rome felt for him that made her free".   [200]
[fol. 10]   Thus they secure unwitting. Then began
            With steady tone the lofty hearted Man.

            "Titus, Tiberius: little needs to say
            "What deed hath here placed you, placed me today
            "This first—Search well—if thou—or thou—shalt
                                                    find
            "One further guilt yet lurking in the mind
            "If yet one particle be lingering there
            "That is—ought else but Shame, Reproach, Despair ⎱
            "Go, cast it forth—forget twas ever there   ⎰
            "Yet no—methinks—could I, could Rome forgive,   [210]
            "Ye, even ye, should, yea, would scorn to live.

            "Now, further hear—the loins from whence ye
                                                    sprung
            "Formed you at first as innocent as young,
            "I gave you honesty, I gave you fame,
            "And ye have wrought them into guilt & shame;
            "I for Rome's service bade you live & grow,
            "And ye have lived to labour for her foe;
            "Therefore the gift I gave I here reclaim,
            "And I from whom the public evil came
            "That wrong I did my country will atone   [220]
            "When first I bade you live & be mine own.
[fol. 11]   "Thou, therefore now—go, lictor, bind & slay
            "A sovereign Judge gives sentence here today,

[h] poor

216

"A Voice beyond appeal—Go bind & kill,
* "These are my Sons, & this their Father's will

   "My Countrymen, who would my sons should live!
"The gift ye should not, now ye cannot give.
"Give rather this—dare ye as I have dared
"As these are spared not, so let none be spared
"Die young & old who plotted! one & all!   [230]
"License & lust & tyranny to recall:
"So perish alway, Rome, who work thee ill
"So judge the father, die the children still!"

   O Roman Consul! well some future day
She whom thou savedst shall the debt repay
Thou amidst doubt & anguish, while the rest
Dissuade, entreat, with thine high thought possessed
Following the witness of thine own clear breast
With eye fixed firmly on thine aim sublime
Hast cast this day thine acorn into time.   [240]
[fol. 12] The shower shall fall—the Early rain & late,
The varying Seasons on its nurture wait,
The soft sun shine, the bracing tempest blow
And the young plant thou plantedst surely grow;
Yea, the trunk widen, & the boughs expand,
And the huge shadow darken all the land
O first, best, Consul! Many a toilsome year
Of trial fiery, & test severe
Thou shalt thyself in others' deeds outlive
And dead shalt life & strength to others give   [250]

   For this a new Lucretia to the knife
Of stern Virginius[6] gave her spotless life;—
For this the high-souled Decii undeterred
Spoke in mid fight the sacrificial word,

* [on fol. 10ᵛ] That Brutus condemned his Sons by the Right of a Father, from which there coᵈ be no appeal, & for the purpose of security against the pity of the Comitia to which the case might have been referred from the Consul's Judgment—& that therefore the other Conspirators were equally firmly dealt with—is the Account given by Niebuhr. It is wholly passed over in Livy: to Dionysius I have been unable to refer. (Niebuhr I. 488)
With regard to the light in which Niebuhr has placed the Story of Brutus, it has been thought most fitting to abide by the Livian representation: not however wholly to the exclusion of the character with which this Part of Roman History was invested in the Early Roman Poetry—those lays namely, alluded to below, which Niebuhr believes to have been composed in the City's 4th Century (Vol I p. 256–7) & in the Brutus, for instance, of the dramatic Poet Attius in a later period. (v. Niebuhr I 511)[5]

And died devote[7];—for this in peaceful days
Poets full heart[8] poured forth the patriot lays;—
Quirinus there[9]—and Numa just & good[10],
And righteous Servius[11] born of lowly blood,
Lucretia, Mutius—and in loftiest song—
With solemn form, amid the hero-throng,   [260]
Thou movest there, & silent speakest still
Of high endurance & energic will,
[fol. 13] Whose hand for Rome when Rome was young & new,
For Freedom, known & valued of the few,
For prospects high which scarce the boldest eye
In the dim distance faintly dared descry,
For thoughts sublime yet vague, yet unexpressed
And great hopes barely to thyself confessed,
For all then doubtful, & secured today
Dared, nobly dared thy loving Sons to slay.   [270]

    Spirit of Brutus! If in mortal guise
Thou dwellest yet beneath our Earthly skies,
Come, teach these hearts, howbeit frail & weak,
These coward hearts the magic word to speak
"Off, idle doubts, thou double heart away,
"Arise, shrunk arm, ye, wearied limbs obey,
"In His high name, who with this temporal bound
"Of stern probation girt our being round
"Who set the strife & bade the race be run
"The deed shall be, the duty shall be done"!   [280]
Spirit of Valour mighty een in death,
Of Courage, Patience, Constancy & Faith,
[fol. 14] If yet thou live, and live thou dost indeed
Come, raise us, nerve us, aid us in our need!

Duff MS.   c. March 1840

Selected Bibliography

PRIMARY WORKS

PUBLISHED

Clough, Arthur Hugh. *The Bothie of Toper-na-Fuosich: A Long-Vacation Pastoral*. Oxford, 1848.

———— *A Consideration of Objections Against the Retrenchment Association*. Oxford, 1847.

———— "Contemporary Literature of America," *Westminster Review*, LX (Oct. 1853), 604–605.

———— *The Correspondence of Arthur Hugh Clough*, ed. Frederick L. Mulhauser. 2 vols. Oxford, 1957.

———— [Letters to *The Balance* signed M.A.O.].

"Letter to the Editor," *The Balance* (Jan. 23, 1846), p. 26.

"Political Economy," *The Balance* (Jan. 30, 1846), p. 34.

"The Militia," *The Balance* (Feb. 6, 1846), p. 42.

"Expensive Living," *The Balance* (Feb. 13, 1846), p. 50.

"A Few Practical Hints," *The Balance* (March 6, 1846), p. 77.

"The Spirit of Trade," *The Balance* (March 20, 1846), pp. 93–94.

———— [Letters to *The Spectator* signed Alpha.].

Letter about Francis W. Newman's Speech at London University College, Oct. 13, 1847, *The Spectator*, 1010 (Nov. 6, 1847), 1066.

Letter about Francis W. Newman's Speech at London University College, Oct. 13, 1847, *The Spectator*, 1012 (Nov. 20, 1847), 1118.

———— "Letters of Parepidemus," *Putnam's Monthly*, II (July 1853), 72–74.

———— "Letters of Parepidemus," *Putnam's Monthly*, II (August 1853), 138–140.

———— *Letters and Remains of A. H. Clough*. London, 1865.

———— "Recent Social Theories" [running title], *The North American Review*, LXXVII (July 1853), 106–117. [This is a review by Clough of Charles Norton's anonymous *Considerations on Some Recent Social Theories*. Boston: Little, Brown and Co., 1853, 16 mo., pp. 158.]

———— *Oxford University Commission. Report of Her Majesty's Commissioners Appointed to Inquire into the State, Discipline, Studies, and*

Revenues of the University and Colleges of Oxford. Appendix and Evidence. London, 1852. pp. 211–216.

—— "Oxford University Commission" [running title], *The North American Review,* LXXVI (April 1853), 369–396.

—— *Plutarch's Lives, the Translation Called Dryden's Corrected and Revised by A. H. Clough.* 5 vols. Boston, 1857.

—— "The Poems and Ballads of Goethe," *Fraser's Magazine,* LIX (June 1859), 710–717.

—— *Poems . . . With a Memoir* [signed by F. T. Palgrave]. Cambridge and London, 1862.

—— *The Poems and Prose Remains of Arthur Hugh Clough: With a Selection From His Letters and a Memoir,* edited by his wife. 2 vols. London, 1869.

—— *Prose Remains of Arthur Hugh Clough: With a Selection From His Letters and a Memoir,* edited by his wife. London, 1888.

——*The Poems of Arthur Hugh Clough,* ed. H. F. Lowry, A. L. P. Norrington and F. L. Mulhauser. Oxford, 1951.

—— "Recent English Poetry," *North American Review,* LXXVII (July 1853), 1–30.

—— [A Review of] *"Considerations on Some Recent Social Theories,"* *Westminster Review,* LX (Oct. 1853), 604–605.

—— *Selected Prose Works of Arthur Hugh Clough,* ed. Buckner Trawick. University, Alabama, 1964.

Clough, Arthur Hugh and Thomas Burbidge. *Ambarvalia.* London, 1849.

UNPUBLISHED*

Clough, Arthur Hugh. College Essays, 1837–1839, 1839, 1840. Three Notebooks containing 34 essays. Bodleian MS. Eng. Misc. d.513–515.

—— "Conversations of the Earth with the Universe" ["Conversations Between the Sun and the Moon"]. Bodleian MS. Eng. Misc. d.512, fols. 96–118.

—— "Fragment on America." Bodleian MS. Eng. Misc. d.512, fols. 173–174.

—— "An Ill World Indeed." Bodleian MS. Eng. Misc. d.512, fols. 163–164.

—— "The Judgement of Brutus." Duff MSS.

—— Letters. Houghton Library, Harvard University.

—— "Letter to the *Christian Socialist*" [formerly known as "Address on Socialism"]. Bodleian MS. Eng. Misc. d.512, fols. 120–132.

—— "Letter on the Rights of Property." Bodleian MS. Eng. Misc. d.512, fols. 134–135.

—— "Letter on University Reform" Bodleian MS. Eng. Misc. d.512 fols. 146–151.

---

* I have consulted but not listed separately Clough's other MSS in the following collections: Balliol College, Oxford; Beinecke Library, Yale; Bodleian Library, Oxford; British Museum, London; Dr. Williams's Library, London; Duff MSS, London; Houghton Library, Harvard; Oriel College, Oxford.

——— "Letters of Parepidemus." Bodleian MS. Eng. Misc. d.512, fols. 48–75.
——— "Notes on the Religious Tradition." Bodleian MS. Eng. Poet. d.140, fols. 21ᵛ–12ᵛ reversed.
——— "Paper on Expenditure." Bodleian MS. Eng. Misc. d.512, fols. 78–95.
——— "Paper on Religion." Bodleian MS. Eng. Misc. d.512, fols. 39–40.
——— "Petition on University Reform." Bodleian MS. Eng. Misc. d.512, fols. 144–145.
——— "Review of a Book on Progress." Bodleian MS. Eng. Misc. d.512, fols. 136–139.
——— "Review of Mr. Newman on the Soul." Bodleian MS. Eng. Misc. d.512, fols. 24–38, 41–46.
——— Roma Notebook. Balliol College.
——— "Salsette and Elephanta." Duff MSS.
——— "A Sunday Morning Contemplation." Bodleian MS. Eng. Misc. d.512, fols. 154–162.
——— "The Young Cur." Bodleian MS. Eng. Misc. d.512, fols. 165–166.

SECONDARY WORKS

Anon. *An Appeal to Members of the University Whether Graduates or Undergraduates.* Oxford [Jan. 23], 1847, 13 pp.
——— "Balliol Scholars, 1840–43," *Macmillan's Magazine* (Mar. 1873).
——— "Christian Fellowship," *Prospective Review,* No. 3 (1845), 392–415.
——— "Memories of Arnold and Rugby Sixty Years Ago, by a Member of the School," *Parents' Review,* 1896.
——— "Philosophy of History," *British Critic,* XXI (Jan. 1837), 140–167.
——— "Recent French Social Philosophy," *North American Review,* IX (1848), 115–135.
——— *The Student's Guide to a Course of Reading Necessary for Obtaining University Honours.* Oxford: Henry Slatter, 1837.
Abel, Darrel. "Strangers in Nature—Arnold and Emerson," *University of Kansas City Review,* XV (1948), 205–213.
Allott, Kenneth. "Matthew Arnold's Reading List in Three Early Diaries," *Victorian Studies,* II (March 1959), 254–266.
——— [Review of *Selected Prose Works of A. H. Clough*], *Notes and Queries,* n.s. XII (Aug. 1965), 316–317.
Arnold, Matthew. *Civilization in the United States: First and Last Impressions of America.* Boston, 1888.
——— *Culture and Anarchy.* London, 1938.
——— *Discourses in America.* London, 1885.
——— *Essays in Criticism: Third Series.* Boston, 1910.
——— "George Sand," *Fortnightly Review,* 27 (June 1877), 767–781.
——— *Letters of Matthew Arnold,* ed. George Russell. 2 vols. New York, 1895.
——— *The Letters of Matthew Arnold to Arthur Hugh Clough,* ed. H. F. Lowry. London, 1932.
——— *The Poetical Works of Matthew Arnold,* ed. C. B. Tinker and H. F. Lowry. London, 1950.

———— *Unpublished Letters of Matthew Arnold,* ed. Arnold Whitridge. New Haven, 1923.

Arnold, Thomas, D. D. *Christian Life . . . Sermons Preached Mostly in tions: I. of Personal Identity; II. of the Nature of Virtue.* London, 1736. 1878.

———— *History of Rome.* 3 vols. London, 1838–43.

———— [Letters to the *Sheffield Courant,* on the Social Distress of the Lower Orders.] Sheffield [1832]. [n.t.p., n.d.]

———— "Oxford Malignants and Dr. Hampden," *The Edinburgh Review or Critical Journal,* LXIII (April–July 1836), 225–239.

———— *Principles of Church Reform.* London, 1833.

Arnold, Thomas, [Jr.]. "Arthur Hugh Clough: A Sketch," *The Nineteenth Century,* 251 (Jan. 1898), pp. 105–116.

———— *New Zealand Letters of Thomas Arnold the Younger,* ed. James Bertram. London & Wellington, 1966.

———— *Passages in a Wandering Life.* London, 1900.

Backstrom, Philip N., Jr. "The Practical Side of Christian Socialism in Victorian England," *Victorian Studies,* VI (June 1963), 305–324.

Bagehot, Walter. *Literary Studies,* ed. R. H. Hutton. 3 vols. London, 1906.

———— "Mr. Clough's Poems," *The National Review,* XV (Oct. 1862), 310–326.

Balliol College Examination Register. (MS).

Balliol Fellowship 1838 Examination Papers. (MS).

Bamford, T[homas] W[illiam]. *Thomas Arnold.* London, 1960.

Barish, Evelyn. "A New Clough Manuscript," *Review of English Studies,* XV (May 1964), 168–174. [See also Greenberger, Evelyn Barish.]

Barry, Alfred, D. D. [ed.]. *The Teacher's Prayer Book Being the Book of Common Prayer, with Introductions, Analyses, Notes, and A Commentary Upon the Psalter.* London [n.d.].

Baum, Paull F. "Clough and Arnold," *Modern Language Notes,* LXVII, (Dec. 1952), 546–547.

Beach, Joseph Warren. *The Concept of Nature in Nineteenth-Century English Poetry.* New York, 1936.

Benn, Alfred William. *The History of English Rationalism in the Nineteenth Century.* 2 vols. London, 1906.

Berger, Harold L. "Emerson and Carlyle: The Dissenting Believers," *Emerson Society Quarterly,* No. 38 (1965), 87–90.

Berthoff, Rowland Tappan. *British Immigrants in Industrial America 1790–1950.* Cambridge, Mass., 1953.

Briggs, Asa. *The Age of Improvement 1783–1867,* 2nd impression with corrections. London, 1960.

Briggs, Asa, ed. *Chartist Studies.* London, 1959.

Brilioth, Yngve. *The Anglican Revival: Studies in the Oxford Movement.* London, 1925.

Brinton, Crane. *English Political Thought in The Nineteenth Century.* London, 1933.

Brogan, D. W. *The French Nation From Napoleon to Pétain, 1814–1940.* London, 1957.

Brooke, Stopford Augustus, LL.D. *Four Poets: Clough, Arnold, Rossetti, Morris.* London, 1913.

Brooks, Van Wyck. *The Malady of the Ideal: Obermann, Maurice de Guerin and Amiel.* Philadelphia, 1947.

Browne, Edward George Kirvan. *History of the Tractarian Movement.* Dublin, 1856.

Burke, Kenneth. *Counter-Statement.* Los Altos, California, 1953.

Butler, Joseph. *The Analogy of Religion, Natural and Revealed, to the Constitution and Course of Nature. To Which Are Added Two Brief Dissertations: I. of Personal Identity; II. of the Nature of Virtue.* London, 1736.

Butler, Joseph. *The Whole Works of Joseph Butler, LL.D.* London, 1850.

Campbell, R. J., D. D. *Thomas Arnold.* London, 1927.

Cannon, Walter. "The Problem of Miracles in the 1830's," *Victorian Studies,* IV (Sept. 1960), 5–32.

Carlyle, Thomas. *Chartism.* London, 1841.

—— *Critical and Miscellaneous Essays; On Heroes, Hero-Worship, and the Heroic in History; Past and Present: The Works of Thomas Carlyle,* ed. H. D. Traill, Centenary ed. 30 vols. New York, 1896–1901. Vols. XXVIII, V, X.

—— *Sartor Resartus.* 20 vols. Boston, 1884. Vol. I.

Carpenter, Frederick Ives. *Emerson and Asia.* Cambridge, Mass., 1930.

Carpenter, J. Estlin. *James Martineau: Theologian and Teacher: A Study of his Life and Thought.* London, 1905.

Cecil, David. *Lord M: The Later Life of Lord Melbourne.* London, 1954.

Chadwick, Owen, ed. *The Mind of the Oxford Movement.* London, 1960.

Chorley, Katharine. *Arthur Hugh Clough: The Uncommitted Mind.* Oxford, 1962.

Christensen, Torben. *Origin and History of Christian Socialism: 1848–54.* Acta Theologica Danica. Vol. III. Copenhagen, Universitetsforlaget I Aarhus, 1962.

The Christian Socialist: A Journal of Association. Vols. I–II (Nov. 2, 1850–Dec. 27, 1851).

Church, R[ichard] W[illiam]. "Arthur Hugh Clough," *The Christian Remembrancer,* XLV (Jan. 1863), 61–89.

—— *Life and Letters of Dean Church,* ed. Mary C. Church. London, 1895.

—— *The Oxford Movement, Twelve Years, 1833–45.* London, 1891.

Clark, G. Kitson. *The Making of Victorian England.* Cambridge, 1962.

Clough, Blanche Athena. *A Memoir of Anne Jemima Clough.* London, 1897.

Cockshut, A. O. J. *The Unbelievers: English Agnostic Thought 1840–1890.* London, 1964.

Cole, G. D. H. *Chartist Portraits.* London, 1941.

Coleridge, Ernest Hartley. *Life and Correspondence of John Duke Lord Coleridge.* 2 vols. London, 1904.

Conington, John. *Miscellaneous Writings of John Conington . . . with a Memoir by H. J. S. Smith,* ed. J. A. Symonds. 2 vols. London, 1872.

Conroy, Sir Edward. MS annotations to *The Oxford University and City Guide,* new ed. Oxford, 1829. (MS. Balliol College Library.)

SELECTED BIBLIOGRAPHY

Conway, Moncure Daniel. *Autobiography, Memoirs and Experiences.* 2 vols. London [1904].

———— *Emerson at Home and Abroad.* Boston, 1883.

Cornish, Francis Warre. *The English Church in the Nineteenth Century.* 2 vols. London, 1910.

Curgenven, John P. "Theodore Walrond: Friend of Arnold and Clough," *The Durham University Journal,* XLIV (March 1952) (N.S. Vol. XIII, No. 2), 56–61.

———— "Thyrsis," *Litera,* IV (1957), 27–39; V (1958), 7–16.

Dalglish, Doris N. "Arthur Hugh Clough: The Shorter Poems," *Essays in Criticism,* II (Jan. 1952), 38–53.

Davies, Horton. *Worship and Theology in England:* Vol. III: *From Watts and Wesley to Maurice, 1690–1850;* Vol. IV: *From Newman to Martineau, 1850–1900.* Princeton and Oxford, 1961–1962.

Davis, H. W. C. *Balliol College.* London, 1899.

———— *A History of Balliol College,* rev. ed. by R. H. C. Davis, R. Hunt, *et al.* Oxford, 1963.

DeLaura, David. "Arnold and Carlyle," *PMLA,* LXXIX (March 1964), 104–129.

Disraeli, Benjamin. *Coningsby, or The New Generation.* 3 vols. London, 1844.

Driver, Cecil. *Tory Radical: The Life of Richard Oastler.* New York, 1946.

Drummond, James and C. B. Upton. *The Life and Letters of James Martineau.* 2 vols. London, 1902.

Dunn, Waldo Hilary. *James Anthony Froude: A Biography.* 2 vols. Oxford, 1961.

Elliott-Binns, L. E., D. D. *Religion in the Victorian Era.* London, 1936.

Ellis, W. Paterson. *Extracts From Jackson's Oxford Journal Illustrating Oxford History 1753–1850: Chronologically Arranged from p. 23 to p. 278 by W. Paterson Ellis with Index* [n.p., n.d.].

Emerson, Ralph Waldo. *The Correspondence of Emerson and Carlyle,* ed. Jos. Slater. New York, 1964.

———— *Emerson-Clough Letters,* ed. Howard F. Lowry and Ralph Leslie Rusk. Cleveland, 1934.

———— *Essays: With a Preface by Thomas Carlyle.* London, 1841.

———— *The Heart of Emerson's Journals,* ed. Bliss Perry. London, 1927.

———— *Journals and Miscellaneous Notebooks of Ralph Waldo Emerson,* ed. Wm. H. Gilman, Alfred R. Ferguson, Merrell R. Davis. 5 vols. Cambridge, Mass., 1960–1965.

———— *Journals of Ralph Waldo Emerson,* ed. Edward Waldo Emerson and Waldo Emerson Forbes. 10 vols. Boston, 1909–1914.

———— *The Letters of Ralph Waldo Emerson,* ed. Ralph L. Rusk. 6 vols. New York, 1939.

———— Notebook, No. 109. Unpublished MS. Houghton Library, Harvard.

———— *The Works of Ralph Waldo Emerson: with a General Index and a Memoir,* ed. James E. Cabot. 14 vols. Boston, 1883–1887.

Encyclopaedia of Religion and Ethics, ed. James Hastings. 12 vols. and indexes. Edinburgh, 1908–1926.

Faber, Geoffrey. *Jowett*. London, 1957.

――― *Oxford Apostles: A Character Study of the Oxford Movement,* 2nd ed. London, 1936.

Fairchild, Hoxie Neale. *Religious Trends in English Poetry: IV: 1830–1880.* New York, 1957.

Fejtö, François, ed. *The Opening of An Era: 1848: An Historical Symposium.* London, 1948.

Fields, J. T. *Yesterdays with Authors.* Boston, 1872.

Fisher, H. A. L. *An Unfinished Autobiography.* London, 1940.

Flanagan, John T. "Emerson and Communism," *New England Quarterly,* X (June 1937), 243–261.

Froude, James Anthony. "The Oxford Counter-Reformation," *Short Studies on Great Subjects,* Ser. 4, London, 1883.

――― *Thomas Carlyle: A History of his Life in London, 1834–1881.* 2 vols. London, 1884.

――― *The Nemesis of Faith.* London, 1849.

Fulweiler, Howard W. "Tractarians and Philistines: The *Tracts for the Times* Versus Victorian Middle-Class Values," *Historical Magazine of the Protestant Episcopal Church,* XXXI (March 1962), 36–53.

Garrod, H. W. "Clough," *Poetry and the Criticism of Life.* Cambridge, Mass., 1931, pp. 109–127.

Gaskell, [Elizabeth C.] Mrs. *Mary Barton: A Tale of Manchester Life.* London, 1911.

Gerber, John C. "Emerson and the Political Economists," *New England Quarterly,* XXII (Sept. 1949), 336–357.

[Gladstone, William E.] [Review of *Life of Blanco White*], *The Quarterly Review,* LXXVI (June 1845), 164–203.

Gollin, Richard M., Walter E. Houghton, and Michael Timko. *Arthur Hugh Clough: A Descriptive Catalogue.* New York, 1967.

――― "Arthur Hugh Clough's Formative Years: 1819–1841" (unpub. diss., University of Minnesota, 1959).

――― "The 1951 Edition of Clough's *Poems:* A Critical Re-Examination," *Modern Philology,* LX (Nov. 1962), 120–127.

――― "Clough Despite Himself," *Essays in Criticism,* XII (Oct. 1962), 426–435.

Goulburn, Edward M. *The Book of Rugby School: Its History and its Daily Life.* Rugby, 1856.

Gray, H. D. *Emerson: A Statement of New England Transcendentalism as Expressed in the Philosophy of its Chief Exponent.* Stanford, 1917.

Greenberger, Evelyn Barish. [See also Barish, Evelyn.] " 'Salsette and Elephanta'; An Unpublished Poem by Clough," *Review of English Studies,* n.s. XX (Aug. 1969), 284–305.

――― "Clough's 'The Judgement of Brutus': A Newly Found Poem," *Victorian Poetry,* VIII, No. 2 (Summer 1970).

Grosskurth, Phyllis. *John Addington Symonds: A Biography.* London, 1964.

Guyot, Edouard. *Essai sur la formation philosophique du poète Arthur Hugh Clough: pragmatisme et intellectualisme:* Paris, 1913.

Hale, Edward Everett. *James Russell Lowell and His Friends.* [A series of articles appearing in 1898 in *The Outlook*, pp. 21–627 and 27–49, in the Bodleian Library under title above, n.t.p., n.d.]

Halévy, Elie. *A History of the English People In the Nineteenth Century—IV: Victorian Years: 1841–1895*, trans. E. I. Watkin. Supp. by R. B. McCallum. London, 1961.

Hammond, John Lawrence and Barbara. *The Bleak Age*, rev. ed. West Drayton, 1947.

Hawthorne, Nathaniel. *The English Notebooks of Nathaniel Hawthorne*. New York, 1941.

Hertz, Robert N. "Victory and the Consciousness of Battle: Emerson and Carlyle," *The Personalist*, XLV, 60–71.

Hopkins, Vivian C. *Spires of Form*. Cambridge, Mass., 1951.

Houghton, Walter E. "Arthur Hugh Clough: A Hundred Years of Disparagement," *Studies in English Literature*, I, IV, 35–61.

——— [A Review of] "*Arthur Hugh Clough: The Uncommitted Mind*," *Victorian Studies*, VI (Sept. 1962), 91–92.

——— *The Poetry of Clough: An Essay in Revaluation*. New Haven, 1963.

——— "The Prose Works of Arthur Hugh Clough: A Checklist and Calendar, With Some Unpublished Passages," *Bulletin of the New York Public Library*, 64 (July 1960), 377–394.

——— *The Victorian Frame of Mind: 1830–1870*. New Haven, 1957.

Hovell, Mark. *The Chartist Movement*, ed. T. F. Tout. 2nd ed. London, 1925.

Hughes, Thomas. *Tom Brown at Oxford*. 3 vols. Cambridge, 1861.

——— *Tom Brown's Schooldays*. 3rd ed. Cambridge, 1857.

Hutton, Richard Holt. *Criticisms on Contemporary Thought and Thinkers*. 2 vols. London, 1894.

——— *Essays in Literary Criticism*. Philadelphia [1876].

Inglis, K. S. *Churches and the Working Classes in Victorian England*. London, 1963.

Ireland, Alexander. *Ralph Waldo Emerson, His Life, Genius, and Writings*. London, 1882.

Johari, G. P. "Arthur Hugh Clough at Oriel and at University Hall," *PMLA*, LXVI, 405–425.

Johnson, E. D. H. *The Alien Vision of Victorian Poetry*. Princeton, 1952.

Johnson, W. Stacy. "Parallel Imagery in Arnold and Clough," *English Studies*, XXXVII, 1–11.

King, Bolton. *Mazzini*. London, 1902.

Kingsley, Charles. [A Review of *The Bothie*] *Fraser's Magazine*, XXXIX (1849), 103–110.

Knight, William Angus. *Principal Shairp and his Friends*. London, 1888.

Ladu, Arthur I. "Emerson: Whig or Democrat," *New England Quarterly*, XII (Sept. 1940), 419–441.

Lake, Katharine, ed. *Memorials of William Charles Lake, Dean of Durham 1869–1894*. London, 1901.

Levy, Goldie. *Arthur Hugh Clough: 1819–1861*. London, 1938.

Lillibridge, G. D. *Beacon of Freedom: The Impact of American Democracy Upon Great Britain 1830–1870*. Philadelphia, 1955.

Lockwood, H. D. *Tools and the Man. A Comparative Study of the French Workingman and the English Chartists in the Literature of 1830–48.* New York, 1948.

Lowell, J. R. *My Study Windows.* Boston, 1871.

MacCarthy, Desmond. *Portraits.* London, 1949.

Maccoby, S. *English Radicalism: 1832–1852.* London, 1935.

Mallet, Sir Charles Edward. *A History of the University of Oxford.* 3 vols. London, 1924.

Masson, David. *Memories of London in the 'Forties.* Edinburgh, 1908.

Mathieson, William Law. *English Church Reform: 1815–1840.* New York, 1923.

Maurois, André. *Lélia: The Life of George Sand.* London, 1953.

Mayhew, Henry. *London Labour and the London Poor.* 2 vols. London, 1851.

McCarthy, Patrick J. *Matthew Arnold and the Three Classes.* New York, 1964.

Mill, John Stuart. *Autobiography of John Stuart Mill,* ed. R. Howson. New York, 1924.

——— *Essays on Some Unsettled Questions of Political Economy.* London, 1844.

——— *The Letters of John Stuart Mill,* ed. H. S. R. Elliott. 2 vols. London, 1910.

——— *A System of Logic, Ratiocinative and Inductive; Being a Connected View of the Principles of Evidence and the Methods of Scientific Investigation.* 2 vols. London, 1843.

——— *Principles of Political Economy, with Some of Their Applications to Social Philosophy.* 2 vols. London, 1848.

Miller, Perry. "Emersonian Genius and the American Democracy," *New England Quarterly,* XXVI (March 1953), 27–44.

——— *The Transcendentalists.* Cambridge, Mass., 1950.

Minnick, Wayne C. "Matthew Arnold on Emerson," *Quarterly Journal of Speech,* XXXVII (Oct. 1951), 332–336.

Morison, Samuel Eliot and Henry Steele Commager. *The Growth of the American Republic.* 5th ed. Vol. I. New York, 1962.

Morley, John. *The Life of William Ewart Gladstone.* 3 vols. London, 1903.

Mossner, Ernest Campbell. *Bishop Butler and the Age of Reason.* New York, 1936.

Mozley, Thomas. *Reminiscences of Oriel College and the Oxford Movement.* 2 vols. London, 1882.

Neff, Emery. *Carlyle.* London, 1932.

——— *Carlyle and Mill: An Introduction to Victorian Thought.* 2nd ed. New York, 1926.

Neimann, Fraser. "The Zeitgeist of Matthew Arnold," *PMLA,* LXXII, 977–996.

Newman, Francis William. *The Soul, her Sorrows and her Aspirations: an Essay Towards the Natural History of the Soul, as the True Basis of Theology.* 2nd ed. London, 1849.

[Newman, John Henry.] *Loss and Gain, The Story of a Convert.* London, 1848.

Newman, John Henry. *Newman's Apologia Pro Vita Sua—The Two Versions of 1864 and 1865* . . . , ed. Wilfrid Ward. Oxford, 1913.

[Norton, Charles Eliot.] "Arthur Hugh Clough," *North American Review,* CV (Oct. 1867), 434–477.

—— *Considerations on Some Recent Social Theories.* Boston, 1853.

—— *Letters of Charles Eliot Norton.* 2 vols. Boston, 1913.

Osborne, James Insley. *Arthur Hugh Clough.* London, 1920.

Oxford Society for the Suppression of Mendicity and Relief of Distressed Travellers. Annual Reports. Oxford, 1831–1849.

Oxford University Commission. Report of Her Majesty's Commissioners Appointed to Inquire into the State, Discipline, Studies, and Revenues of the University and Colleges of Oxford. Appendix and Evidence. London, 1852.

Packe, Michael St. John. *The Life of John Stuart Mill.* London, 1954.

Palgrave, G. F. *Francis Turner Palgrave: his Journals and Memories of his Life.* London, 1899.

Palmer, F. W. "The Bearing of Science on the Thought of Clough," *PMLA,* LIX (Mar., 1944), 212–225.

—— "Was Clough a Failure?" *Philological Quarterly,* XXII (Jan. 1943), 58–68.

Palmer, Paul. "Benthamism in England and America," *American Political Science Review,* XXXV (Oct. 1941), 855–871.

Pattison, Mark. *Memoirs.* London, 1885.

Paul, Sherman. *Emerson's Angle of Vision.* Cambridge, Mass., 1952.

Pelling, Henry. *America and the British Left: From Bright to Bevan.* London, 1956.

Pochmann, Henry A. *German Culture in America.* Madison, 1957.

The Prospective Review; A Quarterly Journal of Theology and Literature, Vol. I, London, 1845.

Prothero, Rowland E. *Life and Letters of Dean Stanley.* 2 vols. London, 1893.

The Publishers' Circular and General Record of British and Foreign Literature Containing a Complete Alphabetical List of All New Works Published in Great Britain and Every Work of Interest Published Abroad. Vol. XII, London, 1849.

Raleigh, John Henry. *Matthew Arnold and American Culture.* Berkeley, 1957.

Rannie, David W. *Oriel College.* London, 1900.

Reid, T. Wemyss. *The Life, Letters, and Friendships of Richard Monckton Milnes.* 2 vols. 2nd ed. London, 1890.

Richards, George C. and Charles L. Shadwell. *The Provosts and Fellows of Oriel College.* Oxford, 1922.

Ritchie, Anne Isabella [Thackeray, Lady]. *Chapters From Some Memoirs.* London, 1894.

—— *Records of Tennyson and Robert and Elizabeth Browning.* London, 1892.

Roach, J. P. C. "Victorian Universities and the National Intelligentsia," *Victorian Studies,* III (Dec. 1959), 131–158.

Robinson, Henry Crabb. *Henry Crabb Robinson on Books and their Authors,* ed. Edith J. Morley. 3 vols. London, 1938.

———— MS letters and Journals, Dr. Williams's Library, London. Also in this collection: the Minute Books of the Trustees of University Hall.

Robson, John M. "Victorian Liberals," *University of Toronto Quarterly,* XXXI, 242–245.

Rudman, Arthur. *Mazzini: Patriot and Prophet.* London, 1922.

Rudman, Harry W. "Clough: 'Say Not the Struggle,' " *Notes and Queries,* CXCVIII, 261–263.

Rusk, Ralph L. *The Life of Ralph Waldo Emerson.* New York, 1949.

[Russell, G. W. E.] *Collections and Recollections.* New York, 1899.

St. John-Stevas, Norman. *Walter Bagehot: A Study of His Life and Thought Together With a Selection from his Political Writings.* London, 1959.

Sandford, E. G., ed. *Memoirs of Archbishop Temple by Seven Friends.* 2 vols. London, 1906.

Santayana, George. "Emerson," *Little Essays From the Writings of George Santayana,* ed. L. P. Smith. New York, 1920.

Schlegel, Friedrich von. *The Philosophy of History,* trans. with a memoir by Jas. B. Robinson. 2 vols. London, 1835.

———— *Essai sur la langue and la philosophie des Indiens,* trans. M. A. Mazure. Paris, 1837.

Schlesinger, Arthur Meier. *Political and Social History of the United States: 1829–1925.* New York, 1927.

Schlesinger, Arthur M. [Jr.] *The Age of Jackson.* Boston, 1946.

Scudder, Townsend, III. "A Chronological List of Emerson's Lectures on His British Tour of 1847–1848," *PMLA,* LI (March 1936), 243–248.

———— "Emerson in London and the London Lectures," *American Literature,* VIII (March 1936), 22–36.

———— "Emerson's British Lecture Tour, 1847–1848," pt. I: *American Literature,* VII (March 1935), 15–36; pt. II: *American Literature,* VII (May 1935), 166–180.

———— *The Lonely Wayfaring Man: Emerson and Some Englishmen.* London, 1936.

Selfe, Lt. Col. Sydney G. F. *Notes on the Characters and Incidents depicted by the Master Hand of Tom Hughes in "Tom Brown's Schooldays." Together with Some Supplementary Information as to Rugby School in the Days of Thomas Arnold, D. D. 1828–1842.* Rugby, 1909.

Shackford, Martha Hale. "The Clough Centenary: His *Dipsychus,*" *The Sewanee Review,* XXVII (Oct. 1919), 401–410.

Shairp, John Campbell. *Aspects of Poetry.* London, 1881.

Sidgwick, Henry. "The Poems and Prose Remains of Arthur Hugh Clough," *The Westminster Review,* N.S. XXXVI (Oct. 1869), 363–387.

Sikes, Enoch Walter and Wm. Morse Keener. *The History of North America.* Vol. XIII. Philadelphia, 1905.

Smith, William, D. D., ed. *Dictionary of Greek and Roman Biography and Mythology.* 3 vols. 1844–1849.

Spectator, The, Nos. 1008, 1010, 1012 (Oct. 23, Nov. 6, Nov. 20, 1847).

Stanley, Arthur Penrhyn. *The Life and Correspondence of Thomas Arnold, D. D.* 2 vols. London, 1844.

Statham, Reginald. "Arthur Hugh Clough," *National Review* (April 1897), 200–212.

Strachey, Marjorie. *Mazzini, Garibaldi and Cavour.* London, 1937.
Strauss, Dr. David Friedrich. *The Life of Jesus: Critically Examined,* translated from the Fourth German Edn. 3 vols. London, 1846.
Super, R. H. "Emerson and Arnold's Poetry," *Philological Quarterly,* XXXIII (Oct. 1954), 396–403.
Symonds, John Addington. "Arthur Hugh Clough," *The Fortnightly Review,* N.S. IV (Dec. 1868), 589–617.
Tener, Robert H. "Clough, Hutton and University Hall," *Notes and Queries,* n.s. VII, 456–57.
Thistlethwaite, Frank. *The Anglo-American Connection in the Early Nineteenth Century.* Philadelphia, 1959.
Thompson, Cameron. "John Locke and New England Transcendentalism," *The New England Quarterly,* XXXV (Dec. 1962), 435–457.
Thompson, Frank T. "Emerson and Carlyle," *Studies in Philology,* XXIV (1927), 438–453.
Thomson, David. *England in the Nineteenth Century (1815–1914).* Harmondsworth, 1950.
Ticknor, Caroline. *Glimpses of Authors.* Boston, 1922.
Ticknor, George. *Life, Letters and Journals,* ed. [Anna Ticknor]. 10th ed. 2 vols. Boston, 1880.
Tillotson, Geoffrey and Kathleen. *Mid-Victorian Studies.* London, 1965.
Tillotson, Kathleen. "Matthew Arnold and Carlyle," *Proceedings of the British Academy,* XLII (1956), 133–153.
Times, The. No. 19,681 (Oct. 15, 1847).
Timko, Michael. "Amours de Voyage: Substance or Smoke?" *English,* XIII (1960), 95–98.
―――― "Arthur Hugh Clough: A Portrait Retouched," *Victorian Newsletter,* 15 (Spring 1959), 24–28.
―――― "Corydon Had a Rival," *Victorian Newsletter,* 19 (Spring 1961), 5–11.
―――― *Innocent Victorian: The Satiric Poetry of Arthur Hugh Clough.* Ohio Univ. Press: n.p., 1966.
―――― "The 'True Creed' of Arthur Hugh Clough," *Modern Language Quarterly,* XXI, 208–222.
Trevelyan, George Macaulay. *British History in the Nineteenth Century and After (1782–1919).* 2nd ed. London, 1937.
―――― *Garibaldi's Defence of the Roman Republic 1848–9.* London, 1949.
Trilling, Lionel. *Matthew Arnold.* New York, 1955.
Tuckwell, W[illiam]. *Pre-Tractarian Oxford: A Reminiscence of the Oriel "Noetics."* London, 1909.
―――― *Reminiscences of Oxford.* London, 1907.
―――― "Reminiscences of Oxford: *Addendula Quaedam,*" *The Oxford Magazine* (May 24 and June 7, 1905), p. 339.
Tulloch, John. *Movements of Religious Thought in Britain During the Nineteenth Century.* London, 1885.
Turberville, A. S. *The House of Lords in the Age of Reform 1784–1837: With an Epilogue on Aristocracy and the Advent of Democracy, 1837–1867.* London, 1958.

Veyriras, Paul. *Arthur Hugh Clough: 1819–1861.* Paris, 1964.
Waddington, Samuel. *Arthur Hugh Clough: A Monograph.* London, 1883.
Wallace, Elisabeth. "The Political Ideas of the Manchester School," *University of Toronto Quarterly,* XXIX, 122–138.
Ward, Maisie. *The Wilfrid Wards and the Transition.* 2 vols. London, 1934.
Ward, Mrs. Humphrey. *A Writer's Recollections.* London, 1918.
Ward, Wilfrid. *William George Ward and the Oxford Movement.* London, 1899.
Ward, W[illiam] R[eginald]. *Victorian Oxford.* London, 1965.
[Ward, William George.] "Arnold's *Sermons,*" *The British Critic and Quarterly Theological Review,* XXX (Oct. 1841), 298–364.
[Ward, William George.] "Church Authority," *The British Critic and Quarterly Theological Review,* XXXIII (Jan. 1843), 202–233.
Watson, John Gillard. "Arnold and Oxford," *The Quarterly Review,* CCXCIV (Jan. 1956), 44–54.
Wellek, René. *Confrontations: Studies in the Intellectual and Literary Relations Between Germany, England, and the United States During the Nineteenth Century.* Princeton, 1965.
Wemyss, Rosslyn. *Memoirs and Letters of the Right Hon. Sir Robert Morier, G. C. B. From 1826 to 1876.* 2 vols. London, 1911.
[Whately, Richard]. *Historic Doubts Relative to Napoleon Buonaparte,* new ed. London, 1865.
Whately, E. Jane. *Life and Correspondence of Richard Whately, D. D.* London, 1875.
Wheeler, G. W."Bodleian Press Marks in Relation to Classification," *The Bodleian Quarterly Record,* I, No. 10 (July 31, 1916), 280–292.
Whicher, Stephen E. *Freedom and Fate.* Philadelphia, 1953.
White, Joseph Blanco. *The Life of the Rev. Joseph Blanco White,* ed. John H. Thom. 3 vols. London, 1845.
Wilbur, E. M. *A History of Unitarianism in Transylvania, England and America.* Cambridge, Mass., 1952.
Willey, Basil. *Nineteenth Century Studies.* New York, 1966.
Williams, S. T. "Clough's Prose," *Studies in Victorian Literature,* London, 1924.
Williamson, Eugene L., Jr. *The Liberalism of Thomas Arnold.* University, Ala., 1964.
Woodham-Smith, Cecil. *The Great Hunger: Ireland 1845–1849.* London, 1962.
——— *Florence Nightingale: 1820–1910.* London, 1950.
Woodward, Sir Ernest Llewellyn. *The Age of Reform: 1815–1870.* 2nd ed. Oxford, 1962.
Woodward, Frances J. *The Doctor's Disciples. A Study of Four Pupils of Arnold of Rugby: Stanley, Gell, Clough, William Arnold.* London, 1954.
Young, G[eorge] M[acaulay]. *Early Victorian England: 1830–1856.* 2 vols. London, 1934.
——— *Victorian England: Portrait of an Age.* 2nd ed. London, 1953.
——— *Victorian Essays,* ed. W. D. Handcock. Oxford, 1962.

Notes

INTRODUCTION

1. Arthur Penrhyn Stanley, *The Life and Correspondence of Thomas Arnold, D. D.* (London, 1844), II, 24. Cited thereafter as Stanley.

2. Katharine Chorley, *Arthur Hugh Clough: The Uncommitted Mind: A Study of His Life and Poetry* (Oxford, 1962). Cited hereafter as Chorley.

3. Michael Timko, *Innocent Victorian: The Satiric Poetry of Arthur Hugh Clough* (Ohio Univ. Press, 1966), p. 7 *et passim*. Cited hereafter as Timko, *Innocent Victorian*. He credits Lionel Trilling's *E. M. Forster* (Norfolk, Conn., 1943), pp. 22, 23 with the phrase.

4. "Arthur Hugh Clough, A Hundred Years of Disparagement," *Studies in English Literature*, I (Autumn 1961), 35–61.

5. *The Poems and Prose Remains of Arthur Hugh Clough, With . . . a Memoir*, ed. [Blanche M. S. Clough] (London, 1869), I, 37, 40–42. Cited hereafter as *P.P.R.* [Walter Bagehot], "Mr. Clough's Poems," *The National Review*, XV (Oct. 1862), 310–326. Cited hereafter as Bagehot, "Mr. Clough's Poems."

6. *The Poems of Arthur Hugh Clough,* ed. H. F. Lowry, A. L. P. Norrington, and F. L. Mulhauser (Oxford, 1951), pp. 49 and 54–60. Cited hereafter as *Poems*.

7. Timko, *Innocent Victorian,* pp. 48–50.

8. Stanley T. Williams, "Clough's Prose," *Studies in Victorian Literature,* (London, 1924), p. 238. Williams here is referring to the excisions from Clough's letters; his article does not in fact discuss Clough's prose essays as distinct from his correspondence.

9. *Selected Prose Works of Arthur Hugh Clough,* ed. Buckner B. Trawick (University, Ala., 1964). Cited hereafter as *S.P.*

10. Kenneth Allott in his review severely censures both the principles of selection and the editorial practices. *Notes & Queries,* n.s. XII (Aug. 1965), 317.

11. The following, omitted by Trawick and Mrs. Clough, are drawn on in this study: "Contemporary Literature in America," "Conversations of the Earth with the Universe" (previously titled "Conversations Between the Sun and the Moon"), "Fragment on America," "An Ill World," a "Letter of

233

Parepidemus," "Paper on Expenditure," "Petition on University Reform," "Review of a Book on Progress," "Roma Notebook," "The Young Cur," twenty-nine undergraduate essays (see Appendix A and Chapter I) and various manuscript letters. The poems "Salsette and Elephanta," and "The Judgement of Brutus" have also been useful and are printed in Appendix B. Other MSS (see Bibliography) have also been consulted. Like other scholars, I have not had access to the Clough materials loaned to Prof. Mulhauser by Clough's heir, Miss K. L. Duff, in 1952.

12. See n. 2; Paul Veyriras, *Arthur Hugh Clough: (1819–1861)* (Paris, 1964). Cited hereafter as Veyriras.

13. For typical criticisms, see Frances J. Woodward, *The Doctor's Disciples: A Study of Four Pupils of Arnold of Rugby: Stanley, Gell, Clough, William Arnold* (London, 1954), p. 8 (cited hereafter as F. J. Woodward); Samuel Chew, "The Nineteenth Century and After," *A Literary History of England,* ed. A. C. Baugh (New York, 1948), p. 1405; and Chorley, pp. 192, 349–361. A thorough review of Clough's reputation appears in Chapter One of Walter E. Houghton, *The Poetry of Clough: An Essay in Revaluation* (New Haven, 1963). Cited hereafter as Houghton, *Revaluation.*

14. *P.P.R.,* I, 1–54. Attributions of the "Memoir" have been various, but her authorship has been settled by her co-editor, J. A. Symonds. See n. 17 below.

15. *The Correspondence of Arthur Hugh Clough,* ed. Frederick L. Mulhauser (Oxford, 1957), I, 301. Cited hereafter as *Correspondence.* See also Bodelian MS Eng. Lett. e. 77, fol. 66.

16. *Correspondence,* I, 275.

17. Phyllis Grosskurth, *John Addington Symonds* (London, 1964), pp. 130–133. Mrs. Grosskurth believes that Symonds in fact helped write the "Memoir" but that the degree of his aid is uncertain. Cited hereafter as Grosskurth.

18. Grosskurth, p. 133.

19. *P.P.R.,* I, 34–35.

20. Chorley, p. 263, n.; Evelyn Barish, "A New Clough Manuscript," *Review of English Studies,* n.s. XV, (May 1964), 168–174. Cited hereafter as Barish. See also Richard M. Gollin, "The 1951 Edition of Clough's *Poems:* A Critical Re-Examination," *Modern Philology,* LX (Nov. 1962), 120–127.

21. Chorley, p. 137, and Veyriras, p. 430. *"Ses idées sociales ont assez peu évolué par rapport à celles de 1848."* Veyriras acknowledges that Clough's ideas in 1853 were *"légèrement en retrait,"* but this does not reveal the degree of his reaction.

22. *Correspondence,* I, 296.

23. *P.P.R.,* I, 37.

24. *P.P.R.,* I, 37, 40–42.

25. *Correspondence,* II, 402–403. "It is horrid," she wrote of his poetry. "[The poems] seem to me full of honest coarse strength and perception. I don't mean to blame, but I don't like it. I don't like men in general; I like women—why was not the world made all women—*can* there not be strength without losing delicacy . . . I did hardly know that good men were so rough and coarse."

NOTES TO PAGES 9–16

26. Houghton, *Revaluation,* p. 228.

27. Walter Houghton, reviewing Chorley's biography in *Victorian Studies,* VI (Sept. 1962), 91–92, wrote "Lady Chorley is not interested in Clough's mind but in his psyche." Richard M. Gollin reviewed it in greater detail and even more severely in "Clough Despite Himself," *Essays in Criticism,* XII (Oct. 1962), 426–435.

28. See n. 21 above and my review of Veyriras's book in *Review of English Studies,* n.s. XVIII (May 1967), 219–222.

29. Timko, *Innocent Victorian,* pp. 87–90, discusses Clough's "concept of liberty" as mediating for him the major social and personal antinomies man faces, but he relies only on one of Clough's latest writings (1853), which is not representative of his earlier thought. As Frank Thistlethwaite has pointed out, moreover, even British Benthamites (far more doctrinaire reformers than Clough), were antipathetic to Lockean concepts of natural rights, tending to believe "in strong government by the enlightened few in the interests of the greatest number, not in limited government and diffused rights." *The Anglo-American Connection in the Early Nineteenth Century* (Phila., 1959), pp. 73–74. Cited hereafter as Thistlethwaite. Clough and his mentors, Arnold and Carlyle, were if anything more certain of this than the Utilitarians, and "Liberty" is not a word he stresses. See Chapters I (n. 14) and II below.

30. *The Balance,* no. 5 (Jan. 30, 1846), p. 34; *S.P.,* p. 211.

31. *P.P.R.,* I, 351.

32. *Poems,* p. 276.

CHAPTER I: THE HIGHER LINE

1. *Correspondence,* I, 283–284.

2. *Poems,* p. 295.

3. Stanley, II, 152.

4. Blanche Athena Clough, *A Memoir of Anne Jemima Clough* (London, 1897), p. 7. Cited hereafter as *Anne Clough.* This work and the "Memoir" in *P.P.R.,* I, 1–10 are the primary sources of Clough family history.

5. Thistlethwaite, pp. 76–77, and Chapters One and Two, *passim.*

6. *Poems,* pp. 85–87.

7. *Anne Clough,* p. 7.

8. *P.P.R.,* I, 8.

9. *Correspondence,* I, 65.

10. "To the energetic members of the Sixth, it was more than a magazine, it was a message." Thomas W. Bamford, *Thomas Arnold* (London, 1960), pp. 104–105. Cited hereafter as Bamford.

11. *Correspondence,* I, 35.

12. *Correspondence,* I, 19–20.

13. *Correspondence,* I, 20.

14. *Correspondence,* I, 29. See also Clough's letter to his sister Anne, expounding Arnold's theory of Church and State, and attacking the "dreadful"

and "shocking" ideas of liberty and independence held in America, where Anne still lived. *Correspondence,* I, 33.

15. *P.P.R.,* I, 12.

16. [Thomas Hughes], "In Memoriam," *Spectator* (Nov. 23, 1861), 1285. Samuel Waddington attributes the anonymous article to Hughes in *Arthur Hugh Clough: A Monograph* (London, 1883), p. 52.

17. The most detailed discussion of the group is the Rev. William Tuckwell's *Pre-Tractarian Oxford: A Reminiscence of the Oriel Noetics* (London, 1909). Cited hereafter as Tuckwell. See also John Henry Newman, *Newman's Apologia Pro Vita Sua. . . ,* ed. Wilfrid Ward (Oxford, 1913), pp. 114–116. Cited hereafter as *Apologia.* On Whately, see E. Jane Whately, *Life and Correspondence of Richard Whately* (London, 1875).

18. *Apologia,* pp. 496–497.

19. For the members of the Noetic party, see Francis Warre Cornish, *The English Church in the Nineteenth Century* (London, 1910), 188–189 (Cited hereafter as Cornish); Tuckwell, vii; and L. E. Elliott-Binns, *Religion in the Victorian Era* (London, 1936), p. 48. Cited hereafter as Elliott-Binns. There is slight disagreement on the identity of minor members.

20. Tuckwell, p. 59.

21. *Apologia,* pp. 232, 493, 498–501. A. W. Benn agreed with Newman on the Liberals' importance at Oxford and held that they constituted the mainstream of Anglican thought. Alfred William Benn, *The History of English Rationalism in the Nineteenth Century* (London, 1906), II, 81–82. Cited hereafter as Benn.

22. According to one source, Newman's use of Butler caused the latter to be banished from the Oxford syllabus in 1845 when Newman was converted. *Encyclopedia of Religion and Ethics,* ed. James Hastings (Edinburgh, 1908–1926), III, 50. Cited hereafter as *Encyclopedia of Religion.* Ernest C. Mossner, however, in *Bishop Butler and The Age of Reason* (New York, 1936), p. 219, says that Butler was dropped "around 1860" at the instigation of Mark Pattison and others. The full title of Butler's most influential work is *The Analogy of Religion, Natural and Revealed, to the Constitution and Course of Nature* (Oxford, 1849). Cited hereafter as *Analogy.* He was also the author of *Fifteen Sermons.* Arnold set even schoolboys to reading Butler, as Clough's Rugby Notebooks show, and Clough was also assigned Butler's sermons at Balliol in Lent term (January–April), 1840. Duff MSS and the Balliol College Examination Register, cited hereafter as B.C.E.R.

23. *Analogy,* p. 183.

24. Benn, I, Chs. VII–IX *et passim;* Cornish, I, 186.

25. Stanley, II, 51–52.

26. *Apologia,* p. 117.

27. Stanley, I, 182.

28. Stanley, I, 259.

29. Stanley, I, 243.

30. Basil Willey, *Nineteenth Century Studies: Coleridge to Matthew Arnold* (New York, 1966), p. 53ff. Cited hereafter as Willey.

31. Stanley, I, 259–267, 357. Many of Arnold's most radical proposals were contained in his early "Letters to the *Sheffield Courant,*" (title supplied

by Stanley), especially Nos. I, III, and XII. Cited hereafter as "Letters to the *Courant.*" His advice to young clergymen is in *Christian Life* . . . *Sermons* (London, 1878), III, xiii–xiv.

32. "Letters to the *Courant,*" No. XI, p. 30, and *Principles of Church Reform* (London, 1833), p. 7. Cited hereafter as *Principles.*

33. Stanley, I, 257.

34. Lytton Strachey, *Eminent Victorians* (New York, 1963), pp. 197–231. "Skilful and very readable . . . falsification," in Willey's words (p. 51).

35. Oriel College MSS Letters, II, 199.

36. John Henry Newman, *Loss and Gain* (London, 1848), pp. 20–21. "To put up images in England in order to create the religious feeling is like dancing to create music . . . Shaw, Turner, and Brown . . . pupils of Dr. Gloucester—you know whom I mean— . . . tell us that we ought to put up crucifixes by the wayside, in order to excite religious feeling." See also Stanley, II, 384.

37. Stanley, II, 98–99, 35.

38. Stanley, I, 20.

39. James Martineau, *Essays, Reviews, and Addresses,* I. Cited by F. J. Woodward, p. 2.

40. Benn, I, 324–325.

41. Bamford, p. 60.

42. Stanley, I, 258–259, 266.

43. See *Correspondence,* I, 33, in which Clough writes his sister a homily on America's barbaric notions of independence vs. the ideal "Christian State." For the references to democracy and Horne Tooke see Stanley, *Arnold,* I, 53, 102. For one of his comments on independence, see *Sermons,* III, 213: "The feeling of independence is . . . a wish . . . in which there is nothing at all noble or admirable, except in the face of the fear of danger."

44. Eugene L. Williamson, Jr., *The Liberalism of Thomas Arnold* (University, Ala., 1964), p. 20. Cited hereafter as Williamson.

45. F. J. Woodward, p. 6.

46. [William George Ward], "Arnold's Sermons," *The British Critic* . . . , XXX (Oct. 1841), 304.

47. *P.P.R.,* I, 294. In *S.P.,* p. 278, a corruption gives the penultimate "they" as "to." Cf. Bodleian MS, Misc. d. 512, fols. 24–38; 41–46.

48. Stanley, I, 186.

49. "The Oxford Malignants and Dr. Hampden," *Edinburgh Review,* LXIII (April 1836), 234.

50. Stanley, II, 42.

51. *Principles,* p. 85.

52. Thomas Arnold, *History of Rome* (London, 1838–43), I, xii; Stanley, II, 57.

53. *Introductory Lectures on Modern History,* p. 62. Cited by Woodward, p. 7.

54. H. W. C. Davis, *et al., A History of Balliol College,* rev. ed. (Oxford, 1963), p. 150. Cited hereafter as Davis (1963).

55. H. W. C. Davis, *Balliol College* (London, 1899), p. 205. Cited hereafter as Davis (1899).

56. There were thirteen fellows, including the Master, and sixty-five students living in college in 1837, although during the four-year period there were about one hundred and twenty individuals in residence. *The Oxford University Calendar* (Oxford, 1837), pp. 187–193.

57. There were over forty boys in the school's fourth form, the school's largest, "too large for any one man to attend to properly." Thomas Hughes, *Tom Brown's Schooldays* (Cambridge, 1857), pp. 177 and 179.

58. Davis (1963), pp. 182–183, 185.

59. Davis (1899), pp. 184 and 203; Wilfrid Ward, *William George Ward and the Oxford Movement* (London, 1889), p. 36. Cited hereafter as Wilfrid Ward.

60. Benjamin Jowett, cited by Wilfrid Ward, *Apologia,* p. 437.

61. See Appendix A for a full list of the essays, the tutors who heard them, dates, etc. The essays are contained in three notebooks in the Bodleian Library, MS Eng. Misc. d. 513–515.

62. Davis (1963), p. 184.

63. Wilfrid Ward, pp. 118–119.

64. *DNB, s.v.* Tait, Archibald.

65. Wilfrid Ward, pp. 429–430; and *Oxford University Calendar* (Oxford, 1838), p. 179.

66. William Tuckwell, "Reminiscences of Oxford: *Addendula Quaedam,*" *The Oxford Magazine* (May 24, 1905), p. 339.

67. *Correspondence,* I, 67.

68. For Jenkyns's comment, see the title of Essay 23 (Appendix A): "From an Examination of the First Book of Aristotle's Politics Point Out the Imperfect View of Society Taken by the Wisest of the Greeks." The B.C.E.R. shows that Clough read Aristotle in eight out of his twelve terms, while Plato was omitted entirely from the syllabus (in fact he had read the *Ethics* twice over). For Clough's private reading of Plato, see *Correspondence,* I, 91. "Very little was known of Plato," wrote Jowett, "The philosophy of that day was contained in Aristotle's *Ethics* and *Rhetoric* and Butler's *Analogy* and *Sermons* . . . There was very little true interpretation of any book in those days. Hampden alone was a real Aristotelian scholar. For political economy, for Locke, and for utilitarian philosophy a supreme dislike and contempt was entertained. Coleridge and even Wordsworth were also regarded with suspicion, as in the tendency of their writings likely to be adverse rather than favorable to the Tractarian movement." Wilfrid Ward, p. 432.

69. Wilfrid Ward, pp. 102–103.

70. For Clough, see B.C.E.R., Michaelmas 1838 through Lent term, 1841; for Jowett, Easter term, 1837; for Arnold, Lent 1842 through Michaelmas term, 1843.

71. *Correspondence,* I, 234.

72. I found these in the course of my researches. Both are edited and appear in Appendix B. The first, or 1839 attempt, was published as " 'Salsette and Elephanta': An Unpublished Poem by Clough," *Review of English Studies,* n.s. XX (Aug. 1969), 284–305. For Clough's references to this poem, see *Correspondence,* I, 90, and 102. Reference to the Hertford Latin prize is made in *Correspondence,* I, 68. For the Powell prize, see B.C.E.R., *passim.*

73. See Appendix A for Jenkyns's comments.

74. *The Letters of Matthew Arnold to Arthur Hugh Clough,* ed. H. F. Lowry (London, 1932), p. 66. Cited hereafter as *Arnold-Clough Letters.*
75. F. J. Woodward, pp. 8–19, 127–179; James I. Osborne, *Arthur Hugh Clough* (Boston, 1920), p. 24. Cited hereafter as Osborne. "In Clough Dr. Arnold found a servant ready to subject his own will completely . . . to . . . his master's purposes."
76. An unwritten essay, the tenth, has been assigned a number because a title and space were allotted for it in Clough's composition book; the essays therefore bear the numbers one to thirty-five.
77. *Poems,* p. 45; see also *Correspondence,* I, 102.
78. *Poems,* p. 295.
79. F. J. Woodward takes the standard position, p. 8. Chorley dissents, holding Clough to have been an empiricist, uninterested in metaphysical questions almost from the beginning (pp. 53–54).
80. Stanley, I, 242.
81. The numbers shown in the text were assigned for convenience by me and correspond to entries in Appendix A where the titles and other information about the essays are given.
82. Stanley, I, 315.
83. Henry Mayhew, *London Labour and the London Poor* (London, 1851), I, 40.
84. *Cf.* the intensely personal "Roused by importunate knocks," in which fantasies, "Vain hopes, wild fancies, fitful joys," absorb and lay waste the speaker's time and emotional energies. *Poems,* pp. 30–31.
85. *Correspondence,* I, 88–89.
86. Friedrich von Schlegel, *Essai sur la langue et la philosophie des Indiens,* trans. M. A. Mazure (Paris, 1837); cited hereafter as *Essai. The Philosophy of History,* trans. J. B. Robinson, 2 vols. (London, 1835).
87. Wilfrid Ward, pp. 107–112.
88. Davis (1899), p. 208.
89. *Correspondence,* I, 80–83, 86–88. Mulhauser (*Correspondence,* I, xviii) points out on the basis of the unpublished notebooks in his possession that Clough felt it his "duty" to respond to Ward, and spent an "astonishing" amount of time with him.
90. *Correspondence,* I, 95, 101, *et passim.*
91. Benn, I, 318.
92. "Arnold's Sermons," p. 304.
93. "Arnold's Sermons," p. 318n.
94. [William G. Ward], "Church Authority," *British Critic* . . . XXXIII (Jan. 1843), 213–214.
95. "Arnold's Sermons," pp. 304–306.
96. See n. 93.
97. This *terminus ad quem* is furnished by his reference in a letter of that date to having completed the poem. *Correspondence,* I, 90.
98. "The view of the different Varieties of Indian Religion [was taken] from F. Schlegel on the Language and Wisdom of India, his French translator Mazure . . . " See Appendix B.
99. The availability of Schlegel's *Philosophy of History* at the Bodleian Library is evident from the first two digits of its pressmark, 35.675, which

represent the year of its accession. See G. W. Wheeler, "Bodleian Press Marks is Relation to Classification," *The Bodleian Quarterly Record,* No. 10 (July 31, 1916), p. 291. Among the many ideas about history found both in Schlegel's *Philosophy of History* and Clough's essays are the belief that the art of rhetoric is dangerous to steady government, illustrated with examples taken from classical history (Essay 32 and Schlegel I, 314); that Aristotle's *Ethics* is deficient in not seeking after higher truths (Essays 15 and 23, and Schlegel I, 311); that the early traditions of Roman history are not credible, but valuable as illustrations of a nation's character (Schlegel, I, 321); that inflexible perseverance and fortitude in battle were the great strengths of the Roman character (Schlegel, I, 326–327 and Essay No. 35); and that each conquering nation is providentially overthrown by a worse one (Schlegel, I, 331—Clough seems to have applied this principle to the realm of the development of philosophy in Essay No. 14).

100. See Robinson's introduction, *Philosophy of History,* I, iii–lxvii, and the *Biographisches Wörterbuch Zur Deutschen Geschichte,* eds. H. Rossler and G. Franz (Munich, 1952), s.v. Schlegel, F.

101. *Philosophy of History,* II, 334–335.

102. *Essai,* p. 106.

103. Schlegel, *Philosophy of History,* I, lxxxi–ii, lxxix, lxxxiii–iv.

104. "Philosophy of History," *British Critic,* XXI (Jan. 1837), 140–167, esp. 151–164.

105. Clough addresses Buddhism and describes the lingering elements of truth in some of its idolatrous doctrines:

> And yet, as wilful children, when they roam,
> Turn oft their hesitating glances home,
> As troubled spirits rove at close of day
> Round the loved precincts where they dare not stay,
> So come with all thine idol forms combined
> Strange conscious hauntings of a purer Mind
> And from afar some rays of glory shine,
> And faintly gleams primeval Truth divine.
> ("Salsette and Elephanta,") See Appendix B, lines 147–154.

106. *Poems,* p. 75.

107. E.g. Edouard Guyot, *Essai Sur la Formation Philosophique Du Poète Arthur Hugh Clough: Pragmatisme Et Intellectualisme* (Paris, 1913). Chorley speaks of his being an "empiricist," p. 54.

108. *Poems,* pp. 28–34.

109. *Correspondence,* I, 98, 101.

110. *Correspondence,* I, 203.

111. *Correspondence,* I, 93, 96, 99–100, 106.

112. Thomas Carlyle, *Chartism* (London, 1841), pp. 54, 19–20, 89. Cited hereafter as *Chartism.*

113. Arnold opposed slavery, but believed that "distinctions of moral breed are . . . natural and . . . just"; and therefore that citizenship should be denied to convicts or even convicts' children in New Zealand. Stanley, II, 46.

CHAPTER II: CITOYEN CLOUGH

1. *Correspondence,* I, 130.
2. Essay No. 13.
3. John Morley, *The Life of William Ewart Gladstone* (London, 1903), I, 334. Cited hereafter as Morley.
4. *Correspondence,* I, 218.
5. *Correspondence,* I, 216.
6. R. W. Church, "Arthur Hugh Clough," *The Christian Remembrancer* (January 1863), p. 67. Cited hereafter as Church.
7. In 1848, Clough's *Bothie* was called "communistic"—*Correspondence,* I, 240. The unnamed assailant was a Tractarian don by the name of Shadforth, described by Tom Arnold as a "dear man" but very conservative; Shadforth also praised a Victorian epic poem as being "the equal of *Paradise Lost* as poetry, and *much more orthodox!*" Thomas Arnold, "Arthur Hugh Clough: A Sketch," *Nineteenth Century,* No. 251 (Jan. 1898), 109–110; and *Passages in a Wandering Life* (London, 1900), p. 149. Cited hereafter as *Passages.* For Bonamy Price's inferences, see Bodleian MS. Eng. Lett. C. 190, fols. 109–116 and the discussion below. See Osborne, pp. 65ff. for the view of Clough as a victim of Carlyle's ideas.
8. *Correspondence,* I, 116.
9. His income may have been slightly more, as he had probably saved something from his summer tutoring, and he continued to hold his £60 exhibition until 1843. *Correspondence,* I, 104, 112, 114.
10. Waldo Hilary Dunn, *James Anthony Froude* (Oxford, 1961), I, 95. Cited hereafter as Dunn.
11. *Correspondence,* I, 123.
12. *Dictionary of Greek and Roman Biography and Mythology,* ed. William Smith, 3 vols. (London, 1844–49). See Richard M. Gollin, Walter E. Houghton, and Michael Timko, *Arthur Hugh Clough: A Descriptive Catalogue* (New York 1967), p. 47. Cited hereafter as Gollin, *Catalogue.*
13. *Correspondence,* I, 125.
14. *Oxford University Calendar* (Oxford, 1844), pp. 250–251.
15. *Oxford University Calendar* (Oxford, 1848), p. 269.
16. *Oxford University Commission. Report of Her Majesty's Commissioners Appointed to Inquire Into the State, Discipline, Studies, and Revenues of the University and Colleges of Oxford. Appendix and Evidence* (London, 1852). Cited hereafter as *O. U. Commission Report.* The life of a less successful coach, however, could be a straitened one.
17. *Correspondence,* I, 135.
18. *O. U. Commission Report,* p. 33.
19. *The Prime Minister* (London, 1961), p. 17. Clough helped support his mother, and this of course was a drain on his income.
20. Joseph Arch, *Free Trade Versus Protection* (Coventry and London, 1884), Preface, Ch. X. Cited by Herman Ausubel, *The Late Victorians: A Short History* (New York, 1955), p. 110.

21. Crane Brinton, *English Political Thought in the Nineteenth Century* (London, 1933), p. 87.

22. Asa Briggs, *The Age of Improvement: 1783–1867,* 2nd ed. (London, 1960), pp. 302–306. Cited hereafter as Briggs.

23. Elie Halévy, *A History of the English People in the Nineteenth Century, IV: 1841–1895,* trans. E. I. Watkin (London, 1961), pp. 12ff. Cited hereafter as Halévy.

24. John L. and Barbara Hammond, *The Bleak Age,* rev. ed. (West Drayton, 1947), p. 120. Cited hereafter as Hammonds.

25. *Correspondence,* I, 94; untitled MS notebook of Anne Clough for 1839–1845, Duff MSS.

26. Halévy, p. 30.

27. S. Maccoby, *English Radicalism: 1832–1852* (London, 1935), p. 442.

28. *English Historical Documents XII (1): 1833–1874,* ed. G. M. Young and W. D. Handcock (London, 1956), pp. 834–835.

29. John Stuart Mill, *Political Economy* (London, 1848), I, 129–130.

30. Ernest Llewellyn Woodward, *The Age of Reform: 1815–1870,* 2nd ed. (Oxford, 1962), pp. 448ff. Cited hereafter as E. L. Woodward.

31. *The Spectator* (Aug. 8, 1846), p. 757; (Oct. 30, 1847) p. 1044–1045.

32. Lionel Robbins, *The Theory of Economic Policy in English Classical Political Economy* (London, 1952), pp. 34–67. Cited hereafter as Robbins.

33. E. L. Woodward, p. 16.

34. Morley, I, 102–103.

35. Morley, I, 91–92.

36. Torben Christensen, *Origin and History of Christian Socialism: 1848–1854* (Copenhagen, 1962), pp. 71ff. Cited hereafter as Christensen. K. B. Smellie quotes Macaulay in *A Hundred Years of English Government,* 2nd ed. (London, 1950), p. 37.

37. Halévy, p. 118.

38. E. L. Woodward, p. 447.

39. David Cecil, *Lord M: Or the Later Life of Lord Melbourne* (London, 1954), p. 253.

40. Young, *English Historical Documents,* pp. 132, 140–141.

41. G. M. Young, ed., *Early Victorian England: 1830–1865* (Oxford, 1934), I, 131–138.

42. Briggs, p. 304.

43. E. G. Sandford, ed., *Memoirs of Archbishop Temple by Seven Friends* (London, 1906), I, 82.

44. See Disraeli's *Coningsby* (London, 1844) and George Eliot's *Felix Holt the Radical* (London, 1866).

45. John Stuart Mill, *Autobiography,* ed. R. Howson (New York, 1924), p. 137.

46. *Chartism,* p. 89.

47. *Autobiography,* pp. 150–153.

48. *OED, s.v.* socialism.

49. *Passages,* p. 64.

50. Briggs, p. 311.

51. E. L. Woodward, p. 126.

52. Christensen, p. 104.

53. *Passages,* p. 58.

54. Young, *English Historical Documents,* p. 447.

55. Young, *Early Victorian England,* I, 65, 66.

56. *DNB, s.v.,* Price, Bonamy; and Clough, Bodleian MS Eng. Lett. d. 175, Sept. 23, 1845: "Price . . . is Director of two railways and on the managing committee of at least one more . . . He is sadly railway-bitten I fear."

57. See the report of Gladstone's Select Committee of 1844 on railways, Young, *English Historical Documents,* p. 248.

58. *Correspondence,* I, 130.

59. Morley, I, 329.

60. *Correspondence,* I, 130.

61. *Correspondence,* II, 384–385, 430.

62. Houghton, *Revaluation,* p. 36.

63. *Correspondence,* I, 106.

64. *Correspondence,* I, 96.

65. Veyriras, p. 141.

66. Chorley, p. 134, quoting John Holloway, *The Victorian Sage* (London, 1953), p. 23. Cited hereafter as Holloway.

67. Review of a Book on Progress. Bodleian MS Eng. Misc. d.512, fols. 136–139.

68. *Chartism,* p. 53.

69. Thomas Carlyle, *Past and Present,* ed. H. D. Traill, Centenary edn., *Works,* 30 vols. (New York, 1896–1901), X, 215.

70. See Chapter I above.

71. *Cf.* Louis Cazamian, *Carlyle,* trans. E. K. Brown (New York, 1932), pp. 169–180. Cited hereafter as Cazamian.

72. Letter of Parepidemus; see below, Chapter V, n. 35.

73. *Correspondence,* I, 140.

74. *Sator Resartus,* Ed. de luxe (Boston, 1884), I, 158–160.

75. *Correspondence,* I, 141.

76. *Poems,* p. 34; and see n. 67.

77. The full name of the organization was the Oxford Society for the Suppression of Mendicity and Relief of Distressed Travellers. The following citations from its annual reports will use the abbreviation *O.S.S.M.*

78. *O.S.S.M.,* 1841–1848.

79. Tuckwell, *Pre-Tractarian Oxford,* p. 46.

80. *O.S.S.M.,* 1837–1840, 1831.

81. *O.S.S.M.,* 1844, p. 6.

82. *Correspondence,* I, 127.

83. *Memorials of William Charles Lake, Dean of Durham: 1869–1894,* ed. Katharine Lake (London, 1901), p. 38.

84. John Duke, Lord Coleridge, *Life and Correspondence,* ed. E. H. Coleridge (New York, 1904), I, 76–77.

85. "Your sanguine friend still puts his trust in master manufacturers, as in those olden days when the face of Fortescue shone triumph in the Decade"; Clough about himself to Tom Arnold, 1849; *Correspondence,* I, 280, 243.

86. *DNB, s.v.* Fortescue, Chichester.

87. *DNB, s.v.,* Conington, John. For his secretaryship of the Decade, see "Memoir," *P.P.R.,* I, 31. H. J. Smith in his "Memoir" sees Conington's early politics as liberal rather than radical. He may be right, or he may have retouched his portrait for reasons similar to Mrs. Clough's in view of Conington's later standing. *Miscellaneous Writings of John Conington . . . with a Memoir,* ed. J. A. Symonds, 2 vols. (London, 1872).

88. *P.P.R.,* I, 25, 31.

89. The record shows that Clough spoke on at least nine occasions at the Decade; probably, since the records are not complete, he was more active than this. Tom Arnold, *Passages,* p. 59; *P.P.R.,* I, 25–32.

90. *P.P.R.,* I, 31.

91. Morley, I, 329, 334, 335.

92. E. L. Woodward, 153–155.

93. *Spectator* (March 6, 1847), p. 217.

94. *Passages,* p. 59.

95. *Correspondence,* I, 126–127.

96. *Chartism,* pp. 52, 92, 113, *et passim.*

97. *P.P.R.,* I, 31.

98. *Correspondence,* I, 243.

99. *Political Economy,* I, 284–285.

100. *Prospective Review,* IV (1848), 460.

101. *The Lowell Offering: Written, Edited and Published by Female Operatives Employed in the Mills,* IV (1844), 282.

102. *Correspondence,* I, 130.

103. Thistlethwaite, p. 40.

104. "Vulgar" was the term that Arnold and *The Spectator* alike applied to American representatives abroad; G. S. Venables, leader-writer for *The Times* knew, sight unseen, that America "would not be a country for a gentleman and I for one would be quite a stranger in it." *Arnold-Clough Letters,* pp. 71, 66; *The Spectator* (April 4, 1846), p. 326; and Henry M. Pelling, *American and the British Left,* p. 3.

105. *Correspondence,* I, 167.

106. *The Balance,* No. 1 (Jan. 2, 1846), 1.

107. The column ceased to be printed in April; the last issue was that of May 15, 1846. With a proto-Alger ethic, a typical column tells the story of the success through industry and thrift of a poor lad who is revealed as Benjamin Franklin only in the last sentence.

108. Emery Neff, *Carlyle and Mill: An Introduction to Victorian Thought,* 2nd ed. (New York, 1926), pp. 25, 41.

109. No. 4 (Jan. 23, 1846) p. 26; *S.P.,* pp. 208–210.

110. Trawick believes it is "difficult to ascertain" whether Clough wrote the passage of ninety-three words in which this quotation appears, and relegates it to a footnote (*S.P.* p. 343, n. 9) because it appears out of context between "my-" and "self" in the text. The ideas expressed in this crux are important in Clough's thought, however, and the problem deserves further study. Trawick himself grants that the passage is "obviously relevant to the topic," the style is clearly like Clough's, and the prima facie evidence is that it was written by Clough but marred by a typographical error.

I think the crux may be resolved if we accept the conjecture that the excluded ninety-three words were intended as an insertion by Clough, probably meant as a penultimate paragraph preceding the one which begins "With regard." The insertion's lacking most of a final sentence or sentences may be explained by positing that the printer received the insertion on a separate piece of paper whose last lines were illegible, written overleaf, or in some way less accessible to him. Working in haste and not knowing, because of unclear instructions, where to insert the new material, he followed only roughly a mark, perhaps hastily drawn, and instead of placing the addition correctly as a separate paragraph above the first line of the last paragraph he began it after setting that first line. He then set as much of the inserted material as he could read and returned to the original text without bothering to check for coherency.

This theory of an insertion also explains why, as Trawick notes, "the remainder of the letter reads smoothly" without these ninety-three words: they were composed not as a closing paragraph but to elaborate the point Clough makes in the preceding paragraph about the "spiritual welfare" of the people. The emended text, missing the lost lines at the end of the insertion, would read: "Political economy has for its legitimate object the lawful increase of wealth and national welfare; and I must rate very low the intellect or knowledge of any man, who is not aware that physical well-being, domestic comfort, such an exemption from the miseries and moral degradation of want as shall give a man respect in his own eyes, and confidence in the laws, must be the basis of national morality. Improvement in these important points is the end of political economy, and, as such, it is the minister of religion. Doubtless, its conclusions . . .

"With regard to the Corn-laws, it may very well be (for myself I believe it is so) that the reasons for the repeal, the evils to be escaped, and the benefits to be hoped for are as much social as economical. But social changes of some kind assuredly there will be; nor will they, of course, be unmixedly either good or evil. It is but prudence to think beforehand what they will be on either side, and seek to be prepared to avail ourselves of the good, and provide against the evil."

111. *The Balance*, No. 5 (Jan. 30, 1846), p. 34. *S.P.*, pp. 211–213.

112. Mill wrote in *Political Economy*, I, 284, that competition had been overrated as being the sole principle of political economy because only on its basis "has political economy any pretension to the character of a science."

113. *Essays on Some Unsettled Questions of Political Economy* (London, 1844), pp. 123–125. Cited hereafter as Mill, *Essays*.

114. *Correspondence*, I, 126: "We have all been reading also a grand new philosophy-book, Mill on Logic—very well written at any rate, and 'stringent' if not sound."

115. *Cf.* Carlyle, "Mirabeau," *Works*, XXVIII, 471.

116. Bagehot, "Mr. Clough's Poems," 325–326. Cited hereafter as "Mr. Clough's Poems."

117. Mill, *Essays*, pp. 48–49.

118. Benjamin Disraeli, *Sybil* (Oxford, 1925), p. 360.

119. *The Balance*, No. 7 (Feb. 13, 1846), p. 50. *S.P.*, pp. 217–221.

120. Young, *English Historical Documents,* pp. 207–209.
121. *The Balance,* No. 10 (Mar. 6, 1846), p. 77. *S.P.,* pp. 221–223.
122. *The Balance,* No. 12 (Mar. 20, 1846), pp. 93–94. *S.P.,* pp. 223–225.
123. *Political Economy,* I, 285.
124. E. L. Woodward, p. 16.
125. "Jacob," *Poems,* p. 85.
126. Essay, No. 15: "Examine How Far Aristotle's View of the Virtues in his Fourth Book of Ethics is Deficient;" MS Eng. Misc. d.513.
127. Robbins, p. 159.
128. *Autobiography,* p. 162.
129. Arthur Hugh Clough, *A Consideration of Objections Against the Retrenchment Association* (Oxford, 1847), p. 12; cited hereafter as *Retrenchment; S.P.,* 226–242.
130. Church, p. 67.
131. Grosskurth, pp. 132–133.
132. Gollin, *Catalogue,* p. 49.
133. The nature of the writing paper and the references to the cholera, which was endemic from 1847 to 1849, as well as the quality of the handwriting, suggest the date of c. 1847 for the MS. The paper used in this MS (Eng. Misc. d.512, fols. 163–164) is exactly similar to, and the writing and ink are also like those of another "Right of Property" MS (Eng. Misc. d.512, fols. 134–135), which has been dated (*Catalogue,* p. 49) "1847?" No other example of this paper is to be found among the Clough MSS in the Bodleian collection. The two sheets are folios which when open measure 8¾" × 14¼". The maker's mark, ⁹⁄₁₆" in diameter, is an embossed crown set in circles of lines and dots; above and below the crown are, respectively, the words IMPERIAL and SUPERFINE. The paper is lightweight, gray, without chain-lines, and is watermarked with three feathers. For the anticipation of the cholera, see *The Spectator,* (Aug. 8, 1846) p. 757. See also Young, *English Historical Documents,* 751, 775.
134. *Correspondence,* I, 203.
135. *Poems,* p. 269.
136. *Correspondence,* I, 301. For a view of this pamphlet as a mainly Carlylean work, see Timko, pp. 73–76.
137. Cecil Woodham-Smith, *The Great Hunger: Ireland 1845–1849* (London, 1962), p. 410. Cited hereafter as Woodham-Smith.
138. When Clough, for example, wrote to Arnold's old friend, Whately, now Archbishop of Dublin, for information about conditions in Ireland, the latter replied that he could understand England's distrust of reports "from a land so infested with falsehood," although the distress was real and great. *Correspondence,* I, 175.
139. Woodham-Smith, pp. 162–163.
140. Woodham-Smith, pp. 410–411.
141. *Correspondence,* II, 389.
142. John Holloway, p. 27.
143. *Retrenchment,* pp. 18, 10. Subsequent references to this pamphlet will be included in the text.
144. Holloway, pp. 3, 9.

145. Cazamian, pp. 197–209.
146. *Works,* X, 212.
147. *Ibid.*
148. See Timko, *Innocent Victorian,* pp. 73–76 for a somewhat different view.
149. Morley, I, 91.
150. Young, *English Historical Documents,* p. 448.
151. See n. 122.
152. MS. Eng. Lett. c. 190, fols. 109–116. Subsequent leaf numbers will be included in the text.
153. "My dear Clough: Stanley sent me your pamphlet—you should have done so yourself." *Ibid.,* fol. 109.
154. *Retrenchment,* p. 12.
155. MS. Eng. Lett. c. 190, fol. 134.
156. MS. Eng. Lett. c. 190, fol. 135.

CHAPTER III: THE MORALS OF INTELLECT

1. Chorley, p. 352 and Chapter XIII, *passim.* Clough's life, she believes, was dominated by an unresolved Oedipal conflict (using Jungian terminology, she does not employ this name) which gave him a pervasive sense of guilt. The source of this guilt lay "in the boy child's longing with all the force of his hidden instinctive drives for complete and exclusive possession of his mother. And this longing may have become all the more fearful for him because his father stood as a figure of love." Later Lady Chorley implies that Clough suffered from latent homosexuality; again she does not use the words, but this is clearly the import when she writes that he did not dare to feel the aggressive *animus* of love, but could imagine without danger "the receptive role of the *anima*" (p. 354). Elsewhere she stresses the description of him looking upon Dr. Arnold with "an almost feminine tenderness," evidently also to support this.
2. A. H. Clough, *The Spectator,* No. 1010 (Nov. 6, 1847), p. 1066.
3. HCL, bMS. Eng. 1036 (5), *P.P.R.,* I, 351.
4. See n. 2.
5. Dunn, I, 98.
6. *Correspondence,* I, 218, 219.
7. W[illiam] R[eginald] Ward, *Victorian Oxford* (London, 1965), p. 80. Cited hereafter as W. R. Ward, *Victorian Oxford.*
8. Alfred Barry, D. D., *The Teacher's Prayer Book, Being The Book Of Common Prayer, With Introduction, Analyses, Notes And A Commentary Upon the Psalter.* (London [n.d.]), pp. 280 a–280 l. Cited hereafter as Barry.
9. The Anabaptists' doctrine of communal property, for example, is singled out for condemnation in Article 38. Moreover, in Barry's view, Articles 9–18, which define the Church's position relative to Calvinistic and Lutheran views, especially those on free will, justification by works, and predestination, were "unsatisfactory to the Calvinistic party." Antipathy to the Roman Catholic Church is most evident in Articles 19–36, dealing with the Church and the

sacraments, and containing "from the nature of the case . . . the strongest protests against the usurpations of Rome." Article 31, for instance, denies the validity of the propitiatory mass celebrated by Roman Catholics, calling such a mass "blasphemous fable and dangerous deceit." Barry, 280 a–k.

10. *Apologia,* pp. 226–232.

11. Morley, I, 315.

12. In Trollope, for example, doctors are barely admitted to county society, and lawyers scarcely ever appear except peripherally.

13. "Guy's Hospital Maurice" was Frederick D. Maurice, who had been converted to Anglicanism from Unitarianism, and who had published in 1834 a pamphlet called *Subscription No Bondage.* He was to be one of the founders of Christian Socialism, but at the time was Chaplain at Guy's Hospital.

14. *Correspondence,* I, 124.

15. W. R. Ward, *Victorian Oxford,* pp. 89–90, 120–122, and Chapters V–VI, *passim.*

16. It lies at the heart, too, of the series of proceedings against Hampden, Newman, Pusey, Maurice, and Colenso which, Gladstone's biographer has written, "constitute a chapter of extraordinary importance in the general history of English toleration." Morley, I, 316.

17. "To combine is good" Clough wrote in a letter to *The Spectator,* on university reform quoted further below. "To separate is good also." The idea of the new university should not be utterly to divorce moral and intellectual training, but to free it from "the timid intolerance of a worn-out dogmatism." The older universities needed from the nation at large "assistance or even compulsion to self-reform." *The Spectator,* No. 1012 (Nov. 20, 1847), 1118.

18. *Correspondence,* I, 140.

19. *Correspondence,* II, 393.

20. *Correspondence,* I, 140.

21. W. R. Ward, *Victorian Oxford,* pp. 128–129, quoting the *Christian Observer* and the liberal, Goldwin Smith.

22. David Friedrich Strauss, *Das Leben Jesu Kritisch bearbeitet,* 2 vols. (Tubingen, 1835–1836).

23. Joseph Blanco White, *The Life of the Rev. Joseph Blanco White,* ed. J. H. Thom, 3 vols. (London, 1845). Cited hereafter as White.

24. As early as 1839 he had been reading Goethe and Schiller in the original (*Correspondence,* I, 98).

25. Duff MSS No. XIX. Subsequent quotations from Anne's journals refer to this MS.

26. David Friedrich Strauss, *The Life of Jesus: Critically Examined* (London, 1846), III, 426.

27. *Correspondence,* I, 155.

28. Gladstone and Mozley attacked the book in leading journals, and the *Prospective Review,* the leading Unitarian organ, defended it. Whately was so upset by the publicity given the free-thinking views of his former protégé that he told people he had proof that White was mad, but Clough remarked of Whately at the time that "one seldom need believe that swearing old

Arch-bishop." See *Correspondence,* I, 155 and 158, and J. Estlin Carpenter, *James Martineau: Theologian and Teacher* (London, 1905), pp. 162–163. Cited hereafter as Carpenter.

29. White, I, 493.

30. White, II, 71–86.

31. *Correspondence,* I, 155.

32. It was at the house of the Unitarian Samuel Bulley (presumably Clough's "seul ami Unitarien") that Emerson first met Clough's sister and had Clough's pamphlet read to him. And it was under Emerson's aegis that Clough came to America in 1852. Clough's wife (whom he met through her cousin Florence Nightingale and R. Monckton Milnes) was also a Unitarian, and came from one of the sect's leading families. Cecil Woodham-Smith, *Florence Nightingale* (London, 1950), p. 109.

33. See James Drummond and C. B. Upton, *The Life and Letters of James Martineau,* 2 vols. (London, 1902); cited hereafter as Drummond.

34. *Correspondence,* I, 168.

35. *Correspondence,* I, 234.

36. Theodore Parker, *Discourse of Matters Pertaining to Religion* (Boston 1842).

37. Drummond, I, 176.

38. "Christian Fellowship," *The Prospective Review,* I (No. 3, 1845), 395, 400.

39. Roma Notebook. Balliol College MS 441 (α), fols. 3^v–4^v. Subsequent quotations from this piece of writing all refer to this MS.

40. Ralph Waldo Emerson, "Harvard Divinity School," *The Works of Ralph Waldo Emerson,* ed. James E. Cabot, 14 vols. (Boston, 1883–1887), I, 142. Cited hereafter as *Works.*

41. Here Clough refers to the article cited in n. 38.

42. A draft of a letter dated October 30th [1850] [Mulhauser and watermark of 1850] for example, complains that members of the Council had been questioning the servants behind Clough's back. Bodleian MS. Eng. Lett. d.176, fols. 200–207.

43. Bodleian MS. Eng. Poet. d.140, fols. 21^v–12^v reversed. "Notes on the Religious Tradition," *S.P.,* pp. 289–293.

44. *Correspondence,* I, 186.

45. R. W. Emerson, *Essays With a Preface By Thomas Carlyle* (London, 1841).

46. Duff MSS, No. XIX.

47. *Correspondence,* I, 186.

48. Townsend Scudder, *The Lonely Wayfaring Man: Emerson and Some Englishmen* (London, 1936). Cited hereafter as Scudder. R. L. Rusk, *The Life of Ralph Waldo Emerson* (New York, 1949). Cited hereafter as Rusk.

49. The exception is Veyriras (pp. 206–212). He, however, believes that their relationship ended, so far as influence goes, in a "spiritual impasse" and on an essentially negative note only some three months after their first meeting. He bases this view on Clough's journal entry (*Arnold-Clough Letters,* p. 83) that although Emerson's talk was healing it was not the same as his own sense of God's immanence, the "Power whose name is Panacea . . .

who itself is Prescription and Recovery." Some readers, however, might find this passage itself so notably Emersonian both in its individualistic and intuitional premises and in its language as to furnish evidence for the opposite conclusion. I would interpret Clough's remarks simply as an eminently sane response to protracted contact, with its innate temptations to dependency, and his balanced tone as the best guarantee of future stability in their friendship. If Clough had in fact turned to Emerson as a surrogate for God or a Universal "Panacea," the "spiritual impasse" M. Veyriras refers to would indeed have occurred, and rapidly.

50. Veyriras, pp. 206–207.

51. Scudder, p. 61.

52. Scudder, pp. 72–73.

53. "Miracle . . . is Monster." "Harvard Divinity School," *Works,* I, 128. Rusk, pp. 160–165.

54. Strauss, "Concluding Dissertation," III, 396–446, esp. pp. 396 and 445–446.

55. "The Over-Soul," *Works,* II, 265.

56. "Spiritual Laws," *Works,* II, 138, 136, 132.

57. "Compensation," *Works,* II, 99.

58. Scudder, p. 97.

59. "Self-Reliance," *Works,* II, 57, 55; "The Over-Soul," *Works,* II, 277.

60. "The Over-Soul," *Works,* II, 267, 265–266.

61. "Self-Reliance," *Works,* II, 51–52, 55.

62. "The Over-Soul," *Works,* II, 271.

63. "Self-Reliance," *Works,* II, 51–52.

64. Dunn, I, 99.

65. Ralph Waldo Emerson, *Journals of Ralph Waldo Emerson* (Boston 1909–1914), VII, 387 n. Cited hereafter as *Journals.*

66. Moncure Daniel Conway, *Autobiography, Memories and Experiences,* 2 vols. (New York, 1904), I, 109–110.

67. Frank T. Thompson, "Emerson and Carlyle," *Studies in Philology,* XXIV (1927), 438–453; René Wellek, *Confrontations* (Princeton, 1965), pp. 187–212; Henry A. Pochmann, *Culture in America* (Madison, 1947), 153–207, cited hereafter as Pochmann; Arthur I. Ladu, "Emerson: Whig or Democrat," *New England Quarterly,* XII (Sept. 1940), 419–441.

68. Dunn, I, 99.

69. "Self-Reliance," *Works,* II, 50, 60, 51–52.

70. *Correspondence,* I, 233, 316.

71. Pochmann, pp. 156–157.

72. My researches and Veyriras's, p. 208, are parallel on Clough's use of "History."

73. *P.P.R.,* I, 32.

74. "History," *Works,* II, 41.

75. "History," *Works,* II, 36, 31.

76. *P.P.R.,* I, 26.

77. Tuckwell, *The Oxford Magazine* (June 21, 1905), p. 412. "Tufts" were so called because the gold tassel on their academic caps distinguished them from other students who, as "commoners," were not permitted this dressing up.

78. Sir Edward Conroy's annotations in Balliol College's copy of *The Oxford University and City Guide,* new ed. (Oxford, 1829), pp. 10–12 and 169–186. Conroy was the son of the Irish courtier, Sir John Conroy, whose association with Queen Victoria's mother, the Duchess of Kent, created a scandal.

79. *P.P.R.,* I, 26.

80. "Manners," *Works,* III, 118–119.

81. *P.P.R.,* I, 26.

82. "Manners," *Works,* III, 131, 128.

83. *P.P.R.,* I, 26.

84. *Correspondence,* I, 124.

85. "What right have our MA's to say whether statements x, y, z agree or not with the Articles . . . ? If the Church does not settle it, the University has no business to do so. If you ask who *should* settle it, Price answers the Court of Arches, i.e., Sir Herbert Jenner-Fust and the Privy Council. And if you complain of being referred thither [to a secular body] why then let the necessity for something better declare itself, and force itself on people's minds—and then we shall get something better in the way of ecclesiastical supreme administration established." *Correspondence* (I, 143—December 31, 1844).

86. *Correspondence,* I, 161–165.

87. *Correspondence,* I, 182.

88. "Over-Soul," *Works,* II, 266–267.

89. W. R. Ward, *Victorian Oxford,* p. 133.

90. Bodleian MS Eng. Misc. d.512, fols. 144–145. Gollin, *Catalogue,* p. 56, dates it later, 1853–54.

91. See *The Spectator,* No. 1010 (Nov. 6, 1847), 1066. *Selected Prose* titles the material "Two Letters About Francis W. Newman's *The Soul.*" *The Soul* was not published until two years after these letters appeared in 1847, and they might better be called "Letters to *The Spectator.*" They are printed in *S.P.,* pp. 273–276.

92. *The Times,* 19,631 (Oct. 15, 1847), 3.

93. *The Spectator,* 1008 (Oct. 23, 1847), 1022–23.

94. *Correspondence,* I, 187.

95. *Correspondence,* I, 88–89.

96. *The Spectator,* 1010 (Nov. 6, 1847), 1066. All subsequent quotations from this letter refer to this source.

97. *The Spectator,* 1012 (Nov. 20, 1847), 1118.

98. *Correspondence,* I, 191.

99. *Correspondence,* I, 193, 192–197.

100. *Correspondence,* I, 219.

101. *Correspondence,* I, 248.

102. *Correspondence,* I, 249.

103. "History," *Works,* II, 31.

104. *Correspondence,* I, 249.

105. *Correspondence,* I, 296.

106. *Correspondence,* I, 297.

107. *Correspondence,* I, 290.

108. *Correspondence,* I, 277.

109. *Correspondence,* I, 215–216.

110. *The Letters of Ralph Waldo Emerson,* ed. Ralph L. Rusk (New York, 1939), IV, 48. Cited hereafter as Emerson, *Letters.*

111. "I leave England with an increased respect for the Englishman . . . I forgive him all his pride. My respect is the more generous that I have no sympathy with him, only an admiration.—I have seen . . . persons in England of the American type, and, what is curious, not easily distinguishable from Americans in speech. Do you remember how decisive and unmistakable is the English voice? Yet at Oxford . . . I conversed as with countrymen with young men whom I think I should have met without remark in Boston or Concord . . . Froude . . . and Clough . . . have been valuable to me." Three years earlier John Chapman, the publisher, had proposed to Emerson that he take a part in a transatlantic journal (which without him eventually materialized as the *Prospective Review*) but Emerson had refused. On meeting Froude and Clough, however, the idea began to interest him, and he gave serious thought to joining them in such a venture: "Froude and Clough," he wrote, "would gladly conspire" but he feared America would be apathetic to the idea. *Letters,* IV, 62, 56.

112. Dunn, I, 119.

113. *Journals,* VII, 428, 427.

114. *Journals,* VII, 560.

115. *Journals,* VII, 295–296.

116. They dined together daily, often at midday, and then spent the evenings together. Rusk, *Emerson,* p. 346.

117. Clough attended the meetings of these new clubs (*Correspondence,* I, 213). This is also evident from Emerson's unpublished account books at Harvard which show that he went with Clough to three of them, the Club des Femmes, the Blanqui and Basles Clubs, paying one franc each time. He also borrowed thirty-three francs from Clough, which weighed on his conscience enough to note it three times until it was discharged by John Chapman, the publisher, on June 3, 1848. Houghton MS. Notebook No. 109.

118. *Journals,* VII, 560.

119. *Correspondence,* II, 611, 391, 420.

120. Edward Everett Hale, "James Russell Lowell and His Friends," *The Outlook* (1898), p. 46.

CHAPTER IV: THE WORLD'S ARENA

1. Bodleian MS Eng. Lett. c.190; Feb. 20, 1848, March 26, 1848.

2. François Fejtö, ed., *The Opening of an Era: 1848: An Historical Symposium* (London, 1948). Cited hereafter as Fejtö; the chapter on France, however, is by Georges Bourgin.

3. Fejtö, p. 22.

4. Fejtö, pp. 74, 75.

5. *Cf.* Christensen, pp. 111–113.

6. Fejtö, pp. 35, 86, 89, 90.
7. Fejtö, pp. 90–91, 98–99, 101–106, 110.
8. *Correspondence*, I, 256, 244.
9. *Correspondence*, I, 214.
10. *Correspondence*, I, 213.
11. One hundred and seventy-one newspapers sprang up at one point in the course of a few weeks. Fejtö, pp. 25–31, 96. MS Eng. Lett. c. 190, fol. 236, May 29, 1848.
12. *Correspondence*, I, 206.
13. Fejtö, pp. 87, 89.
14. *Correspondence*, I, 206.
15. *Correspondence*, I, 206–207.
16. "Stooping, I saw through the legs of the people the legs of a body. / You are the first, do you know, to whom I have mentioned the matter." *Poems*, p. 193.
17. *Correspondence*, I, 278.
18. *Correspondence*, I, 207.
19. *Ibid.*
20. *Ibid.*
21. *Correspondence*, I, 208.
22. *Correspondence*, I, 209.
23. *Correspondence*, I, 214.
24. *Ibid.*
25. *Correspondence*, I, 215.
26. *Correspondence*, I, 244.
27. George Macaulay Trevelyan, *Garibaldi's Defense of the Roman Republic, 1848–9* (London, 1949), pp. 16, 51–59, 56n. 3. Cited hereafter as Trevelyan.
28. Rosslyn Wemyss, *Memoirs and Letters of the Right Hon. Sir Robert Morier, G.C.B. From 1826 to 1876* (London, 1916), I, 75–76.
29. Bodleian MS. Eng. Lett. d.176 fols. 81–85.
30. Bodleian MS. *Ibid.* Mill also had been interested in a *métayer* system for the leasing of land.
31. Trevelyan, pp. 72, 86, 106, 113.
32. See n. 29.
33. *Ibid.*
34. *Correspondence*, I, 255, 257, 256, 268.
35. *Correspondence*, I, 257, 252; *Poems*, p. 185.
36. *Correspondence*, I, 315, 280. His Roma Notebook gives evidence of some twelve meetings between them, and a subsequent letter from her, very open and personal in tone, indicates that she hoped for further communication. *Correspondence*, I, 280–282.
37. *Correspondence*, I, 253.
38. *Ibid.*
39. *Correspondence*, I, 256, 252, 261.
40. *Correspondence*, I, 260.
41. *Correspondence*, I, 261.
42. MS. Eng. Lett. e. 77, fol. 123.

43. *Correspondence,* I, 224.
44. *Correspondence,* I, 290.
45. *Correspondence,* I, 141.
46. Letters. Dr. Williams's Library MS., 74.5.8. (Nov. 25, 1848).
47. Clough's friend, J. P. Gell, who had had insuperable difficulties himself in the same sort of work in New Zealand, examined University Hall's statutes for Clough and warned him in advance that the governing Council held all the power. Bodleian MS.; *Correspondence,* I, 288; Chorley, p. 224.
48. Osborne, p. 90.
49. *Correspondence,* I, 282; II, 393.
50. Barish, pp. 169–170, emending *Correspondence,* I, 278.
51. *Correspondence,* I, 312, 217.
52. See Tom Arnold, *Passages,* pp. 149ff, and *New Zealand Letters of Thomas Arnold The Younger,* ed. James Bertram (London & Wellington, 1966), pp. xxixff.
53. *Correspondence,* I, 290.
54. *Correspondence,* I, 279.
55. *Correspondence,* I, 243.
56. *Correspondence,* I, 284.
57. "Epilogue" to *Dipsychus, Poems,* p. 295.
58. Bodleian MS. Eng. Misc. d.512, fols. 24–38, 41–46; *S.P.,* pp. 277–286.
59. "Paper on Religion," Bodleian MS. Eng. Misc. d.512, fols. 39–40; *S.P.,* pp. 287–288; *P.P.R.,* I, 301, at the break to the fifth line from the bottom of p. 302. Now generally regarded as a separate piece, the "Paper on Religion" is conflated in *P.P.R.* and in the MSS with the "Review of Mr. Newman's *The Soul.*" See Gollin, *Catalogue,* p. 54. "Notes on the Religious Tradition" is Bodleian MS. Eng. Poet. d.140, fols. 21^v–12^v reversed; also *S.P.,* pp. 289–293.
60. "Notes on the Religious Tradition"; see n. 59.
61. "Review of Mr. Newman's *The Soul*"; see n. 58.
62. *Ibid.*
63. *Ibid.*
64. *Ibid.*
65. Francis William Newman, *The Soul; Her Sorrows and Her Aspirations: An Essay Towards the Natural History of the Soul, As the True Basis of Theology,* 2nd ed. (London, 1849), p. 148. Cited hereafter as *The Soul.*
66. *The Soul,* pp. 180, 209.
67. "Review of Mr. Newman's *The Soul,*" Bodleian MS.
68. See n. 59.
69. "Review of Mr. Newman's *The Soul,*" Bodleian MS.
70. "Paper on Religion," Bodleian MS.
71. *Ibid.*
72. "Review of Mr. Newman's *The Soul,*" Bodleian MS.
73. "Paper on Religion," Bodleian MS.
74. "Review of Mr. Newman's *The Soul,*" Bodleian MS.
75. See n. 59.
76. Chorley, p. 132.
77. "Notes on the Religious Tradition," Bodleian MS.

78. *Ibid.*

79. *Correspondence,* II, 392.

80. Bodleian MS. Eng. Misc. d.512, fols. 96–117. This title, which has been used by Clough scholars ever since, appears in pencil on the sheet that enfolds this MS. The handwriting is the same as that identified by Norrington in *Poems,* p. 528, as that of Mrs. A. H. Clough, Jr.

"Conversations of the Earth with the Universe" has been dated 1846 by Gollin *et al* (*Catalogue,* p. 48) because in it Clough refers to Neptune having "just" been discovered, as it was in that year. He could, however, have used this phrase for a number of years after so historically significant a discovery, and the paper he used suggests rather that the "Conversations" can be dated rather closely to the period December 1851–January 1852. The paper is identical with some used by Clough for letters in those two months and not, so far as I can determine, at any other time. (MSS Eng. Lett. d.177, fols. 28–37 [Dec. 12, 1851, *Correspondence,* I, 299]; d.177, fols. 37–38 [Jan. 3, 1852, unpub. MS Mulhauser No. 551]; e. 77, fols. 23–34, 35–40, 42–44 [January 1852, unpub. MSS to Blanche Smith]). The paper is in folios, measuring (open) $8^{13}/_{16}'' \times 7^{3}/_{16}''$, of a darkened cream, and bearing rather faint chain lines. All the examples of this paper show precisely the same degree of flexibility and the same texture. This paper also is without either watermark or stationer's imprint, although one or the other of these marks is usually present on this sort of folio stationery as used by Clough. The profoundly questioning tone and the gentle, almost distant satire on the sexes' psychology also suggest a date later than the period of Clough's greatest political activism (1844–1848), and closer to the date of his engagement to Blanche and his less buoyant London years.

81. Bodleian MS. e. 77, fol. 77 (Feb. 1852). For the frequent early misunderstandings that marked the courtship of the lovers, see MSS Eng. Lett. e. 77–81.

82. See n. 80. Subsequent quotations from "Conversations" will refer to this MS source.

83. Bodleian MS. Eng. Misc. d.512, fols. 120–132; *S.P.,* 243–248. The *S.P.* text errs in its title (cf. below and Gollin, p. 50) and in its reading of "homes" for the correct "horses," p. 247, ninth line from the bottom. Compare MS fol. 129^{v}.

84. Bodleian MS. Eng. Misc. d.512, fols. 165–166.

85. Bodleian MS. Eng. Lett. e. 77, fol. 64 (Jan. 21, 1852).

86. Christensen, pp. 71–92.

87. Edward C. Mack and W. H. G. Armytage, *Thomas Hughes* (London, 1952), pp. 56–57.

88. Christensen, pp. 111, 124–131.

89. The journal was published under this title until Dec. 27, 1851, after which Thomas Hughes edited it as *The Journal of Association.*

90. Gollin *et al.,* p. 50, have titled the MS "Letter on Christian Socialism."

91. *Christian Socialist,* I (Nov. 2, 1850), 1.

92. *Christian Socialist,* I (Dec. 2, 1850), 1.

93. See n. 83.

94. Bodleian MS.

95. Bodleian MS.
96. *The Balance* (Feb. 13, 1846), p. 50.
97. "Letter to the *Christian Socialist*," Bodleian MS.
98. *Ibid.*
99. *Ibid.*
100. *Ibid.*
101. *Ibid.*
102. See n. 84.

CHAPTER V: THE HOPEFUL COUNTRY

1. *Correspondence,* I, 299, 301.
2. Bodleian MSS. Eng. Lett. e. 77–78; *Correspondence,* I, 312.
3. *Correspondence,* I, 309, 318, 303, 312.
4. *Correspondence,* I, 315.
5. *Correspondence,* II, 364; I, 316; II, 322, 329.
6. *Cf.* Chorley, pp. 279–290.
7. *Correspondence,* II, 454.
8. *Correspondence,* II, 395, 343, 390, 391.
9. *Correspondence,* II, 420.
10. *Correspondence,* II, 342, 344.
11. *Correspondence,* II, 407.
12. *Correspondence,* II, 380, 337, 364.
13. See n. 15; *Correspondence,* II, 409.
14. "Letters of Parepidemus," Bodleian MS. Eng. Misc. d.512, fols. 48–75; *S.P.,* pp. 172–186, 249–257, 317–323. For the translation of "Parepidemus," see Gollin, *Catalogue,* pp. 53–54.
15. All were printed in *The North American Review,* as "Oxford University Commission," LXXVI (April 1853), 369–396; "Recent Social Theories," and "Recent English Poetry," LXXVII (July 1853), pp. 106–117 and 1–30.
16. *Correspondence,* II, 367. *Plutarch's Lives, the Translation Called Dryden's Corrected and Revised by A. H. Clough,* 5 vols. (Boston, 1857).
17. Bodleian MS. Eng. Misc. d.512, fols. 136–139.
18. *Correspondence,* II, 349. Gollin (*Catalogue,* p. 53) suggests that Clough had already given this lecture in England.
19. "Recent Social Theories," see n. 15; *S.P.,* pp. 258–269.
20. Bodleian MS. Eng. Misc. d.512, fols. 63–64.
21. *Correspondence,* II, 421, 336, 334, 371, 376.
22. Richard Holt Hutton, *Essays in Literary Criticism* (Philadelphia, 1876), p. 158.
23. Arthur Meier Schlesinger, *Political and Social History of the United States: 1829–1925* (New York, 1927), pp. 121–129. Cited hereafter as Schlesinger, Sr.
24. *Correspondence,* II, 334–335.
25. Arthur M. Schlesinger, Jr., *The Age of Jackson* (London, 1946), p. 397 defines Old Hunkers as the conservative wing of the Democratic party who were supposed to "hanker" after office.

26. *Correspondence,* II, 340.
27. *Correspondence,* II, 341.
28. *Correspondence,* II, 356.
29. *Correspondence,* II, 354.
30. Schlesinger, Sr., p. 109.
31. George Ticknor, for example, a distinguished American who had travelled much abroad, tried in 1850 to explain to Prince John, Duke of Saxony, that a recent "piratical expedition" against Cuba had really been an act of private enterprise which the U.S. Government, lacking a secret police, could not forestall, and which had been carried out mostly by foreigners anyway. George Ticknor, *Life, Letters and Journals,* 10th ed. (Boston, 1880), II, 267–268.
32. Schlesinger, Sr., p. 109.
33. *Correspondence,* II, 341.
34. Schlesinger, Sr., p. 139.
35. Bodleian MS. Eng. Misc. d.512, fols. 65–72; *S.P.,* pp. 249–255.
36. *Ibid.*
37. *Ibid.*
38. *Ibid.*
39. *Ibid.*
40. *Ibid.*
41. *Ibid.*
42. *Ibid.*
43. Bodleian MS. Eng. Misc. d.512 fols. 73–75; *S.P.,* pp. 256–257.
44. The quotation from Dante, "Caina attende chi vita ci spense," is from *Inferno,* V, 107.
45. *Correspondence,* II, 415–416.
46. *Correspondence,* II, 389. "Oxford University Commission," *The North American Review,* LXXVI (April 1853), pp. 369–396. Cited hereafter as "O. U. Commission." Only the last four pages of this article have been reprinted in *S.P.*
47. Bodleian MS. Eng. Misc. d.512, fols. 144–145. I would tentatively assign this a somewhat earlier date than the "1853–54" given by Gollin *et al.,* p. 56, although not necessarily as early as the date of 1848 I previously suggested, 1849 or 1850 being possible. It is not likely that Clough would have written the draft of a petition after the Commission had published its findings, or indeed after it had been established. The agitation and drafting of petitions such as these was most vigorous in the two or three years preceding the government's establishment of the Royal Commission in 1850 under various pressures, some of it from friends of Clough. See W. R. Ward, *Victorian Oxford,* pp. 152–153 and Chapter VII *passim.*
48. See n. 16, Chapter II.
49. "O. U. Commission," 392–393.
50. "O. U. Commission," p. 396.
51. *Ibid.*
52. See n. 6. To Lady Chorley's account, however, one must add the evidence of Blanche's reluctance (see e.g., *Correspondence,* II, 425), and of Clough's and her own concern for the delicacy of her feelings (e.g., the

contretemps following her unsanctioned reading of his private papers, and his sense that American society might not do for her. *Correspondence,* II, 350, 402).

53. *Correspondence,* II, 337, 440.

54. "Fragment on America" is Bodleian MS. Eng. Misc. d.512, fols. 173–174. The last quotation is from "Contemporary Literature in America," *Westminster Review* LX (Oct. 1853), 604–605. Clough acknowledges his authorship of this portion of the *Westminster's* survey in *Correspondence,* II, 468, and the brief essay should be added to his canon. It is a much shorter version of his July review of Norton's book (see below and n. 19).

55. *P.P.R.,* I, 41.

56. See n. 15.

57. Bodleian MS. See n. 17.

58 Thistlethwaite, p. 77.

59. [Charles Eliot Norton], *Considerations on Some Recent Social Theories* (Boston, 1853), pp. 26 and 154. Cited hereafter as Norton. For the attribution of the anonymous work to him see *DAB,* and also *Correspondence,* II, 435.

60. Norton, pp. 60, 143, 48.

61. Timko, *Innocent Victorian,* pp. 14, 67–68, 81, 87–90.

62. "Recent Social Theories," 106.

63. Bodleian MS. See Chapter I.

64. "Recent Social Theories," 107.

65. "Recent Social Theories," 108.

66. Bodleian MS., Essay No. 31.

67. *Correspondence,* I, 300.

68. "Recent Social Theories," 110–111.

69. "Recent Social Theories," 111–112.

70. *Poems,* pp. 327–328.

71. "Recent Social Theories," 112.

72. "Recent Social Theories," 115.

73. *The Balance* (Jan. 23, 1846), p. 26.

74. *Apologia,* pp. 491–502, esp. p. 499 item 6.

75. Bodleian MS. See n. 17.

76. "Recent Social Theories," 115.

77. *Correspondence,* I, 256.

78. See n. 3, Chapter III.

79. *Correspondence,* II, 392.

80. "Letters of Parepidemus on Board the 'Canada,'" Bodleian MS. Eng. Misc. d.512, fols. 49–62; *S.P.,* pp. 317–324.

CHAPTER VI: THE BATTLE BY NIGHT

1. *Arnold-Clough Letters,* pp. 95–96.

2. *Arnold-Clough Letters,* p. 96.

3. Fraser Neiman, "The Zeitgeist of Matthew Arnold," *PMLA,* LXXII, 996.

4. Michael Timko, "Corydon Had a Rival," *Victorian Newsletter,* XIX (Spring 1961), 5–11.

5. *Correspondence,* I, 140; *The Balance* (Jan. 23, 1846), p. 26.
6. W. R. Ward, *Victorian Oxford,* p. 133.
7. Matthew Arnold, "Obermann," *Essays in Criticism: Third Series* (Boston, 1910), pp. 115–116. Cited hereafter as "Obermann."
8. "Obermann," p. 132.
9. Van Wyck Brooks, *The Malady of the Ideal* (Philadelphia, 1947), p. 42.
10. Lionel Trilling, *Matthew Arnold* (New York, 1955), pp. 28–30. Cited hereafter as Trilling.
11. *Cf.* Chauncy B. Tinker and Howard F. Lowry, *The Poetry of Matthew Arnold: A Commentary* (Oxford, 1950), pp. 65–66.
12. *Unpublished Letters of Matthew Arnold,* ed. Arnold Whitridge (New Haven, 1923), pp. 18–19.
13. Trilling, pp. 24–25.
14. E. D. H. Johnson, *The Alien Vision of Victorian Poetry* (Princeton, 1952), pp. ix, x, xv, 217–219, 217.
15. *Arnold-Clough Letters,* p. 66.
16. David Masson, *Memories of London in the 'Forties* (Edinburgh, 1908), pp. 77–81.
17. *Correspondence,* I, 290, 284.
18. Bodleian MS Letter to Blanche. Eng. Lett. e. 77, fol. 64. See n. 85, Chapter IV.
19. "Review of a Book on Progress," Bodleian MS, Eng. Misc. d.512, fols. 136–139.
20. Timko, *Innocent Victorian,* p. 90.
21. "Self-Reliance," *Works,* II, 51.
22. *Correspondence,* I, 301.
23. *Poems,* pp. 273, 250–251.
24. Clough interestingly treated the sexual theme twice more, in *Dipsychus* and "Christian," *Mari Magno.* In the latter he portrayed the dilemma of a simple, sexual love followed—in an almost Lawrentian way—and not preceded by a profounder love between two young people of different classes. Although trammeled by convention, they are ultimately not punished but rather rewarded for their affair with an illegitimate son. Christian, the woman, who is implicitly a successor to that other Christian pilgrim, marries happily and wealthily. The son of the illicit union finds his true father, and the tutor-hero marries a wealthy older woman—who proves to be barren. It is, by Victorian standards, an immoral poem. *Poems,* pp. 368–382.
25. *Correspondence,* I, 260, 278.
26. *Poems,* p. 517.
27. *Poems,* p. 193.
28. *Poems,* p. 294.
29. *Poems,* p. 276.
30. *Poems,* p. 250.
31. *Poems,* p. 251.
32. "Bothie" is Scots for hut.
33. *Poems,* p. 264. He refers here to "Easter Day, Naples, 1849."
34. *Woman:* I wanted, money, bread, all things, 'tis true,
    But wanted above all things, to see you.

Dipsychus: This cannot be . . .
Woman: . . . I came to see you only . . .
Dipsychus: . . . yet I stinted still my ease—
    Curtailed my pleasures—toil still extra toil—
    To repay you for that you never gave . . .
Woman: You pay us with your miserable gold . . .
Dipsychus: Six weeks tomorrow you shall see me again;
    Now you must go. Do you need money? here,
    It is your due: take it . . . .

                      (*Poems,* pp. 298–299)

35. Kenneth Burke, "Psychology and Form," *Counter-Statement* (Los Altos, Calif., 1953), pp. 29–44.
36. *Poems,* p. 272.
37. *Correspondence,* I, 284.
38. *Poems,* p. 170.
39. *Poems,* p. 276.
40. "A compliment is to my feeling the next thing to an impertinence, and I never can utter praise to anybody." Bodleian MS. Eng. Lett. e. 77, fol. 58. Clough is answering Blanche's charge that his "honesty" in expressing his views on marriage was "insulting" to her.

APPENDIX B: SALSETTE AND ELEPHANTA

1. Clough evidently added two lines between lines 125 and 150, and then deleted ten between 150 and 175, later making a fair copy but forgetting to alter his original numbering. Since ten lines is the median length of a stanza in this work, it is reasonable to conjecture that Clough did delete an entire stanza, possibly after line 162 (the only place between lines 150 and 175 where a stanzaic break occurs). It is interesting that this occurs at just the point where Clough's poem shows most clearly the influence of Schlegel's ideas about a pre-Christian revelation of Truth: it is not impossible that Clough cut out a stanza which on second thought he felt might seem rationalistic to such intensely orthodox and High Church judges as John Keble.

2. The motto under which the poem was submitted: "What God is uncertain, but a god dwells there," *Aeneid,* viii.352.

3. Arnold H. L. Heeren, *Researches Into the Politics, Intercourse, and Trade of the Principal Nations of Antiquity,* 4th edn., vol. iii: *Asiatic Nations, Indians* (Oxford, 1833).

4. Friedrich von Schlegel [Frédéric Schlegel], *Essai sur la langue et la philosophie des Indiens,* trans. and ed. by M. A. Mazure (Paris, 1837).

5. James Douglas (of Cavers), *Errors Regarding Religion* (Edinburgh, 1830).

6. Schlegel, *Essai,* pp. 100–53 *et passim.*

7. This note by Clough appears on fol. 3ᵛ opposite 11.20–23. The cited sources refer to Hugh Murray, J. Wilson, R. K. Greville, *et al., Historical and Descriptive Account of British India,* 3 vols. (Edinburgh, 1832), which bears on its spine the name of the bookseller's series, "Edinburgh Cabinet

Library," by which Clough refers to it, and Capt. Robert Hall, *Fragments of Voyages and Travels,* 2nd Ser., 3 vols. (2nd edn., Edinburgh, 1832).
"Buckingham" is probably James Silk Buckingham's *Sketch of Mr. Buckingham's Life, Travels, and Political and Literary Labours* (London, 1829).
8. *Sic.*
9. This note appears on fol. 6ᵛ opposite l. 98.
10. This quotation eludes all attempts at identification.
11. *Sic.*
12. "My former thoughts returned: the fear that kills / And hope that is unwilling to be fed," Wordsworth, "Resolution and Independence" (11.113–14), *The Poetical Works of Wordsworth,* ed. E. De Selincourt, rev. edn. (Oxford, 1936, 1959), p. 156.
13. Final identification of this quotation has not been possible.

APPENDIX B: THE JUDGEMENT OF BRUTUS

1. τέτλαθι δή, κραδίη· καὶ κύντερον ἄλλο ποτ' ἔτλης.
"Bear up, my soul, a little longer yet; / A little longer to thy purpose cling!" Homer, *Odyssey,* XX, 18.
2. Brutus here addresses the slave Vindicius.
3. Brutus supposes Vindicius telling his story to the Tarquins.
4. Lucretia's avengers were Tarquinius Collatinus, Spurius Lucretius, Publius Varius, and Lucius Junius Brutus.
5. Niebuhr's theory that lost popular lays or ballads formed a basis for Livy's work is discussed in my article cited above.
6. Verginia was traditionally slain by her own father [Verginius] to save her from the cupidity of the decemvir Appius Claudius." The story was probably based on Lucretia's. *Oxford Classical Dictionary.*
7. Both Livy and Plutarch mention the acts of three heroes named Publius Decius Mus. All acted as the first had done in battle, ensuring Roman victory "by solemnly 'devoting' himself . . . and then charging into the enemy ranks to his own death." *Oxford Classical Dictionary.*
8. Clough may mean either "Poets full-heartedly poured fourth," or "Poets['] full heart[s] poured forth . . . " I think the first reading the more likely, for had he meant the second Clough could have added the plural "s" to "heart." The omission of the apostrophe after "Poets," however, would not necessarily make the second reading less probable, for he omitted it not infrequently in MS. The names mentioned in the next lines (11.257–259) are those of heroes who would have figured in the presumed "lays."
9. A Sabine god, the equivalent of Mars.
10. "A great reputation for justice and piety was enjoyed by Numa Pompilius," *Livy,* I, 63. Numa, an early king, was supposed to have organized the priestly colleges and reformed the calendar.
11. Servius Tullius was supposed to have been the child of a maidservant and to have been found as an infant in the palace of the Tarquins. He became sixth king of Rome.

Index

"Manners" (Emerson), 111–112
Martineau, Harriet, 102
Martineau, James, 20, 101, 102;
  Clough on, 103
Mary Barton (Gaskell), 58
Masson, David, 170
Maurice, Frederick D., 98, 114; and
  Christian Socialism, 142
Mayhew, Henry, 32
Mazzini, Giuseppe, 66, 123, 126;
  Clough on, 127, 163
Melbourne, Lord, 60
"Memoir" (Mrs. Clough), 4–9;
  Symonds on, 5–6; suppressions in,
  7–9; Clough a failure in, 8, 9
Menu, 117, 137
Mexican War, 154, 158
Mill, John Stuart, 59, 60–61, 72; on
  competition, 77, 80; on distribution
  of wealth, 78; Clough compared
  with, 82–83, 92
Milman, Joseph, 17, 18
Milton, John, 12, 35, 114, 138
Mind Among the Spindles, 72
Mirabeau, Comte, 77, 90
Miracles, Biblical, 117, 134
Missouri Compromise, 153
Mohometanism, 117
Monroe Doctrine, 155
Morality, questioned by Clough, 177
Morley, John, 89, 97
"Mystery of the Fall," 138–139
Myths, place of, 33

Natura Naturans, 6, 105
Necessity, Clough on, 164
Neff, Emery, 74
New Poor Laws, 59
New Zealand, 132
Newcastle, Duke of, 59, 89
Newdigate prize, 28, 38
Newman, Frank W., 20, 114, 134.
  See also "Review of Mr. Newman's
  The Soul"
Newman, John Henry, 16, 93, 113,
  115, 165; and the Noetics, 17, 20;
  Tract 90, 17, 25, 97; influence of
  on Clough, 27, 29; conversion of,
  99; Emerson compared to, 119
Newmanites, 26
Newton, Isaac, 136
Niboyer, Mme., 123
Niebuhr, B. G., 33

Nietzsche, Friedrich Wilhelm, 173,
  175
Nigger Question, The (Carlyle), 74
Nightingale, Florence, 2, 148
Noetics, 68, 101; Thomas Arnold as
  follower of, 16; described, 17; and
  subscription, 98
North American Review, 151, 158
Northcote, Stafford, 70
Norton, Charles Eliot, Clough's re-
  view of, 6, 151, 161–165
"Notes on the Religious Tradition,"
  131, 134, 137

Obermann (Sénancour), 167
O'Brien Most Disconsolate of Men,
  201–202
"On the Effect of Dramatic Repre-
  sentations on the Taste and Morals
  of a People," 51
Opium, 156
Oriel College, 7; Noetics at, 16–17;
  contrasted with Balliol, 24;
  Clough's posts at, 56
Osborne, James L., 131
"Over-Soul, The" (Emerson), 106
Owen, Robert, 61, 94
Oxford Mendicity Society (Oxford
  Society for the Suppression of
  Mendicity: O.S.S.M.), 66–67
Oxford University: Liberals at, 16;
  Clough at, 56, 95; question of sub-
  scription at, 96–98; concept of the
  gentleman at, 111; attempts to re-
  form, 113; Commission Report on,
  158–159. *See also* Balliol College;
  Oriel College
"Oxford University Commission,"
  158–160

Palgrave, F. T., 127
Pantheism, 122, 136
Papal States, 126
"Paper on Religion," 133, 136, 138
Paris, Clough in, 116, 119, 123
Parker, Theodore, 102–103, 153
Parties, political, 60
Past and Present (Carlyle), 59, 66
Payne, P. S. H., 25, 26
Peel, Robert, 61, 85
Perfectibility, 146
"Petition on University Reform,"
  158

Philosophy of History (Schlegel), 35, 39
Picasso, Pablo, 130
Pierce, Franklin, 153, 154, 158
Pinter, Harold, 130, 176
Plato, 27, 42, 43
Plutarch's Lives, revised by Clough, 151
Pochmann, Henry A., 108
Poems, Clough's: basic ideas of, 172–178; modern style of, 178–179; sincerity of, 180, *et passim*
Poetry and Prose Remains, 9
Political opinions, Clough's: changes in, 6–7, 10; lack of, in essays, 48, 52; in letters to *The Balance,* 73–83; in "An Ill World," 83–85; in *Retrenchment,* 85–92; summary of, 92–94; development of in America, 153
Politics: English, 60; possibility of career in, 60–61; Clough's writings on, 141–147
Polk, James Knox, 153, 154
Positive naturalism, 1, 171
Pragmatism, 42–45
Price, Bonamy, 62, 73, 79, 83; on Clough's economic views, 90–92
Property, private, an inalienable right, 89–92
Prospective Review, 102
Ptolemy, 136
Puffendorf, Samuel, Baron von, 43
Pusey, Edward Bouverie, 18, 112

Quietism, 137

Radical party, 61
Railways, Gladstone's proposal on, 61–62
Rationalism, 17–18
"Recent Social Theories," 161–165
Reform, university, 114. *See also* Oxford University
Religion, Clough's writings on, 133–141; "Paper on Religion," 133, 136, 138; review of *The Soul,* 135–136; "Notes on Religious Tradition," 134, 137; "Conversations," 137–141
Religious doubt, 7, 52. *See also* Thirty-Nine Articles
Republicanism, 121, 128

Resignation, Clough's, of tutorship, 116; consequences of, 117–118, 132, 148, 171
Retrenchment pamphlet, 10, 49, 64, 83, 85–92, 113, 142; occasion for writing, 85–86; influence of Carlyle in, 86; concept of private property in, 89–92; tendency toward socialism in, 91–92
"Review of a Book on Progress," 151, 161, 163–164, 165
"[Review of] *Considerations on Some Recent Social Theories*" (in *Westminster Review*). *See* "Contemporary Literature of America"
"Review of Mr. Newman's *The Soul,*" 133, 135–136
Revolutions: Clough's interest in, 121–122; French (1848), 122–126; Italian (1849), 126–129
Rhetoric, Clough on, 42
Rintoul, Robert S., 61
Robbe-Grillet, Alain, 176
Robbins, Lionel, 59, 82, 83
Robertson, J. B., 39
Robinson, Henry Crabb, 97, 131
Rome, 51; revolution in, 126–129; in *Amours de Voyage,* 174, 176
Rousseau, Jean Jacques, 112, 164
Rugby, 9; influence of Arnold at, 12; Clough's years at, 14–16; headmastership of, 118, 120
Russell, Lord John, 60, 85–86

St. Ebbe's, 66
Salsette and Elephanta, 38, 41; text of, 202–210
Sartor Resartus (Carlyle), 46, 49, 52, 65
Sartre, Jean Paul, 176
Satire, Clough on, 47–48
Schlegel, Auguste von, 39
Schlegel, Friedrich von, 10, 35, 40; influence of on Clough, 38–39, 110, 117
Schlesinger, Arthur M., Jr., 155
Scotland, universities in, 97
Scott, Robert, 27
Scudder, Townsend, 105
Sellar, William Yonge, 167
Sénancour, Etienne P. de, 168–169
Shairp, John C., 5, 69, 97, 111, 118, 120, 124, 132, 164, 178; as